# THE BEST POLICY?
## Honesty in Education, 1997-2001

by Paul Francis

DISCARD

LIBERTY BOOKS

Published by Liberty Books:
7 Swan Meadow, Much Wenlock, Shropshire TF13 6JQ.

Further copies can be obtained from that address for £8.00
(inc. p. and p.), payable by cheque.

ISBN 0 9520568 4 4

*Many thanks to Maggie Mason for the cover.*

British Library in Cataloguing in Publication Data:
a catalogue record for this book is available from the British Library.

Design and production by Dick Richardson,
Country Books, Courtyard Cottage, Little Longstone, Bakewell, Derbyshire DE45 1NN

This book is dedicated to an idea
– that all children are entitled
to a decent education.

# A NOTE ON THE AUTHOR

Paul Francis taught in comprehensive schools from 1967-1998. He is now a freelance writer, who reads his own poems in local festivals. In 2000 he won the OUSS "Sonnet at the Millennium" competition, and his "Legendary Lives" was "Best Overall Play" in the Play-Writing competition run by the Drama Association of Wales. He is the author of the following books:

*Education*:
Beyond Control?
What's Wrong with the National Curriculum ?
Woodhead on the Block ?

*Talk Materials:*
Working Talkshop
What Do You Say ?
Boys will Be Men
(with Bain and Matthews) Talking to Learn

*Collections of Plays:*
Power Plays
Under Pressure
Looking for the Moon
The play "Witness" is shortly to be published, in a Heinemann collection.

*Collections of Poems:*
Our Class, Frozen Flashbacks, Nuggets in the News;
Snapshot Sonnets, A Shropshire Lass.

*Short Story anthologies* (edited with Gill Murray)
Myths and Legends; Survivors

*CD Rom Study Guides* (for Wordsworth Interactive Editions):
Tess of the d'Urbevilles; Mayor of Casterbridge; Hard Times.

His novel, "Love and Chalkdust" was published in 2000, and is available from Liberty Books, Much Wenlock, TF13 6JQ, at £8.00 (inc. p and p).

# CONTENTS

# INTRODUCTION

"Honesty is the best Policy."

It sounds like good advice, the sort of thing we say to kids. "You should be nice to old people, kind to animals, and always tell the truth." But it's smarter and more interesting than that.

"Policy" doesn't just mean "what you do." For the Elizabethans, policy was streetwise. It was political sense, the advice you would get from Machiavelli. So, "honesty is the best policy" means "If you tell the truth, that will get you the best results."

I was a teacher for over thirty years, and I think that's true. Sometimes with classes, or as a deputy head with teachers or parents, I might not say everything I knew. There is still a case for confidentiality, and tact. But many of the distortions in education cannot be defended on those grounds.

I have also been a student of education. Since I was at university, I have read books, watched TV programmes, and taken cuttings out of the paper. I have followed what politicians and journalists have said and written, and matched their words against the reality of my work.

This book is an analysis of the Labour government's policy on education between 1997-2001, and the way that has been undermined by dishonesty. Sometimes that is a refusal to accept that mistakes have been made, sometimes it's a pretence that things are simpler than they are. But we pay, now and in the future, for the failure to tell the truth. And the eve of an election is a good time to remember that.

I argue that experts should be taken seriously, but this isn't a book for experts. I want parents and pupils and members of the public to be aware of this situation, and to be part of the pressure which makes government see and say more of the truth. This book is aimed at the general reader, in language as clear as I can make it.

There are footnotes which show my sources, and an index, which explains abbreviations and the posts held by the experts that I name. For some readers that information may be helpful, or necessary for their own further work. But it should not get in the way of the main argument, which is that our education system is in desperate need of more honesty from those who claim to be in charge.

This book has been slowly written but published fast. I had planned a patient accumulation of evidence, followed by a period of reflection. But as the postscript makes clear, the imminence of an election, and the government's reponse to that, add a new urgency to the debate. It is now vital now that we all understand what is happening, before decisive changes are made on the basis of distortions and lies.

# Chapter 1:

# IN MARGARET THATCHER'S SHADOW

## THE TORY RAID

We live in the shadow of Margaret Thatcher.

Before her, education was a no-go area. Government might be worried, but it couldn't affect what went on in school. Uusually it didn't matter who the minister was, and education seldom made the news.

All that has changed. Intervention is not only possible, it's frequent, as governments try to show their impact on pupils' learning. There is fuller media coverage and more awareness, as parents read brochures, go to meetings and visit schools. Once their child has started, they will worry about testing and exams.

Margaret Thatcher hated consensus. It was wet and cowardly, the sign that people weren't thinking for themselves. Consensus was how producers kept consumers in the dark. Agreement was seen as weakness, and information could not be neutral. Experts looked after themselves, so government had to find experts of its own. When Kenneth Clarke started the market system in health, he was asked why there was no pilot scheme. He replied that opponents would have tried to wreck it. In his view, there was no such thing as a neutral experiment. It's us against them, so we do as much as we can before they muck it up.

In education, the programme was radical, and the tone was tough. These people have done this job, but they've done it badly. They've tried to keep it quiet, but we'll expose them, and show how they have failed. Tell the truth, and sort them out. That suited the media, and it became the pattern. So opposition got tough with the government, and the government got tough back.

Tories say schools are no good, because Labour wrecked them. Labour say it's the Tories fault. They hammer away at each other, but the only thing that sticks is the idea that schools are no good – because they seem to agree on that. And it looks more scientific if you can throw in a few numbers, like test scores or exam results.

"How is my child doing?" That is the classic question, and it should be. "Leave it to us, they all do fine" is no kind of answer. Good teachers have always wanted to be in touch with parents, to learn from them as well as to report back. But what do you report, and how?

According to the Thatcher government, teachers didn't tell parents enough. So ministers had to intervene, to offer information which teachers could neither conceal nor distort. That was why tests were brought in, and why league tables were made of their results. The media were delighted, because it gave them figures, and regular stories every time the tables came out. Some parents were keen, and some weren't, and many weren't too sure.

Between politicial parties it made things worse. Instead of saying "that lot are rubbish, we'll do better" you could now say "63 percent? That's appalling. It used to be 67%." They blamed each other, and it didn't matter who was in power. You could pick on the previous government, or the present government, the previous council, or the present council, because they were responsible for the decline. Teachers know that praise works better than blame, but in politics and the media they still don't get it.

This example comes from Prime Minister's Question Time, on January 26th., 1996. Tony Blair, leader of the opposition, comments on tests results for 11-year olds:

"These are children born under a Conservative government, sent to school under a Conservative government, educated under a

Conservative government. That failure is not theirs but the Conservative government's."

To which John Major replied: "If it is the Conservative government which has failed, perhaps you can explain why some of your friends remove their children from Labour education authorities and have them educated in Conservative ones?"

Earlier, David Blunkett, shadow education secretary, pointed to a decline in children's performance in their final years at primary school, and on they went, looking for failure, placing blame. They think they're scoring points, but what they are doing is hammering home that things aren't going well.

There was a comic moment towards the end of the Major government when ministers finally saw that it might be an idea to celebrate success, but by then it was too late. The rival gangs can agree about failure, and blame each other. But if one side claims success, then that claim has to be attacked, and the evidence denied.

Little has altered with a change of government. Theresa May, Tory education spokeswoman, gets the hang of opposition: "The Government is pledged to reduce the number of pupils leaving school without any passes at GCSE, yet that number has increased. Having done a great deal to raise education standards over our years in government, we are worried about the decline in the overall pass rate, and those leaving with no passes." [1]

Baroness Blackstone, a Labour minister, thinks things are looking up. "We have reduced by 7,000 the number of school leavers without any qualifications." [2] As a reader's letter pointed out "We shall next be hearing that the government has not only taught the pupils, but sat their exams for them." [3]

The result of this playground fight is to make the politicians important, and to hide the work of teachers and pupils. Passes, results, tables become devalued, so that we can trust neither the information nor the explanations offered by either side. That breeds cynicism, but it also draws attention towards the studios, away from the schools.

It is a relief to turn back to an earlier pattern, before the Thatcher revolution. Edward Boyle was not concerned to identify failure and blame it on the opposition. His concern was to celebrate success. He visited schools, talked to pupils, teachers and parents, and his main message was very simple – "What you are doing matters. We want you to do well, and are delighted when you do."

It sounds old-fashioned, but he put in hours of travel, courtesy and thought to prove that he was serious. He made an impact, because he was concerned with them, rather than himself. If these had been pro-motional tours, where he claimed responsibility for all that had happened, they would have left a sour taste. But because he was open, responding to the work that was going on and the people that he met, his visits were valued and remembered.

Tony Crosland was different. A tough intellectual, he was convinced of the need for British schools to become comprehensive. This was a mixture of personal belief and political realism, based on parents' dislike of the 11 plus. He pushed through laws to effect this change as quickly and effectively as he could. He knew there would be doubts and opposition, but he was prepared to face these directly.

He did not, though, get involved in the teaching. "I didn't regard myself or my officials as in the slightest degree competent to interfere with the curriculum. We're educational politicians and administrators, not professional educationists." [4]

For teachers today that's a nostalgic quote. They will be told "Now things have changed, you have to adapt, live in the real world." But Boyle's unselfish enthusiasm and Crosland's clarity about his role are both more positive and more realistic than the gestures of their successors.

Since Thatcher education ministers have been an assortment, regularly shuffled, but at their worst they have shown:
- a crude, aggressive manner, putting forward their own views and putting teachers down, ignoring expertise or criticism;
- a distaste for evidence, argument and consultation, with a reluctance to look seriously at examples in the past or in other countries;
- a denial of their own responsibility, and the damage they have done.

That isn't party political. It describes the contributions of several ministers from each of the main parties. "The denial of responsibility" sounds vague, but it has to be clearly understood if we want things to get better. A key quote illustrates what I mean.

In 1994, the government made extra money available for technology teaching, but not in LEA schools. An OFSTED report indicated that many of the opted out schools had failed to use the money well. It had been unfairly handed out and badly spent, and many people wanted to know why. A DoE spokesman said: "We have moved on. We have taken the best parts of the city technology colleges and TSI schemes and incorporated them in the new arrangements." [5]

We have moved on. It sounds smooth, the passage of a luxury train, or the gradual aging of a queen. But it wasn't that. It was a retreat from a biased, incompetent reform, which had been opposed at the time, and whose critics had been proved to be right. But there is no apology, no analysis of failure, just keep talking and move on.

Under Thatcher, the civil service was shredded. Their tradition of neutrality and impartial advice was scrapped. They served the Thatcher project, or got out. Many left, and others were replaced by outside advisers or consultants on short-term contracts. Morale was low.

"Look at the cock-ups over the school curriculum... We knew it was daft, but who was going to say that? There were papers written explaining the problems with the curriculum, but stories were planted in the papers saying civil servants were members of the educational establishment determined to wreck the Government's parent-power plans. Guess who planted the stories? It took a brave man to make waves after that." (Grade 3 civil servant) [6]

"John Wiggins and Clive Saville were highly respected DoE officials. They were worried about the proposals for reform of teacher training and said so. A delegation of Tory right-wingers went to see the minister and demanded they be moved. They were moved." (Middle-ranking civil servant.) [7]

"Two thirds of the civil servants at the DfEE say they suffer from low morale and only 6% think their organisation is caring or effective, according to an internal survey circulated by the permanent secretary, Michael Bichard. The civil servants were offered a range of words which might apply to how they feel most of the time in their job. The most popular descriptions were "frustrated" (44%) "disillusioned" (41%) "interested" (35%) and "insecure" (35%)." [8]

The civil servants were not alone. Margaret Tulloch reports on her experience of consultation:

"Even if a reasonable time is allowed it seems little notice is taken of responses. When the Government consulted over scrapping minimum space allocations in the school premises regulations, of 119 reponses only one supported the change. The Government went ahead. 124 responded to the Secretary of State's draft circular proposing selection of up to 15 percent of pupils without publishing statutory proposals. Of these only 15 welcomed the proposals, others opposed selection in principle and were concerned about the impact of provision of school places locally. The DfEE said 'after careful consideration of the results of the consultation exercise, Ministers decided to proceed briefly as planned.' " [9]

And there was an early form of spin. Kenneth Clarke and John Patten were anxious to attack "trendy ideas" which they thought were the cause of failure. Teacher training needed sorting out. They knew that education correspondents might ask awkward questions, or demand actual examples. They therefore fed the stories to tabloid columnists and political correspondents, who knew much less about it. The papers were suddenly full of headlines about trendy ideas in teacher training, written by people who had never been inside a college or met a trainer of teachers.

This did not produce effective government, but it did anger teachers. They knew what was happpening but could do nothing to stop it. The channels of consultation had been deliberately clogged. If you made criticisms you were ignored. If you could see a disaster coming but nobody seemed to care, then it was hard to keep going, to respond to the next phoney consultation, hard almost to bother at all. So many teachers kept their heads down, and hoped for a change of government.


## LABOUR IN OPPOSITION

Well before the election Labour had been changing its approach. At the 1995 Labour Party Conference, there was a debate on grammar schools, and a proposal that they should be brought back into the comprehensive system. The Labour leadership were not keen, but critics were satisfied by David Blunkett – "Read my lips. No selection by examination or interview."

Tony Blair chose to send his son eight miles across London to a grant-maintained school, saying that choice was more important than "political correctness." At the time, this was unusual within Labour. Ann Taylor praised parents at a West Yorkshire school who had voted not to become grant-maintained, and David Blunkett told MPs that grant-maintained schools would be stripped of their status if Labour came to power. [10]

A month later "Labour's education policy was in turmoil yesterday when Tony Blair directed his education spokesman, David Blunkett, to undergo a humiliating volte-face and drop the idea of charging VAT on private school fees, only hours after he had confirmed it was under consideration." [11]

In January 1996, Harriet Harman decided to send her son to a grammar school. This was a great opportunity for the Tories, and a blow to Labour. Tony Blair asked Philip Gould how he should react: "I said 'She has to stay. We cannot allow old Labour to win.'" [12]

The chance to opt out or to be selected became the New Labour badge, the proof that they were in touch with floating voters. That meant edging away from the comprehensive system, teacher unions and leftwing academics, and towards testing, league tables and the acceptance of selection.

It also meant adopting the same kind of approach as Tory ministers. In March 1994, at Highfield Primary School, Yorkshire, there was a sex education lesson which mentioned oral sex and sex with Mars bars. Education minister John Patten immediately ordered an enquiry, and David Blunkett, the shadow health secretary, described the case as a "crass and inappropriate provision of sex education", which "could set us back a very long way in making the case for sensitive and appropriate sex education in schools." [13]

You can sympathise. Reporters are asking for a quote, he doesn't know the details, and he knows the Tories will be hawkish. He can't afford to be soft on sex, any more than he can be soft on drugs, so it seems safest to go for the hard line.

What he doesn't do is look at the facts. In sex education, you either tell, or you talk and listen. If you simply tell, you get across some information, but pupils don't feel that you're talking to them. If you talk and listen, there's more chance of them getting involved, and much more chance that they'll remember and think about what you say.

Sue Brady, the nurse responsible, didn't go into Highfield thinking "Today I need to tell them about Mars bars." But she did offer to answer questions, and one of those questions was about Mars bars. "My belief is, rather than having children going out into the playground and getting a perverted and wrong description about something, I would prefer to tell them, in a sensitive way, the true facts." [14] Mrs. Brady had been a nurse for 23 years and a sex educator for five years. "When this session ended I asked both the class teachers how they thought it had gone. They said it had gone well. They were happy." [15] Anne O'Brien, chair of governors, emphasised that the questions had been dealt with firmly in the context of loving relationships. Her colleagues defended Mrs. Brady's decision to answer the questions openly rather than take individual children on one side to deal with it. [16]

Her NHS manager said "We have completed our investigation and feel Sue has done nothing wrong." [17] Five months later, the official report concluded that "the school nurse handled the situation sensitively and responsibly." [18]

Crass ? Set back sensitive sex education? I was involved in sex education at the time, and I remember two powerful reactions. First, sympathy with Sue Brady; "there, but for the grace of God..." Second, anger at David Blunkett, that he could echo the crude reactions which were themselves setting back the cause of sex education.

I've had the benefit of subsequent coverage and time for reflection, but that's part of the point. The original complaint came from a parent, who went straight to the local paper, rather than talking to the school. Maximum noise, maximum fuss. That's how crises are blown up, and a responsible politician would resist that pressure and calm things down, refusing to make a judgement until he knew what he was talking about. In terms of their personal background, political aims and educational philosophy John Patten and David Blunkett are light years apart, but in their response to this crisis there was nothing to choose between them.

This terror of giving anything away, of leaving the tabloids with an excuse to criticise, was part of a general cowardice. After losing a string of elections, you could see why Labour was careful. But as Eric Hobsbawm points out, there is a difference between winning an election and running the country:

"What separates Labour's intellectuals from its political operators... is the sheer amount of self-censorship and non-truthtelling which is imposed on any party believed capable of winning a general election. But refusing to say the electorally inconvenient, which is just a step away from refusing to think the electorally inconvenient, cannot be an adequate guide for taking care of the destinies of a country." [19]

He gives examples from economics, but it applies equally to education. We've all been to school, we care about what will happen to our kids, so we want to be sure that what we are told is the truth. Over the past twenty years that hunger had been exploited, so it was all the more important that New Labour, offering a fresh start, and a priority of "education, education, education" should also find clear, honest language in which to express their plans.

It needs thinking about, because education is difficult. Sometimes it had suited the Tories to say that it was simple, and in any case their aims were more limited. What they wanted was to break up the system, to free entrepreneurs to profit and succeed. The best will rise, and the worst go to the wall, and parents will accelerate the process by choosing between the two.

Labour talked about education for all, the many not the few, which is more ambitious and much more difficult. It also raised questions about their way of running things. For their partisan raid, the Tories ran a dictatorship. There was no way they could have imposed their tests through genuine consultation. But if Labour were going to heal the wounds, and unite the whole community, that should mean open information and a wider involvement in the making of decisions. As we woke up on May 1st, 1997, to a bright new morning, could we also look forward to honest government?

1 Guardian 28.8.98
2 Guardian 29.10.98
3 Adrian Kozlowski, letter to the Guardian 31.10.98
4 Tony Crosland, in "The Politics of Education" p.173
5 Guardian 17.3.94
✳ 6 TES 29.5.94 ✳
7 TES 29.5.94
8 Guardian 28.9.96
9 TES 22.11.96
10 Guardian 8.12.94
11 Guardian 2.1.95
12 TES 30.10.98
13 Guardian 24.3.94
14 Observer 27.4.94
15 Observer 27.4.94
16 Guardian 23.9.94
17 Observer 27.3.94
18 Guardian 19.8.94
19 Guardian 20.6.96

Chapter 2:

# NEW LABOUR, NEW GOVERNMENT

## SPIN, EXPERTISE AND THE REAL WORLD

Labour won the 1997 election because people were fed up with a tired, corrupt government. But they also won it by targeting marginal seats, having tight discipline, and managing the news.

Peter Mandelson, at the centre of the web, made sure that "spinning" became a familiar word. People accepted the need to present, control and place stories, and there was openness about that deceit, honesty about dishonesty. At first New Labour claimed that Bernie Ecclestone had offered a donation; later, they admitted they had asked for it. At first New Labour said that the biased membership of the hunting committee had been decided by its chairman; later they agreed it had been done "by consultation" between him and the government. The basic line is "Well, you can't blame us for trying".

"Us" is a small, tight group, boys in a box. Mainly young, mainly male, and the sense of a small compact group tightens their sense of their own importance, while making it harder for them to see who or what is outside. They boost the leader, not the party, and stay close to him. Derek Draper is an extreme, excitable example, but he captures their excitement at the power they have gained:

"There are seventeen people that count. To say that I am intimate with every one of them is the understatement of the century." [1] They are not just Labour but New Labour, a fresh creation dating from Year Zero. They really believe that you can start again, with a blank sheet of paper.

They knew that the Tory government had purged the civil service, so to be sure of having things done their way they needed to bring in a large number of advisers from outside. They brought in consultants, turned to think-tanks outside the civil service, and invested heavily in the management of news.

Michael Barber had advised Labour before the election, and written "The Learning Game", which Tony Blair had highly praised. Barber now moved from the London Institute into government, where his articles were generally like those of ministers – a loyal, boring account of what we've done, and why we've got it right. Phil Taylor is a headteacher who had valued Barber's original independence – "one was grateful to know that there was one government adviser who was not a complete fool or an outright charlatan."

As he reads about Barber's speech in Washington, he sees him on the far side of a gulf that separate politicians from teachers in schools. "Now that our New Tory government is so enthusiastically demonstrating its own commitment to imposed solutions, increasing divisiveness, simplistic slogans and tabloid concepts, there are one or two questions which its chief education guru might care to ponder." Taylor then offers eight tough questions about social division, propaganda, teacher supply, ability-setting and school improvement. These were the kind of issues with which Barber used to deal seriously, but now his official position restricts what he can say.[2]

A different kind of guru is Tom Bentley, who attended a comprehensive in one of the most deprived parts of London before getting a degree at Oxford. His middle class background gave him a range of extra-curricular activities, which enabled him to get on with a wide range of people, and to see the need to support learners beyond the school walls.

He went from Oxford to a masters in political theory at LSE, but also worked in the Regent street branch of Gap, which "gave me a grounding in reality." He then advised David Blunkett, and his book "Learning Beyond the Classroom" was published in October 1998. John MacBeath concludes an enthusiastic review "I, for one, will sleep more easily in the knowledge that Tom Bentley is advising our political masters." [3]

Bentley was a member of Demos, and it shows; there are frequent references through the book to Demos publications, and other members of the group, as though this were an intellectual Premier League. It's also teeming with short accounts of current projects, which is useful – but frustrating, because there isn't enough detail to show the reader what it means to run a project like this.

This breathless topicality means it has no sense of the past. As MacBeath says "This book is firmly rooted in the present and the future". The boys in the box never look back. Bentley is arguing for a wider conception of education, rooted in the community and beyond the limits of school days and school buildings. This is fine, but not completely original. For fifty years there has been work like this – Cambridge village colleges, Leicestershire community projects, the work of Eric Midwinter, and a whole lot of others.

I can remember stories of Tory councillors, walking round a school humming with evening activity, gasping "How can we afford it?" I recall colleagues, working themselves so hard in the evenings that their daytime work in school was suffering. Others, lucky to work in an authority which recognised these pressures, did an evening a week and had a morning off instead. I sat once in an evening cinema audience, in the theatre where I taught drama during the day, wondering how responsible I should feel for the teenage lad in the fifth row who might be spitting on the backs of those in front.

None of that stops Bentley exploring the territory again, or pointing out new directions which ought to be explored. But he should at least take account of what's been done, and look closely at the experience of the recent past to see what can be learnt, rather than implying that we start again from scratch.

He wants pupils to have mentors, experienced adults they can talk to, from whose advice they can learn. So do I, and I have run a mentor scheme. It's exciting, and good for the kids – provided that it's run right. But it is time consuming, and it isn't easy. What do you do if mentors give advice you don't agree with? What should mentors do about criticisms of school work and school teachers? How much should mentors offer pupils the benefit of their personal experience, their marriage break-ups, their problems with their children?

I've met each of these questions as a real problem. They don't devalue the mentoring, but they add to the work of whoever's in charge, and if 'someone' is ensuring that all school pupils get mentors, the chances are that that someone is a teacher. The lines between school work and mentor work need drawing carefully, or the two systems clash, and that isn't in the pupils' interests.

When it comes to work in school Bentley is an idealist. In his view, young people should be active in their work, making their own decisions and formulating goals for themselves. They should work as a team, involving others in their thinking. They should review what they have done, and how it could be better. "This kind of development," he adds modestly "requires significant reorganisation of school timetables, assessment and record-keeping." He's right. I've done it, and I know. But what I also know is that the current pressure from government is all the other way, towards short-term, individual tasks, in which pupils have no say and by which they are bored. School work now is duller, and more narrowly geared to short-term testing, than it was five years ago. If Bentley wants to be a useful adviser he could work on that, but my guess is that he won't get far.

This is a government where open-ended enquiry is not welcome. Occasionally they asked for other views, but only on the strictest terms. "LABOUR GAGS ITS UNELECTED ADVISERS" was the TES headline. The article beneath it spelt out the reactions of those involved:

"One member said 'I am more than nervous about this. Things that are going to affect many schools are being discussed confidentially. You feel a bit nobbled at times.'

Another said 'I had some anxieties that it was a political game and I was a pawn in it. Certainly it is an interesting development that the government is willing to do this. I hope it has been for real.' " [4]

But that early interest in other people's views has faded. The government is settling for what they've got, but they lose out twice. They miss advice from people outside. And by muzzling people inside, they lose the chance of independent support. Polly Toynbee, a Labour supporter, describes the process:

"Once inside the tent, the New Labour law of omerta is absolute. Criticism is not permitted. Rapid telephone calls expressing anger, suspicion or hurt follow any whisper of anything less than total support. It is astonishing how many basically Labour people no longer dare voice criticism except in an off the record whisper. This rebounds in the end on the government, because those who dare not criticise are lost to the government as good, independent witnesses who can also offer their endorsement. More healthy and open debate from within the tent would strengthen, not threaten, Labour." [5]

The energy doesn't go into promoting debate, but into broadcasting the message. Those inside the box decide what to say, and beam it out to the rest. In the run-up to the election, David Blunkett argued that spin doctors were essential: "In a world where communication is dominant, a spin doctor can help to avoid such confusion by ensuring that one message and one voice is heard by the electorate. We're not advocating a bogey figure here. Noone wants there to be a figure in the shadows who is unaccountable." [6]

In October 1997, Jonathan Haslam, director information at the DfEE, refused to issue a statement he thought was political hype, and was forced to resign. He was the seventh director of information to leave since the election in May. New Labour's grip tightened, on the way news was announced, and the choice of which journalists to brief.

Mike Baker analysed the stories he had covered for the Six O'clock News. He found that 11 out of 15 of them were based on initiatives by the DfEE. "Teachers, professional educators and university specialists have little influence on the news agenda stories. This dominance by Government sources has increased considerably in recent years, particularly since the election." [7]

David Blunkett depends on the work of Conor Ryan. Ryan is described by Baker in an article headlined "The shadowy figure keeps the press pack on message". Education's most influential invisible man ".. is the one at the heart of the media scrum, nudging journalists. ... he is most likely to say 'actually, I'll think you'll find the real story is...' He is least likely to say 'I admit it. The government got it wrong.' " [8]

As a civil servant, Ryan works for the government, not the Labour party. So Liberal Democrat MPs were surprised to find one of his briefing papers on a Westminster photocopier. It told Labour MPs what to say if they were asked about the shortage of teachers. The consultation document proved that the government was listening, but the PRP proposals were "not a return to payment by results." This was brief no. 84. If they got stuck, they should ring Ryan's office and ask for copies of numbers 60, 69 and 72. [9]

This tough, tight control can win elections. But in government, it carries a high price. They never admit that they got it wrong, because that makes it easy for the other side. But if they say they always get it right then we know they're lying – nobody always gets it right. So, maybe they're lying all the time?

Spin is a media topic, but out there, where real people live, does it make any difference?

It does if you work in local government. Graham Lane described "political advisers, spin doctors and education department officials who are going round briefing that all the fault of underperforming schools lies with local government. When I have met these shadowy people, they did not seem to know very much." [10]

Christine Whatford talked about how the government was keen to test whether LEAs were giving value for money.

"So far we have not baulked at any of this. We have not complained that the government feels it must have a framework in place to make sure that we are meeting our responsibilities. In fact we think that to do so is fair and reasonable. What I do have a problem with is the constant sniping and spinning in speeches and press releases that suggest a lack of faith in our competence to deliver, and that therefore ministers need to be constantly on the alert to find a "third way" to cope with our predicted failure."

She encouraged education officers to protest about the effect of press briefings, which were undermining the morale of their staff.

"The most recent example came with stories being trailed in the press in advance of David Blunkett's recent North of England conference speech saying that his theme would be the privatisation of LEAs.

This was followed by adverts in the national press inviting expressions of interest from the private sector or indeed LEAs, in taking over unspecified services at some time in the future. The powers referred to in the speech were not new... why choose to emphasise this particular part of the legislation and trail stories in the press about it?" [11]

Conor Ryan briefed the MPs that they should mention consultation, as a proof that the government was listening. But to test that you have to go back to the people who were being consulted. Did they think the message got through?

"While genuinely welcoming the opportunity to add their voice to the consultation, many of the participants... were dubious about scope for significant changes to their blueprint for change, set out in Excellence for Schools. Even education minister Estelle Morris made it clear that while the Government's first priority was to listen, many elements of the package were already 'non-negotiable.' " [12] If you are asked for your views, and you give them, but you know that no notice has been taken, then that is worse than never having been asked at all.

This is the climax of an impassioned "Dear Mr. Blunkett.." letter from an experienced teacher, angry at the failure of government to recognise the pressures on their work:

"I have earned a privileged insight into my job the hard way and – unlike some politicians – I know exactly what I am talking about. I am a good teacher, because I appreciate and like children. I enjoy my subject and I admire learning, but I am going to need a lot of help to trust a politician again.

The Government and my management will have to support me in order to get back some of the loyalty and sense of vocation that has been squandered needlessly. The years to retirement are going to be a long hard haul and if I could leave teaching I'd go tomorrow. I'm subsidising a bankrupt society with a lot more than charity, and I'm not sure I have much hope for faith left." [13]

That bitterness is shared by many, and it is fuelled by a lack of honesty – a sense that the work in school has been betrayed by politics. From a different direction comes a similar complaint. This is Dominique Ramsay, a dinner lady: "It's a smashing little school. People have said it has not come up to scratch but it doesn't bother me. They've made a lot of improvements, brought in more teachers and things have got much better." She has experience of working in other schools. "You should see some of them. Pretty awful. But here, they're always doing things – field trips, reading clubs, you name it. and the kids are happy."

But that could not keep South Benwell off a list of the worst 18 schools in the country. Sometimes you get the sense that the government is talking a different language. This parent from Cheltenham would agree:

"I have just learned that the head teacher at our school, regarded by my sons as 'the best teacher in all the world' is to leave because she feels her educational ideals have been betrayed and she can no longer believe in what the government is compelling her and her staff to do."

P. Thomas describes the way government initiatives have restricted creative work in the school, and ends with a plea:

"Please, please, Messrs. Blunkett, Blair and Woodhead listen to us, the real parents in the real world. Get out and see what your policies are doing to ordinary people and ordinary children." [14]

The tone is desperate, of someone who knows that they won't be listened to, but the message is so important that they will attempt to get it across all the same. How did things get this bad?


## THE PRP FIASCO

As an example of what has gone wrong, I want to look at the attempt to introduce performance related pay (PRP) for teachers, during 1999-2000. It wasn't a crazy idea. There is already some variation in how teachers are paid, and there is variation between them in how well they do their job. Some ambitious young teachers are attracted by the prospect of being able to earn more than a basic salary, so maybe some form of PRP would boost recruitment.

The argument for it was aimed outside education, trying to persuade the general public that the government was being tough, getting something for something. It was a belief in "how business works" by people who weren't actually in business themselves.

Professionals who knew about PRP were more cautious. Professor Brian Towers suggested that "research evidence offers six broad conclusions which should be helpful to those in charge of educational policy making at all levels." These concerned the subjective nature of judgements, the frequent decline in employee support after early enthusiasm, the damage of divisive attitudes, the difficulty of sustaining any scheme over the long-term, the superiority of rewarding groups rather than individuals, and the improved quality of appraisal interviews if they are not linked to pay. He asked "Do Messrs. Blair, Blunkett, Woodhead and their advisers know all this?" [15]

Their models are American, and the most successful PRP scheme in American schools is that in Douglas County, which overcame early problems because teachers were actively involved. In a survey of PRP in hospitals and the civil service, David Marsden reported that "a lot of line managers felt that it had raised productivity, but staff felt it has demotivated them." [16] Kevin Satchwell feels that his PRP has been successful, by rewarding teams rather than individuals – and 90% of his staff get extra pay. "It's got to be by negotiation" he says. "A barrel to the head approach means that your staff will leave. They'll lack motivation. They'll be scared." [17]

There's plenty of advice there, for a listening government. The PRP proposals were outlined in a booklet which was sent to all teachers, called "TEACHERS – meeting the challenge of change." This covered training and support as well as pay. It outlined the future shape of the profession, and it attracted great interest. I was one of 41,000 who contributed reactions, and I got a reply from the Green Paper team, assuring me that my views would be taken into account. Then David Blunkett made a speech, before the consultation deadline, insisting that he would be going ahead anyway.

The next little green booklet was "TEACHERS – taking forward the challenge of change." This described the consultation as "one of the most active ever undertaken by Government." It said that there was widespread support for the priorities in the original proposal, and for the intention to raise the status of teachers and support them more fully. It also reported that "about one third of respondents supported and one half opposed the specific proposals on pay and performance management."

29

Just think about it. 41,000 people read a document and generally welcome it, but half of them are against one of its proposals. Maybe it would be worth looking at that proposal to see if the same aim could be achieved in another way?

Not in this document. The detailed summaries make even grimmer reading:

"32% supported threshold assessment based on national standards and 35% further pay progression above the threshold linked to teacher performance. Just below one third (32%) supported some form of School Performance Award Scheme." But what about the rest? What about the 68%, 65% and 68% who don't support these proposals? Aren't their views worth considering? Is it only the numbers that support the government which count ? This is consultation, but not as we know it.

When the government decided to go ahead, they needed some advice. (This in itself was strange. Wouldn't it have made more sense to find out about PRP, and what it might mean for schools, before committing themselves?) They consulted Allan Odden, an American authority. These are Odden's principles for successful PRP. It should actively involve all the interested parties (i.e. include teachers and the public), be supported with adequate funding unlimited by quotas, and be backed up with effective training and a consistent long-term approach.

None of these conditions applied. Blunkett somehow knew that "more than a half" of the eligible teachers would benefit, but the government was only funding the extra payments for two years. After that, teachers were at the mercy of school budgets: successful schools with a surplus could encourage staff, but teachers at struggling schools might have to look elsewhere.

They also asked Hay McBer for help, but they were not encouraging. Headteachers, they reported, weren't used to going into classrooms to assess the teaching competence of their staff. To equip them to do this would be a long-term piece of professional training, not to be rushed."You can't possibly train anybody to observe lessons in a day. Where are they going to get the confidence?" [18]

The government had no time to listen to this. They were too busy to pay attention to the School Teachers' Review Body, which wrote a

100-page report urging them to slow down. The STRB argued that "there was real concern about the need to win teacher support. Change was being attempted too quickly across too broad a front. A huge agenda is reform is being attempted over a short period of time." [19] This is not a union being awkward, but an advisory body doing its job of advising. New Labour did not wish to be advised, and went ahead.

This put pressure on teachers, who had to decide whether or not to apply. It gave heads a huge workload of applications to sift through, and further angered them by providing training which was sometimes poor and rushed. And in the long run it will put further pressure on pupils, who will be subjected to further tests, as their teachers have to provide evidence of the difference that they have made.

Meanwhile, the spinning went on. Number 10 boasted that Tony Blair was taking on the "vested interests" by pushing through performance related pay. This aggressive slant was later toned down, although Estelle Morris made the announcement rather than David Blunkett. There were dark rumours that Blunkett wished to keep himself in opposition to the NUT, because that would play well with the media.

Members at the NUT conference were angry, because they felt that a previous resolution against PRP had been ignored. They then listened to Morris, their former colleague, telling them why PRP was in their best interests, although many of them had already decided for themselves that it was not. Morris later admitted that "If there was a touch of anger, it was over the assumption that we hadn't listened." [20] This is an assumption shared by many teachers, including Simon Burton:

"Not listening properly has a knock-on effect; the government can't listen properly to teachers, teachers have no time to listen to pupils and pupils end up with no experience of what it is like to be listened to and consequently no sense of themselves as powerful individuals with a real part to play in this democracy.

If the government does not engage in real listening and try to learn from teachers about what is really involved in the complex and sensitive business of effective teaching, its drive for higher standards of literacy and numeracy will result, ironically, in even more social exclusions and disaffection." [21]

It's a thoughtful response, but ministers were more interested in scoring cheap points. Morris innocently observed that "I was surprised to learn that the National Union of Teachers plans to use legal action to stop teachers getting a £2,000 pay rise." [22] Blunkett made bluff jokes about the NUT being the first union in history to threaten strike action over getting more pay. The effect of both these is to suggest that what the government is doing is common sense, and that the union are simply thick.

It wasn't as simple as that. In their haste, the government wanted not only to give heads total control over the assessment of their staff, but to demand that teachers contribute to that assessment. Staff would therefore be obliged to tell heads who should or shouldn't be promoted, although they would have no ownership of the assessment procedure. It was to that extra duty that the NUT objected, and at the end of the court case Mr. Justice Jackson agreed. He referred back to the STRB's warnings:

"That same haste and confusion caused the hard-working officials of the DfEE to fall into various errors." The four days allowed for teacher consultation about a crucial new duty was "wholly insufficient." [23]

How on earth could a government, faced with so many warnings and objections, be so insensitive? The answer is in the newspaper files. Every step of the way editorials were saying that this was common sense, that teachers were misguided to resist this move, that the government should hold its nerve and press ahead. So, in Medialand at least, the government got it right.

Medialand and schools are not the same. We have a serious crisis, that the picture of schools in our papers is different from the reality. And our government's insistence on choosing the Medialand version only makes that problem worse.

Whatever the leader columns say, the government can't live there all the time. They have serious lessons to learn. They decided early on what ought to happen. They didn't talk to other people who had done it, or draw up possible plans with those whom it would affect. They plotted secretly, made a fuss about public consultation which they then ignored, and then caricatured those who had different but valid views. There were bodies set up to advise them, but this advice was overridden, and when the whole sorry mess came unstuck they had no-one but themselves to blame.

## THE STARS OF THE SHOW

Tony Blair said that his first three priorities were "education, educa-tion, education" and there has been useful action on school buildings, nursery education and class sizes from 5-7. Some money has been spent, although it's hard to say how much. This government repeats announcements about how much it's spending, and sometimes those amounts include other amounts we've already heard about. Also, they hang on to a lot of money for their own priorities, rather than passing it on to schools.

Nobody would say they have done nothing. In fact, they have done too much, or tried to do it too fast. And frequently there has been action which should be beneficial but which has turned out not to be, because of the way in which it has been managed.

Jenny Page, former chief executive of the Dome, told a select committee:"I made several attempts to persuade ministers that stand-ing back from the dome would be good for them as well as good for the dome." [24] Sadly for the ministers, and for the dome, they didn't accept her advice. The same eager self-centredness shows in their management of education.

In opposition, Stephen Byers had harried the Tories, attacking CTCs as "a scandalous waste of money when our schools are starved of resources." [25] He had pressed for more money for teachers, to cut down class sizes, and to help with the integration of pupils with spe-cial needs. Here, teachers might have thought, is someone who under-stands the pressures.

In government, Byers was a different animal. The new minister cut himself off from fellow MPs, and from the beliefs which seemed to motivate him before he came to power. Byers the critic of privilege and under-resourcing became the prophet of "naming and shaming". This was a New Labour version of an old pattern where naughty pupils were told off or caned in front of the rest of the school.

Byers explains: "We made it clear before the election that we would put educational standards at the top of our priorities, and invest steadily in improvement over the lifetime of the Parliament. If this campaign was to be more than rhetoric, then there had to be zero tol-

33

erance of underperformance." [26]

To him, importance equals publicity. Unless it's in the papers, you don't really mean it. If you didn't publish the names, it would just be talk and no action, rhetoric. And yet what could be more rhetorical than that weary old soundbite "zero tolerance"? Just saying it makes you sound tough.

In Byers' private drama, it's education ministers who are playing the central role: "We acted without fear or favour to anyone. Failure to act would have been irresponsible." [27] Notice how the alternatives are shrunk. It's either this particular brand of humiliation, or "failure to act." He doesn't consider that a more discreet, more precise, more positive approach might also have achieved results.

Eighteen schools were named, but nobody explained that number. Were secondary moderns in Kent left out, in case people started to think about selection? Some of the schools named were already improving, and their hard-working teachers did not appreciate the extra attention. One head described the public shaming as "a devastating kick in the teeth." [28]

Byers, however, was being firm but fair. "Naming them was the most controversial standards decisions we have made. It wasn't easy but it was right." [29] That's a neat, balanced sentence, but where does that confidence come from? How does he know it was right? He wasn't relying on the work of Professor Margaret Maden, whose study of eleven schools showed that academic results began improving only after years of hard work. "The pace is bumpy and uncertain and is often a matter of 'two steps forward, one step back'. Are we allowing in our calculations how much and how quickly ailing and failing schools can improve?" [30]

Byers promised that naming and shaming would go on. "Why should the facts be denied to the public ? I want an education system which is assertive and confident, open and honest. Then we shall be in a position to ensure an increased share of our national wealth comes to education." [31]

I also want an honest system, because I believe in honesty as a virtue, and because it leads to better work. Byers wants honesty because newspaper headlines of success make it easier for him to haggle at the cabinet table; show the achievements of education, and you get more government cash.

But he's wrong to say "Why should the facts be denied to the public?" This list of 18 schools isn't just sitting there, as an ugly truth which soft educationists are trying to conceal. It's been deliberately created by government, and the number has been carefully arrived at – large enough so as not to seem unfair, small enough for the press to grasp. It enables them to focus on particular schools. And such a focus, convenient for the media, can be expensive for those on the receiving end.

"Young children were bullied in the street after their London primary school was named and shamed. Heartbreaking stories written by the year 5 and 6 pupils at St. Mary of the Angels revealed how they were attacked as a result of their school being pilloried nationally. More than 40 children were removed from the Westminster primary by their parents. Among those pupils who remained, many were too ashamed to say which school they went to." [32]

None of which would deter Mr. Byers. "We will put pressure on those schools. They will be exposed. People will know they are falling behind. There will be no hiding-place for under-performance. Every parent will know these figures and judge LEAs on how they meet them." [33]

This grinding determination is merely a triumph of the will. There's no close awareness of how pupils improve, how teachers work, why precisely this method will work better than any of the alternatives. There's no research behind it, but when the research does catch up, from the government's own analysis of examinations, "DFEE figures demonstrate that results often plummet after schools are named as failing." [34]

Two months later, naming and shaming was dead. But the funeral was secret, and it is difficult to date its passing. David Blunkett told the TES "the policy has been subsumed under new procedures which give schools identified as failures two years to turn themselves round before action is taken." A DfEE representative was asked whether naming and shaming had gone for ever, but she wouldn't give a definite reply.

It's the spin doctors' ultimate faith – never apologise, never explain. Stephen Byers, with no backing beyond self-confidence, pushed through a damaging policy, until it was ditched because it didn't work. That's good news for the schools and the country, but it's very bad news for him, because that result undermines all his expressions of confidence. Didn't he suspect it might not work? Were there other people to advise him, who thought that it might not work? Or was he just working on a hunch?

He wasn't acting on his own. David Blunkett shared that blunt determination to push it through. "I make no apology for it and we will continue doing it whatever anyone says." [35] You would expect the heads of failing schools to feel bitter, but you might think that those which succeeded would be glad of the boost. It ain't necessarily so.

Jean Milham was head at Morningside School, Hackney, which was the first of the 18 to come out of special measures. "Ms Milham's reaction was that being named had hindered rather than accelerated the school's progress, which was well advanced anyway... I hope they learn this is not the way to do it." [36]

That sounds like useful feedback, but not to David Blunkett. "Whatever her emotional reaction, Morningside was in real difficulties. It has now accelerated out of failure in just six months." [37]

Does he think she doesn't know that? Why is her reaction more "emotional" than his? She has invested in her management of the school, just as he has invested in naming and shaming, so whose achievement is being celebrated here?

This is not just a verbal quibble. Blunkett's comment shows the hunger for rapid change, for which ministers can claim the credit. Boyle's praise of teachers was powerful because it was genuine – he didn't arrange it so that he looked good in the classroom photographs, or claimed the credit that a school had done well.

But New Labour want achievement that's theirs – short term gains which weren't here six months ago. They announce something, it's proved to be a success, they get brownie points. So there's a big emphasis on extras which can be tacked on, like more homework, or summer schools.

I read in my local paper that five local schools are being given £75,000 of lottery money to run summer schools. Good for them, you might think. More education, education, education. But then the questions start. Why these schools? There are other schools with many more deprived pupils, although their staff may not be as clued into business opportunities. They are targetting "gifted and under-achieving pupils", but why? Is it because many "under-achieving pupils" would choose not to go? Is it because the most gifted will be flattered, and their parents are more likely to support the scheme? I'm all for supporting under-achieving children, and gifted children, but I'd like it done rationally. Many of the teachers at these schools would think it was a better use of this money to convert it into teachers, or assistants, or something which connects with the normal work of the school, but those options weren't considered.

Teachers might have thought it would make a difference to have one of their number holding the levers of power, but Estelle Morris did little to reassure them. She had taught at Sidney Stringer School, Coventry, which is not in a leafy suburb. Teachers there know about the pressures on inner-city teenagers, and the role played by LEAs in backing schools up – support services for behavioural problems, minority languages, music tuition for kids whose parents can't afford to pay. We expect Tory councillors to dismiss LEA expenditure as "bureaucracy", but from Estelle Morris it left a very bitter taste.

That was late in 1998. In the summer of 1999, a select committee of her Parliamentary colleagues reported that in their view Chris Woodhead, HMCI, should be made accountable to a management board. Ms. Morris was not enthusiastic:

"If I was worried about accountability, it might be worth looking at more bureaucracy..." [38]

"If I was worried about accountability..." suggests that she isn't, although her fellow MPs are. But the choice of "bureaucracy", again, suggests that this isn't a real concern. They're fussing over paper-clips, while she's doing the real job.

The real job involves instant miracles : "Between 1993 and April 1997 it took an average of 25 months to turn a school around. For those schools coming into special measures since May 1997, the average time for schools coming out of special measures has reduced to 18 months." [39]

What is this, the 200 metres? Is "turning a school round" a clearly defined event, like throwing the discus or clearing the high jump bar? I know schools which have been turned round and then turned back again; schools where the head has attempted to turn them round but they were fine the way they were; and schools where teachers are working their socks off but where attendance and examination results remain low. Estelle Morris shouldn't pretend that this is a simple matter, where the times can be ratchetted down by willpower.

Education ministers are writing a script in which they have to star. Despite their efforts to dominate media coverage, they still don't trust reporters to do their job. They have not only to secure improvement, but to say it's been secured, and so their speeches have become a succession of boasts. This is David Blunkett, reporting on his first year in office:

"We have shown.. As we have placed... We have backed... We have acknowledged... We have started... We are reducing.. We will be setting... and we will conduct... We have started... We believe... We are acting.. We shall be consulting... We will be introducing... We will be working... We will move... We have made..." [40]

So, as we grammar teachers used to say, who is the subject of this speech? What really matters to the speaker? Why is no attention paid to you,or me, or he, or she, or they? Blunkett's story is about Blunkett, and what he's doing.

That self-centred concern means that other views are seen as a distraction, not worth thinking about. He is dangerously quick to caricature the holders of views which do not match his own. Some argue, for instance, that the literacy programme, by demanding substantial amounts of time for the improvement of reading, is discouraging writing, and the proper development of artistic imagination. That's a genuine argument, by artists as well as teachers, and it should be taken seriously:

"Critics said that the government's emphasis on literacy was a threat to creativity. Do they believe that being unable to read helps you to become a better artist? When critics advocated creativity what they really meant was the ill-disciplined anything-goes philosophy that did so much damage to the last generation." [41]

Is that really what they meant? Or is he distorting their ideas to strengthen his case?

Another example concerns homework for primary pupils. A group of researchers at Durham University matched the amounts of homework done by primary pupils with the scores they achieved in tests. That could help to decide whether or not it was a good idea to encourage primary schools to set more homework. It came up with results which did not confirm government policy. The researchers did not claim that homework was a bad idea, or recommend that it should be set less often, but they still got under Blunkett's skin.

"Critics like these tend to share one important characteristic. They would never apply their views to their own children, only other people's." [42] How can he be so sure that they are hypocrites? If the research was properly conducted, aren't its findings of interest? If the names of 18 shamed schools, and the league tables devised from tests, are important information which should not be denied to the public, why should the impact of homework be any different? Or is he saying that the only important information is government information?

From a general accusation of dishonesty, Blunkett moves to a particular illustration which is simply ludicrous:

"We have researchers who tell us that asking five year olds to count to 10 is putting too much pressure on them. I would like to see them with their own children at the age of three or four when they get to the part when they can count to eight and they say 'so far and no further'." [43]

This is from a speech to the CBI, an audience which would not be able to check Blunkett's cartoon against the reality of the research. He also gave them a generalised analysis of opponents in general. Criticism of government policies was "blatant elitism dressed up as well-intentioned liberalism. Those who resisted reforms hankered after the quiet life of the past when the failure of half of our pupils was taken for granted." [44]

This is not true. Blunkett's fiercest critics are those who supported him in 1995, when he seemed to be ruling out selection. The education system has many teachers who passionately believe that decent education is a universal right, and their opposition to current reforms is rooted, not in lax nostalgia for the past, but in anger that Blunkett in power won't pursue the ideals for the future which he proclaimed in opposition.

His targets are not simply academics or researchers. "Everything we do, there is always a cynic sitting behind some desk somewhere who will put the mockers on it in the staffroom. When we decided to set up the summer schools last year, the number of people who complained that children wouldn't turn up, that the teachers would not want to do it, the parents would be aggrieved, that it was going to be a miserable failure – what a miserable bunch of sneering cynics." [45]

This wasn't what union leaders had in mind when they asked Blunkett to raise morale among teachers. Of course there are cynics around, but they are not as dominant as this caricature suggests. And with that dismissal Blunkett also waves away important questions – What are the gains of summer schools? Can they be made available to all pupils? Are parents and pupils who choose not to take part losing out on something essential, or an optional extra? Attempts in America to make summer schools compulsory have run into serious trouble. Here, massive government investment has created a busy industry for organisers and teachers who want extra pay, but that doesn't prove that it's the best use of resources. Why shouldn't teachers, excluded from that decision, feel entitled to question it?

For Blunkett in battling mode, it's him and them, the fight for improvement where he is the star and the others are just being awkward: "Our job is to ensure that every child in every school is given the opportunity that in the past has been confined to a few. However important they think they are, they will not stand in the way of me and my colleagues delivering the changes to improve the education system." [46]

He doesn't have to be like this. The David Blunkett who worked for Sheffield and kept the Labour Party together believed in quality education for all, and had a genuine willingness to involve all in the development of policy. In his autobiography he wrote "It seems to me that one of the problems besetting politics today is that we have lost the art of persuasion through intellectual debate and tend instead merely to indulge in verbal fisticuffs." [47]

On a good day, he has an appetitite for honesty. Blunkett told the Economic and Social Research Council that it was time to break down "the barriers of mutual suspicion and defensiveness which are part of the unfortunate legacy of the past." He was shrewd about his own shortcomings – "When evidence doesn't back up my prejudices I am immediately agin it, at least at first. There's a long way to go in getting those in government to be entirely open-minded, but we're getting there." [48]

And this was how he started his term of office:

"He promised changes in the culture, ethos and operation of the department, encouraging senior civil servants to speak out more openly on public platforms to assist in the task of creating an enabling government... He promised a new departmental style, seeking to unite, build a consensus and rally all the talent and experience within our country and elsewhere." [49]

So, what went wrong? He may have meant it, but it didn't happen. Instead, the harder he works, the more initiatives are announced, the less willing he is to consider that those who think differently are in fact thinking at all:

"They preach equality of opportunity but then cling on to shibboleths which actually deny diversity, underplay excellence, pour cold water on aspiration and expectation, and accept a dreary, miserably mediocre sameness which has trapped too many children in the most disadvantaged areas........ They are accompanied by the British disease – cynical sneering. In education this means that anything short of pouring vast sums of money into the system and leaving it alone is considered to be either interference or some sort of counter-reaction." [50]

It's very angry, very general and it gives Blunkett an excuse to ignore the argument. If these people are simply lazy or scared, hostile to change for its own sake, then he doesn't need to think about what they're saying.

But the key minister is the Prime Minister. It may sound like tabloid thinking to discuss policy in terms of personalities, but this stress on the lone leader was a key part of the Blair Project, and that is how decisions are made. If you want to track Labour's developing attitude to selection, you won't find it in arguments and debates, the report of commitees and votes at conference. You'll find it in the story of Blunkett and Blair.

Andrew Adonis, when he was a journalist and before he became Blair's personal adviser, suggested that Blair should be his own education minister. There are days when it seems as though he has taken that advice. But the same applies to health, the home office and foreign affairs. Blair suggests flexible hours for doctors, a health advice phoneline, instant fines for hooligans and a last-minute relief of sixth forms. The leaked memos of April 2000 only confirmed what the headlines had already made clear – "I should be personally associated with as much of this as possible." [51]

Well before the election, Blair signalled that his programme would demand a change of thinking from people who worked in education:

"It is time to end dogma and bring in common sense. Modernisation in Labour thinking applies to comprehensive education too." [52]

It sounds tough, but what does it mean ? How do we distinguish "dogma" from "common sense"? On the basis of argument, or research? By looking at evidence, or experience elsewhere? Or is "dogma" what other people think, and "common sense" what Tony thinks? There is no standard offered, for deciding on the future course, and no consideration given to the possibility that he might have got things wrong.

Why does he assume that "comprehensive education" thought it was immune from "modernisation"? Is it change of a particular kind that we should look for (more intelligent? more economical? more efficient? more fair?) or will any modernisation do? There's a worrying mix here, of determined willpower with woolly thinking.

Four months after winning the election, he was photographed at Morpeth Secondary School, smiling by a whiteboard on which he had written "Education No. 1. Priority." He was congratulating a school which had achieved excellent exam results, and improvements in uniform, discipline and extra-curricular activities. Blair was asked if he thought the honeymoon was over:

"People want a government delivering on the things for which it was elected. My vision for this country is that we should be the best educated nation in the western world. If we are able to achieve that, all the rest of it doesn't matter."

It's very competitive – couldn't we settle for being "one of the best", or even "uniformly good"? Even more worrying was that the head of the school, Alasdair Macdonald, already saw danger signals in the details of government thinking.

"We feel the advice Mr. Blair is getting is coming from a narrow group of people and he should listen to a wider range of practitioners. Ministers are fixed around 1978-80 in terms of what is happening in schools. Mr. Blair opposed mixed-ability teaching, but we need to be more flexible, instead of saying there is only one way of teaching young people." [53]

Lots of them say it, but the message doesn't get through. It's simpler to deal with stereotypes, our goodies against their baddies. In 1999 Blair spoke to a conference of new headteachers, and attacked "the culture of excuses which still infects some parts of the teaching profession. This is a culture that tolerates low ambitions, rejects excellence and treats poverty as an excuse for failure. In all reform you meet small c conservatives, left and right, who are suspicious of change and who resist change." [54]

Notice how generalised it is – "In all reform…" This isn't a particular argument about improving learning. It's an eternal war, for or against change, so which side are you on? But you want to say – which change? Change why, achieved how, for what purpose and at what cost?

To take his examples, ambitions should be high, but not unrealistic. Schools, and headteachers, have suffered by trying to do too much too fast. Excellence is fine, but which kind of excellence, and for whom? Some definitions of excellence (good scores in tests) work against other kinds of excellence (pupil initiative; sustained writing; art, music and drama). If you spend your money ensuring that sixth-formers each have a copy of their set text, there won't be much money left for poor readers at keystage 3. Poverty does not stop you trying, but it is a powerful factor which limits choices, influences pupil attitudes and cannot be ignored. These topics should lead into a more precise discussion of what we do and why, but in Blair's rhetoric they head the other way, towards simplification and slogans, heroes and villains.

There's a running commentary which goes "We're making things better... all right, it's not perfect... but it's better than the last lot... better than nothing.. and there's still more to do... so why are you getting in the way?" It's one-way traffic. The New Labour megaphone is fixed on transmit, and it doesn't know how to receive.

It could be different. The rhetoric says "It's us or nothing – our kind of change or back to the dark ages", but that isn't true. There are alternatives, each step of the way, and intelligent leadership will consider them. Consultation should be used, not as a trick to make you look good, but as a way to get the best result, deferring a decision until you see the best that's available. Other people's experience does matter, and must be taken into account.

That means listening as well as talking, delaying the announcement of success so that there's time to think the implications through. Spin would say this is a slow, low impact way to do business, but in the long run it gives you not only a more positive atmosphere, but more intelligent policy, fuller involvement and support from those carrying it out. In the end, it works.

1   Guardian 5.7.00
2   Letter to the TES, 21.7.00
3   TES 23.10.98
4   TES 3.10.97
5   Guardian 11.2.00
6   Guardian 19.8.96
7   TES 28.5.99
8   TES 28.5.99
9   Nick Cohen, in the Observer 25.7.99
10  Guardian 8.1.99
11  TES 29.1.99
12  Guardian 16.9.97
13  TES 6.11.98
14  Letter to the Guardian 13.9.99
15  Letter to the Guardian 28.4.00
16  TES 19.3.99
17  TES 19.3.99
18  TES 4.2.00
19  TES 4.2.00
20  TES 19.500
21  Letter to the Guardian 2.6.00

22   TES 31.3.00
23   TES 21.7.00
24   Guardian 16.6.00
25   Guardian 31.12.93
26   Guardian 18.11.97
27   Guardian 18.11.97
28   Guardian 17.11.97
29   Guardian 18.11.97
30   Guardian 9.11.95
31   Guardian 19.11.97
32   TES 2.10.98
33   Guardian 8.1.98
34   Observer 23.8.98
35   TES 14.11.97
36   TES 14.11.97
37   TES 14.11.97
38   TES 11.6.99
39   Guardian 22.6.99
40   Guardian 7.4.98
41   Guardian 20.7.99
42   Guardian 20.7.99
43   TES 23.7.99
44   TES 23.7.99
45   Guardian 29.9.98
46   Guardian 1.4.97
47   "On a Clear Day" p. 90
48   TES 11.2.00
49   Guardian 6.5.97
50   Guardian 12.5.00
51   Guardian 17.7.00
52   Guardian 24. 6.95
53   Guardian 29.8.97
54   TES 29.10.99

# Chapter 3:

# EDUCATION IN THE MEDIA

When I started teaching, education was treated as a bore. Work in the classroom might be a buzz, but newspapers and TV didn't want to know. Ministers might occasionally chat with union leaders, which might lead to a row over pay. Generally, things ticked over and newspapers were full of other things.

Margaret Thatcher changed all that. Lots of reforms, with new laws, hasty and ill-thought out, which meant further reforms and more laws. GCSE provided a regular excuse for moans about falling standards, while tests and league tables filled up the column inches. The government wading into failing schools, poor teachers and incompetent LEAs provided more drama than any reader could possibly need. Education was news.

I saw the change in my own career. When I started teaching, an ambitious young lad might dream of getting a letter in the local paper. Then I wrote a book about discipline, and was amazed and appalled to read a "Daily Telegraph" story headlined –

"COMPREHENSIVE TEACHERS SLINK HOME IN MISERY." I had tried to take discipline seriously, and in the process gave a hostage to rightwing terror. I had described the bursting of a paper bag as "an explosion", and saw this described as a real bomb. So much for poetic licence.

In my first year as a deputy head, I found myself edging a news-cameraman off the car park. I spoke politely, knowing that if I swore or hit him I would be on the national news. Then I went home and watched the local Tory MP describe the place where I worked as a blackboard jungle. Years later, on a different story, I was trying to edge a different news cameraman away, when my head called him in for a chat. Later, he filmed the school promotion video.

So education now makes news, but only news of a kind. Some things appeal more to the media than others. They like drama, excitement, the short-term happening. They like the star figure, heroes and villains, a timespan of events which their readers won't find too taxing. "Superhead turns school round in a year" will always be a better story than "middle aged woman enjoys working for 20 years." And as a result, some stories don't get properly told – complex ideas, long-term developments, interaction between organisations which can't be simply dramatised. The concept of teamwork can be put across in an hour-long play, but it's hard to cover in three column inches, and photographers get itchy if there's more than three faces involved.

That's only a start. I've mentioned Medialand, as a fantasy distorting the vision of politicians. But it isn't a separate, uniform country. It's a cluster of colonies, covering differences in wisdom, length and tone. To say something intelligent about how the media handle education, you have to look at examples. This chapter deals with six – three newspaper stories, one radio documentary and two TV programmes. There were many others in the period I've covered, and there are always further possibilities beyond what we've actually seen and heard, but you have to start somewhere.

# THE RIDINGS

The Ridings was a tabloid dream. Within a month, you had every element an editor could want: pupils assaulting staff, staff threatening a strike, criticisms of the local authority, a head resigning, an inspection hit squad, worried parents, suspended pupils, a school closure, and the arrival of a superhead to sort it out.

Even better, you could see it coming. As a reporter, you could tell that there was going to be a Ridings story before it came to its peak, so there was time to install camera crews and reporters, to catch it as it happened. The Ridings was nothing like the worst school in the country. Peter Clark, the new temporary head, thought that the situation had been grossly exaggerated: "So far, I haven't seen anything here that you wouldn't see in any school, including independent schools, anywhere in Britain." [1]

Such detachment, however, was rare.

"As journalists gathered on the Ovenden hillside in West Yorkshire to capture the arrival of pupils after half-term, there was a constant supply of youngsters keen to express on camera their views on the school's faults. Linda McDermott has turned up for the benefit of GMTV, even though her two sons are permanently excluded. The 13-year old, she said, had been falsely accused of starting a fire and the 15-year old had been excluded allegedly for slashing tyres and smashing windows." [2] If this were a school at the top of the league tables, she wouldn't be regarded as a reliable source. Why does trouble at the school lower the journalistic standard?

Some reporters seemed to think that if this was the school from hell, then none of the normal rules applied:

(1) "A popular girls' magazine headlined a story about the school with allegations of sex in the toilets – then going on to say much lower down that this rumour was in fact not true. Some of the stories were outright fictions, such as the reports of boys urinating in drinks cans and throwing them at teachers." [3]

(2) "Pupils going into school in the morning and at lunchtime have been accosted by journalists. Some say they have been given money for their stories. They were encouraged by the attention given to them to stay outside while they should have been in lessons. When teachers came out to bring them in and they made rude gestures and comments behind their backs, they were filmed and they were able to watch themselves on television when they got home." [4]

(3) "The staff were appalled to see the BBC's Panorama crew with an enormous 'cherry-picker hoist', the type used in outside sport broadcasts. The camera could now peer right into the classrooms." [5]

(4) "The police forced them to move on, and then they did a deal with a guy who owns some land behind the school and set the gantry up there. Anna White adds that they also 'paid some old people to film from their flats.' Last Monday, the school received a phone call from the manager of a petrol station telling them that another camera crew was bribing children claiming to be from The Ridings for interviews (all sorts of would-be rebels are now, apparently, claiming to be Ridings pupils.)" [6]

At the time, there was graphic video footage, excited headlines and frantic reports. Four years later, with added reflection and analysis, it's still hard to get the full picture. Peter Clark describes an incident involving Karen Stansfield, the previous head:

"Karen had obviously been distressed by the episode of the V-signs which had been widely publicised on television and in newspapers. After asking the photographers to stay outside the school grounds, as she turned her back on the cameras to walk up the now-infamous steps a photographer shouted encouragingly to some of the pupils: "flick some Vs." Two girls enthusiastically obliged, and the moment was recorded for posterity, the lowest of low points in the publicity saga.

....What upset Karen most was that she had accompanied the two girls back to meet the press, and they had apologised tearfully and profusely in front of the cameras, but that interview had only been shown once – and at a time when few people were watching." [7]

So the media just don't care. But maybe they do, or some of them do. This is part of a letter from Mike Baker, replying to Clark's charge that the v-sign incident was fixed:

"Mr. Clark was not there himself but bases his claims on what he was told later by pupils. I was not there either but I did use the pictures in a news report. At BBC News, we debated long and hard whether or not to use the images. We checked with the BBC reporter

– a very experienced education specialist – who was present. She assured us that no one had urged the pupils to misbehave. If we had believed that anyone had urged the pupils to act up for the cameras we would not have used the pictures." [8]

Not every reporter was so scrupulous. The Panorama film showed a scene where a teacher watches her class throwing paper and workbooks around. "This was a newly qualified teacher who had been asked to take a class unaided; the scene was filmed a few minutes after it had been announced that the school was closing, so you can imagine the atmosphere. She is in fact a very good teacher, but she was put in a totally unfair situation." [9]

Peter Clark adds: "What I've learnt from this is how television focuses in on a very small part of reality, and influences it." [10] The media must select, but they have to know that they're selecting, and be aware of what they might have missed. They also have to be honest about the ways in which their very presence – wanting pictures, needing drama, looking for the powerful quote – can make things happen, and make things worse.

There was good reporting, but it took account of the context, and of various viewpoints, and that takes time. Broadsheet reports are not always more reliable or perceptive than tabloid reports, but it is likely that a full account of The Ridings situation will involve a lot of column inches.

Martin Bright wrote an excellent article for the Observer, covering more than half a page. Its immediate focus was Barry Higgins, an excluded 11-year old who would not be going back to school. It featured a large photograph of him, half teeenager, half little kid, with a wistful look on his face. The article took account of the pressures on him (including the recent death of his twin brother in a road accident), but was honest about his disruptive behaviour.

It moved on to chart the rapidity of the changes in the school, while acknowledging the irony that Peter Clark, coming in as superhead, was given the resources denied to his predecessor. The article traced the local effect of the school market, leaving The Ridings at the bottom of the heap. Bright understands entirely why Clark has to impose a new regime quickly, and why that should involve permanent exclusions, even though some of them may have been arguable.

But he returns to Barry and the needs of excluded teenagers, who are thrown out as part of the price of saving The Ridings. What happens to them? "Where do you go when the school for the unwanted doesn't want you? The answer, in Calderdale, is nowhere." [11]

Among the articles written at the time, this stands out. It covers a variety of viewpoints, and contains necessary information, but it is also intelligent, easy to read and full of passionate concern.

One important test is, how do the kids see it? These students of today, citizens of tomorrow, will read newspapers and watch television, and how will this experience have affected what they see?

"At one time The Sun was putting in pictures of us with skinheads, beer cans and big cigarettes. It was pathetic because it's nothing like that." (Eleanor Graham 16).

Louise Roscoe, 18, said "One reporter came into the sixth-form centre and asked what exam results we'd got. We all went through them and Michelle said she got an A star in PE. The reporter said 'Well, we won't bother putting that in.' Michelle said 'yeah, you will, because I worked damn hard to get that.' We all got As, Bs and Cs, but they didn't put any of the grades in. They didn't want to see the good side."

We know that bad news is sexier than good news, but it's still painful to see youngsters learn that, by experience.

"There was nowhere near as much interest as when we were the so-called school from hell. The local papers are showing that we're doing good. They haven't been putting us down, but other papers aren't bothered. It's like, they're doing all right now – bye. They're old news."

Michelle is right. But the worst effect of all is when the dishonesty of the press starts to undermine the honesty of pupils:

"You were constantly getting told Ridings is rubbish – what are you there for? You won't learn anything. And it gets to you. When it happened, we were going to be leaving soon. I thought, 'Oh no, imagine putting The Ridings on your CV.' I lied once or twice. You're talking to someone and they'll say 'Oh, what school are you from?' and you'd say another school because if you said The Ridings School when all the media were here, it was like 'Oh no.'... I used to read the papers and think if it's in the paper, it must have happened. You look at them now in a completely different light." [12]


# THE MAIL ON SUNDAY

In the Mail on Sunday, for March 14th. 1999, there was a double-spread article entitled LUDDITES AT THE SCHOOL GATES. Above that headline was the legend – "A top education policy maker exposes the zealots blocking classroom reforms." They want us to think that we're dealing an expert, someone at the top.

So, why is it anonymous? A previous article had been written, exposing William Hague's shadow cabinet, where "by concealing his – or was it her? – identity the writer could tell the unvarnished truth, without fear of retribution. Since the article appeared, a number of other key figures in Britain's establishment have contacted us to reveal what they really feel about their colleagues." But if they're opposed to their colleagues, why do they stay there, and stay silent? If they are key figures, what retribution do they have to fear?

At the top are pictures of Ted Wragg and Tim Brighouse, lit to look like loonies. Each has a cartoon bubble coming out of their mouths, to make it obvious that they are speaking rubbish. Wragg's says "The curriculum for the future must contain a multi-dimensional hyper-space" and Brighouse's "In schools it is better to measure ipsative progress than apply rigid standards."

This is intellectual slumming. The clear suggestion is "these men are talking rubbish", but it comes from someone who has the patience to read through documents with such words as "multi-dimensional" and "ipsative" to pick the juicy quote, but who won't take the time to make the meaning clear. "Ipsative" is an unusual word, but not a silly one, and Brighouse has inspired many Birmingham teachers by his emphasis that pupils should aim to improve on their own previous best, rather than looking at national averages or ministerial targets. If the writer is bright enough to pick out the quotes, they're bright enough to follow this argument properly.

It's a crude appeal, us against them, inviting readers to mock the claims of experts. We start at the beginning. "Parents want their children to be taught the basics of reading, writing and arithmetic. They want them to leave school with a reasonable knowledge of history and of the literature of their country, together with mathematics and science. They want them to be taught how to behave and to present themselves well in the different situations they will meet in adult life."

That's reasonable enough. Not all parents would put it exactly that way, and some of them want other things as well - they want their kids to be safe, honest, happy, questioning, creative. What isn't reasonable is the suggestion that there is a plot to prevent children from getting these things.

"The education establishment is positively Masonic in its secret webs of power: the private preserve of professors, administrators, union leaders and teacher trainers. It hates anything smacking of common sense. Locked into half-baked, child-centred ideologies and desperate to defend its status and privileges. This establishment continues to do everything it can to frustrate any attempt to raise our schools above mediocrity."

Really? Why do all these people want our children to end up second-rate? How can it be in their interests to be repeatedly criticised for incompetence?

We've left behind the idea of "what all parents want" and moved into professional paranoia. The language is more complicated, and it's fuelled by hatred. Will all readers of the Mail on Sunday, you wonder, share this venom for administrators and teacher trainers?

They may not know what the writer is talking about. So they get instant portraits of the villains, sometimes with a handy little soundbite. Di Bentley, of Sheffield Hallam University, for example: "The fearsome professor wants the teachers she is training to be skilled in 'critique, creativity and challenge' and to engage in 'holistic problematised pedagogies'; surely very little to do with the basic tasks parents want schools to perform."

Well, you can't be sure. They might be closely related. From this quote alone you don't know how the professor teaches her students, but that's not her fault. A closer, longer look might show that her student teachers were very well equipped to satisfy the parents of the children they will teach, but that possibility isn't considered. A crude caricature – "fearsome", a simple contrast of polysyllabic garbage against 'basic' values, and we move on to the next.

Margaret Meek, of the London Institute, is attacked for having questioned some of the assumptions behind the teaching of literacy. "She says 'where learners have a rich experience of texts, they successfully acquire phonological awareness' – as if they could have a rich experience of texts without already having phonological awareness." It's sarcastic and confident, but the relationship between pupil involvement and the ability to translate letters into sounds is not a simple one; it is not the same for all pupils, and it does not always follow the sequence – first learn the letters, then enjoy the reading. But the writer of this article isn't interested in how we learn to read. Nor are they concerned with what Margaret Meek really thinks, as we can tell from the way she is introduced – "according to Margert Meek, archetypally Politically Correct reader emeritus at London's prestigious Institute of Education." Before we hear a word from her, we are invited to dismiss her as pretentious and dishonest.

It's flat-out assault, knock down the targets before the space runs out. The teacher unions, for instance "are clearly oblivious to the fact that GCSE – an exam for the whole population and favoured as such by the education establishment – has, since its introduction in 1987, led to runaway inflation of grades and lowering of standards."

Has it? Do we get any evidence of this? The view is regularly aired, often when the results are announced, but despite a lot of work there's no evidence to support it. And what's so wrong with "an exam for the whole population" anyway? Not only does "the educational establishment" support such an arrangement; so do the government and most parents. They weren't, I remember, all that keen on the 11 plus. Is the writer of this piece really central to the establishment?

This is meant to describe Tim Brighouse's attitude to accountability. "What he wants is not inspection by outside bodies but a cosy type of self-evaluation which glosses over real failings. Yet before the publication of national test results, the general public was left completely in the dark about the standards being achieved in such vital areas as reading, writing and arithmetic."

It's a celebration of the Thatcher raid – before, we knew nothing; now, we know everything. He's not with us, so he's against us – against progress, against effort, against telling the truth. That picture doesn't actually match the news from Birmingham, about Brighouse's attitude to information, the authority's monitoring of progress and the constant encouragement to pupils and staff to aim for better work.

Heather Jones is a head teacher to whom Brighouse makes sense. She says "the idea of improving on our previous best underpins everything that we do", and she is committed to Birmingham council's policy of target-setting as part of a host of initiatives for raising standards. She describes his leadership as "inspirational." [13]

But she is a real person, and this is fantasy. Actual kids, parents and teachers don't intrude into this insider's vision. There is only one educationist who emerges with any credit, and he comes later. Otherwise, this is a Rogues' Gallery, progressives that they love to hate, and of very little interest to most readers. Despite its appeal to simple, powerful values – "I want to know how my child is doing at school" – this article doesn't talk the language of most parents, and it doesn't address the questions they would ask. It preaches a gloomy sermon, slandering professionals with the vague, general charge that they are opposed to the education of children. It's hard to see why anyone would write, or publish such an article, and harder still to see how its publication could make anyone any wiser.

## SCHOOLS IN CRISIS

In September 1999, the Guardian ran a series of articles headed Schools in Crisis. The coverage was unusual: three long articles, published on successive days, each covering a third of the paper's front page, and the whole of pages 4 and 5. The articles were written by Nick Davies, well known for his reports on poverty, published as "Dark Heart", and praised as "required reading" by Jack Straw.

"This is the moment. The teacher with the bleeper has legs like an ostrich and takes the stairs three at a time. Within 30 seconds, he has reached the classroom which has called for help and he wades into the confusion."

It's good, dramatic stuff, and through Bleeper Man, the travelling troubleshooter, we glimpse some of the trouble which afflicts Abbeydale Grange, a school in Sheffield. Straight away we know that we're in an actual school.

As a deputy head for seventeen years, without a bleeper but sharing many of the same problems, I recognise the adrenalin surge, the poignant mix of commitment and despair. And it isn't all gloom; there are victories along the way, for him, for other teachers and for kids. But the overall message is not encouraging:

"The children who are caught up by the bleeper patrol have more stories than Hollywood, but almost all of them have one thing in common. They are poor. And that is what matters. It is a simple thing. Every teacher knows it. There was a time when every government minister admitted it. The banal reality is that the single factor which more than any other determines a school's performance is its intake – the children who go there."

This isn't just opinion. Davies was helped by Dr. Phil Budgell, a trained statistician who used to be chief inspector for Sheffield schools. He analysed the 27 secondary schools in the area, matching indicators of poverty (no earner, no car, overcrowding, single parent, ethnic minority) against academic achievement (average scores, mean scores, A-C, A-G). 90% of the difference in exam results between schools was accounted for by poverty, gender and attendance in the final year.

The approach varies through the article, from the anecdotal to the analytic. It's a detailed complex picture, and you don't take it in all at once. Within this first article was a section on the work of Peter Mortimore, who was part of the team that produced "Fifteen Thousand Hours." This was the report on London research which showed that schools with a similar intake could come up with varying results, that it was possible, through intelligent intervention and communal effort to "make a difference." That was useful work, both as a counter to cynicism and as an encouragement to teachers in difficult circumstances.

But it wasn't a blueprint. Davies quotes Mortimore's book "Road to Improvement": "It is crucial that policy makers desist from claiming that school improvement – by itself and in the absence of extra resources – can solve all the problems. While this might be true in 'advantaged' schools, it is certainly not true in 'disadvantaged' schools."

There is a danger that in trying to make a difference, we depend too heavily on the willpower of teachers. We also need to look at national policies, on poverty and school recruitment. Davies argues that "By sidelining the impact of intake, it permitted policies which focussed on detail in the school and were therefore relatively cheap. Such methods also promised to deliver results quickly and were therefore electorally attractive."

They were certainly attractive to Tory ministers, who ignored Mortimore's warnings, while right-wing journalists accused him of not understanding his own research. With them, and with their successors, he tries to be precise about what can and can't be done:

"Whilst some schools can succeed against the odds, the possibility of them all doing so, year in and year out, still appears remote, given that the long-term patterning of educational opportunity has been strikingly consistent throughout the history of public education in most countries... We must be aware of the dangers of basing a national strategy on the efforts of outstanding individuals working in exceptional circumstances."

This is where The Guardian got the benefits of length and expense. This careful survey of evidence from other countries is very different from the picture of Bleeper Man, racing up the stairs. But it does provide a background, and stops you getting carried away with the excitement. Mortimore isn't saying you can't make a difference, or it's not worth trying. He is saying that you can't presume a pattern of universal, consistent improvement, on the basis of a few exceptional heroes. But that is the basis of government strategy.

In his second article, Davies explored the recent educational history of the area. Grammar schools and secondary moderns, the loss and retention of sixth forms, the changing nature of catchment areas, and the impact of the Tory market in school places – all these are traced, with their effect on the reputation and recruitment of various schools. The key result of all this disruption was that hardly any of the resulting schools are truly comprehensive:

"Here is the truth which almost every teacher knows and almost every politician denies: a school system which becomes as socially polarised as Britain's, is guaranteed to generate failure."

Again, it isn't just Davies talking. A further section quotes Edinburgh University research into the beneficial effects on all children of a balanced intake. Margaret Maden can produce the figures:

"If you have around 20-25% in a class or in a school who are well-motivated and come from homes where it's instilled in them from very early on that education and learning matter and are fun and make a difference to your life, then that makes the progress with less well-motivated children and families much, much easier. When you get a concentration of children – disturbed or disadvantaged – there is a critical mass of children who will wreck any school. I will defy any teacher to teach when you have got more than 30% of kids like that in the school..."

In his third article, Davies went back to the source of this turbulence – Kenneth Baker. As Tory education minister, he introduced parental choice, which is what had led to movement of pupils between schools.

Did he realise, Davies asked, that the introduction of parental choice would polarise the system and effectively kill off the comprehensives? "Oh yes. That was deliberate. In order to make changes, you have to come from several points." This was understandable in a rightwing government. For a Labour government committed to education for the many, not the few, it made rather less sense:

"As long as Lord Baker's system remains untouched, all of Mr. Blunkett's reforms are being fed into a structure which constantly penalises the schools he is attempting to help."

So we end up with a complex picture, which starts from one teacher in a school, and moves out beyond that to the school, the other schools in the town, and the national system. It draws on the observations of a single journalist, and his encounters with the lives of teachers and taught, but it also finds room for the experience of statisticians, researchers and politicians. It's a powerful mix.

It had a huge effect. This series dominated the Guardian postbag for some days. There were criticisms – that Davies too readily assumed a link between social class and intelligence, that Baker exaggerated his own impact on the reforms, that particular details about local schools were inaccurate, and that providing such a view might deter recruits to the profession.

But the vast majority of respondents were enthusiastic, some of them passionately so. There was a massive gratitude from many teachers, not only for a vivid truthful picture, but for one that is rarely presented. A simple summary of many of the letters would go "Thankyou, for telling the truth – at last".

There were articles and symposia, about what solutions might be considered, how varied eminent figures would spend five billion pounds of government surplus, if it was up to them to solve the problems identified in these articles. David Blunkett, however, was not impressed:

"It doesn't take 15,000 words of Guardian prose to tell me or anyone else brought up in one of the most disadvantaged areas of Britain that there is a big divide between the haves and the have-nots in education."

He quotes a recent visit to a successful school in Luton, and the rise in their test results. "This is no accident. It demonstrates some realities about the government's approach to education, which were virtually ignored by Nick Davies this week."

And so, with some grinding of the gears, Blunkett moves into self-praise mode, underlining government achievements and increases in expenditure. According to him, the story isn't about Sheffield, or Davies, or the education system. It's about New Labour, what it's done already, and what it's going to do. He's not fair to Davies, who did pay tribute to Blunkett's commitment and energy, and the substantial number of initiatives which he had launched. He is even less fair, though, to Davies' argument, which was not just about poverty.

There is a crucial link that Davies traced, from poverty – social mix – school market – Labour acceptance of Tory reforms. Blunkett does not confront that logical chain at all. His article was headlined

"Do we want to bus the middle class?", which is a sarcastic evasion of a crucial issue. Nick Davies, he suggests "implies that we should wring our hands in despair and accept that you can't expect poor kids to do better (or otherwise, presumably, he would have us marching or busing middle-class kids from the suburbs into the inner cities as he abolishes parental rights)."

Tucked away in that derisive bracket is a panic about facing this question. No, the Tory reforms can't simply be waved away, and any action would be controversial. But the fact remains that the structure within which many teachers work is loaded against them and the success of their pupils, and the responsibility for that structure lies with government. It was Nick Davies' rare achievement to analyse that abstract concept in so vivid a way that it came alive, so that to read an article about schools was to learn. For once, educational journalism was itself an education.


# FILE ON FOUR

A File on Four documentary doesn't hit the headlines. A mid-day radio programme doesn't command a huge audience, especially if it's about "The inclusion of special needs pupils in mainstream education." Just stringing those words together suggests difficulty and boredom, yet this was a clear programme, illuminating a difficult topic. [14]

The government want inclusion, which in the long run means closing down special schools, and integrating a wide range of pupils into mainstream education. When that happens those pupils should get more support in the form of teachers, assistants and facilities.

The programme gave examples of what this might mean. The Newham authority have had an inclusion policy for ten years and feel comfortable with it. They see social benefits for the majority of pupils, as well as for the minority with special needs.

But not all authorities are like that. Zara has cerebral palsy, which commits her to a wheel chair and switch-activated communication. She lives in Camden, who have given her a statement of need, but this is not accepted by her nearest school, which is run by Barnet. "If she had been a Barnet child, she would not have been statemented" said one official. So her mother has to face a system which accepts physically disabled children, but doesn't accept her child.

In Gloucestershire, there is a revolt by parents and teachers in Stroud. They want to protect an MLD school which provides pupils with a warm, safe environment. Jamie is 15 and was bullied in mainstream education, but feels at home here. The LEA, with a large number of MLD pupils, sees its resources being thinly spread. They want to concentrate them in mainstream, rather than keeping expensive small units open. They are asked if that won't restrict parental choice, and they reply that they're doing that already. Parents who want inclusion in mainstream, properly supported, can't have it – because of the expense of keeping MLD schools open.

In the North East, a similar fight goes on. A proposal to close eight special schools in the Sunderland area was resisted by only one of them – the Barbara Priestman. This has good facilities, and huge parental support. It ran a powerful campaign to fight against closure. As a result, the reorganisation plan was turned down by the government – though it was the government who had told LEAs to promote inclusion in the first place.

You have to feel sorry for the LEAs. They are given guidelines and limited budgets. Because of the budgets, they try to move towards the guidelines by closing special units, but are then stopped by government decisions which they cannot overrule.

Maybe you should also feel sorry for the government. But not that sorry. They were invited onto the programme, but chose not to come. They offered the following mission statement : "We are in favour of inclusion in mainstream where parents want it and where there is appropriate support."

This is so bland as to be useless. To promote inclusion is a tough, challenging commitment, but if you're not prepared to support it by taking difficult decisions you might as well not bother. "Where parents want it" allows parents who don't want it, for whatever reasons, a right of veto.

The same contradiction affects admission to schools. Stephen Jenkins is head of Ayrescroft Primary School in Peterborough. His school takes more than its fair share of children with special needs, which causes his governors some concern. That policy may lead to the loss of able children, whose parents would prefer a less varied intake.

This admirable openness will harm Ayrescroft's SAT results. Schools more worried about their results and less concerned for special needs will decide differently. That will leave Ayrescroft taking in far more than its fair share of such pupils, which may mean that more are excluded. Professor Alan Dyson, of Manchester University, underlined the danger of giving schools too crude a message about what they should be doing. If they have been told that SATs are all that matters, why should they worry about inclusion?

This wasn't a destructive programme. It asked a lot of shrewd questions, and left the listener thinking. It covered a wide range of voices: pupils, parents, teachers, officials and educationists. Mark Whittaker, an intelligent, witty reporter, had the sense to know that he wasn't the main story, so he did a self-effacing, professional job. The issues are complex and important, and they were allowed to speak for themselves, through the concerns of the people they affect. It's a small kind of miracle that such careful, organised pieces of work should be buzzing across the airwaves, with so little apparent response.


## HOPE AND GLORY


"This series is about heroic teachers and making a difference. About people whose profession is a vocation which demands commitment and sacrifice." Lucy Gannon's introduction to "Hope and Glory" came to many teachers as good news. For years I was a "Hill Street Blues" fan who envisaged a smooth translation between police station and secondary school – the same bustle of busy working routine, variety of clients, and intense interaction between the inmates, but with a lower body count. "Cops and docs" has been the cliché criticism of television series, so now the teachers finally get their turn.

But there's a worrying note there, too. That "making a difference" is close to the Blair/Blunkett model of instant change, and Gannon has picked up a lot of the current hype. Ian George, played by Lennie

Henry, based on William Atkinson, is a dangerously simple endorsement of the superhead idea. A "Front Row" interviewer suggested parallels with the Western, and Gannon enthusiastically agreed. As the final image of the opening episode she wanted the picture, shot low down, of the new tough head advancing across the playground, hands by his hips.

Some viewers weren't so impressed. "In episode one, having spent a day evaluating Hope Park, an improbably named slum school earmarked for closure, Lenny returned to his pampered, posh overachievers, idealism recharged.

'If this school makes you feel at any point worthless or second-rate,' he told the kids in assembly, 'I want you to tell me. Tell me, because every one of you matters to me more than anything else I might be doing.'

Five minutes later he had resigned, and was on his way to rescue Hope Park. Presumably, the conclusion 'what a bastard' was not the one intended." (Tapehead, in The Guardian).

My conclusion is different. A head shouldn't be flogging his personality in this indiscriminate fashion. What if all the kids want to see him? Do they come out of lessons? Aren't there any other teachers they could see instead – or is it only Ian George who can provide this distinctive uplifting service? This affects organisation, detachment and the deployment of resources, but those aren't considered in the charisma chase.

The final episode of the first series needed a strong cliff-hanger, and it's a good illustration of the choices being made. Debbie Bryan (Amanda Redman) has been there throughout, hard-working, positive and unfailingly attractive. She is just what Ian George needs, professionally, and maybe personally as well - although when he tries to kiss her she turns him down. Will this rebuff cost her the permanent deputy job? But then there's Cathy Simon, available for this episode only. She turns out to have been George's former girlfriend, from whom he has painfully and messily separated.

For this episode, the detached control freak turns into a shambling lover, promising personality change plus help with her housing difficulties, a new responsibility which shoots to the top of his crowded agenda. So, as we approach the staff meeting, we need to know what will happen. Will he get the girl? Which girl will he get? Then the rabbit comes out of the hat. Neither girl. The star of the suprise ending is his male friend and former colleague, whom George has smuggled in as an extra deputy, over the existing one, over the acting one with whom he tried to have an affair. And his powerful ex-girlfriend is totally forgotten. Roll credits.

I have worked in a school where a deputy was brought in from outside, with no advance warning. It was certainly a dramatic situation, though not pleasant for anyone concerned. But if that's happening in a school, it's worth a look, to see what it does to the people and relationships involved. Here, there wasn't a chance. It was there as a ploy, to give viewers something to think about after they'd switched off. The screen time, the effort, the casting money, went on the same old values that have done the business since Jane Austen and the Brontes – will he get the girl?

This isn't a surprise. A lot of television drama works in this way, but it does mean that the claims for dealing with teachers at work must be taken with a pinch of salt. For much of the time, it's teachers and their private lives, or head teachers and their scheming. Teaching as an activity doesn't get a look-in.

The treatment of the job is very vague. Ian George wants to make a difference, so he gets rid of the old desks and gets in new ones, and hangs on to the sixth form even though it's been closed down. People who talk about money are just boring; what they need is the faith to support a vision. I've been in a school which lost its sixth form. For some kids, and some teachers, that was a serious blow, but for the school as an institution it was a gain in educational focus, a fairer use of resources and, eventually, a boost to morale. It may not always be, but it is a serious issue, with complex arguments attached, and not simply an opportunity for defiant gestures.

Headteachers also found the picture over-simplified. "We understand that the head managed to turn round a dreadful school, placing it among the top ten in the country after just three years. That is very misleading." (William Atkinson). "Turning a school round isn't just the efforts of one man, it is about teamwork." (Richard Warne). "It was portrayed as one person, a super-head, turning things round. You need strong leadership but it really has to be about teamwork." (Anna White).

And when it did take up serious issues, they were fudged. One episode featured a teacher under pressure, a married woman whose husband was leaving her. She came to school late, got no satisfaction from her job and was often on the edge of tears. When she walks out of invigilating an exam which will affect the league tables, she's obviously gone too far. Debbie shows her management potential by talking the teacher into going quietly, and the problem is solved.

Many cases are not so clear cut. There are teachers who are very good at some parts of their work, and terrible at others. There are teachers who know they are bad, but are terrified of any of the alternatives, and will cling like grim death to their jobs. What do you do about them? In this series there's a crude line drawn between the goodies (who work ludicrous hours and make sharp jokes but when it comes to it will back Ian George's hunches), and the others (who think he may not be all he's cracked up to be and believe that they have a right to go home). I'm with the others every time.

The TES urged sceptical teachers not to mock too soon. "The profession's public relations problem is deep-seated, fuelled by the tabloids, politicians on the make, and bad memories of school which still rankle with many adults. One drama won't change the world. But along with the Teaching Awards...we might see the beginning of a new appreciation of what teachers do achieve." [15]

I'd love to think so, but this isn't the series to do it. We need something less impressed by fashionable rhetoric, more willing to grapple with the issues and more attracted to the intrinsic drama of the job.


## MAKING THE GRADE

Firfield School, in Newcastle-on-Tyne, was part of the government's Fresh Start programme. Carol McAlpine took over as head, with a £2.4 million boost. Then she was offered the chance to have Channel 4 cameras in the school for a period of months,with them retaining editorial control. McAlpine admitted "It was a very risky thing to be involved with. We had to have confidence in their professionalism." [16]

She accepted, partly because of the research value of the exercise, partly because it might help local recruitment. The result was the documentary series "Making the Grade", shown on Channel 4 in November and December 1999.

The filming swung between the school and the community in which it is set, although the selection of "home background" was tilted strongly towards the truant and criminal end. McAlpine said "there is a lot of deprivation in the community. I think that that comes through." [17] As The Ridings also demonstrated, it really does matter which kids you talk to. It was not surprising that Channel 4 should go to the tough extreme, the kids who didn't want to attend, and while that can provide powerful viewing it can also feel like skewed evidence.

Any school has an uphill task trying to educate kids from this background. The noise, aggression and lack of direction is depressing, and you start to feel sorry for everyone involved. But then the doubts set in. Craig Cornish's parents are filmed explaining how a teacher came with a form, saying that all they had to do was sign, and there would be no further trouble over non-attendance.

The form meant that the school were disowning the pupil, since the parents were agreeing to take responsibility for educating him at home. To see them, and his home, did not make you hopeful that much education would take place. Judy Clayton, the welfare officer, later confirmed to Channel 4 News that "there were about 10 or 12 students who were approached in that particular manner, and that she wasn't very happy about it." [18]

Firfield was established on an educational bet. The authority puts in a lot of money, a perimeter fence is built, a lot of old teachers are got rid of and Carol McAlpine gets to choose the teachers with whom she is going to turn the school around. In return, she has to deliver certain attendance figures, test scores, exam results. These are not set by her and her staff, but their acceptance is the condition on which the school is set up.

The documentary shows the pressures of this deal. McAlpine is keen on PR. She shows Estelle Morris round, and it's obvious that these two are kindred spirits, busy, ambitious individuals on the way up. She lectures to conferences about how the magic is being worked. We watch her tell an impressed gathering of junior heads that attendance was around 60% and is now in the 90s. The TES reported that it had gone from 70% to 87%. And yet on the day Morris visited over 100 out of just over 400 were absent, and this was said to be the same as usual.

As exam time approaches, the senior staff realise that the targets are too tough. They want them reduced, but the LEA won't budge. Those were terms of the deal. But if we know we won't reach them, isn't it better to say so now, they argue. We've spent all the money, and you can't have anymore, the authority reply, with a stunning non-sequitur. They're not asking for money, they're asking for honesty, but that is beyond price.

And that's what this documentary did. It drew you into the situation, made you think and care about the people involved, respond to the arguments advanced. At times it was unfair, in its easy switches between home and school, and it dwelt for too long on the background misery. But as an insight into current education politics, and the contradictions implicit within Fresh Start, it was totally absorbing. You can't avoid taking sides. You flinch at the ludicrous demands which are imposed on this headteacher, and then passed on by her to her staff. Surely, you feel, there has to be a better way?

If I were a head, I would never have admitted cameras in this fashion. But since she did, I'm glad to have had the experience of watching it, and it provides evidence you could not obtain in any other way.

It's a very varied picture. Education does get covered much more than it did, and the best of that coverage is impressive, moving and intellectually stimulating. But that's rare, and one striking feature is how little of this is about thinking. Despite the massive increase in coverage, we don't get much more about how teachers teach, how pupils learn. All the old traps are still there – the impatience with complexity and development, the simplification of ideas, the search for heroes and extremes.

This frustration at being misrepresented is one that many teachers share, and it is not simply a case of bashing the media.

"The cruellest part of the Easter ritual is that the people who present us so crassly are members of our own profession. The teacher unions, conscious of the opportunities afforded by a seasonal lack of hard news, get their publicity machines into top gear and off they go, giving the tabloids a field day. As a result we're depicted as inhabiting some "Please, Sir" world of elbow pads and bumbling amateurishness. Here's this year's crop of headlines:

DISASTER, DISASTER, DISASTER
LITERACY HOUR "BURDEN"
PUPILS SHUN TEACHING OVER "LOW PAY AND STRESS"
ROUGH RIDE FOR BLUNKETT
TEACHERS BACK INDUSTRIAL ACTION
TEACHERS REJECT £31 BILLION PAY PACKAGE." [19]

It's not a good time to be a union leader. They have a tough job, they get no encouragement and very little power. But they do, all the same, look dull.

"Some things, however, don't change. The cast list of the main unions' spokesmen is identical to what it was seven years ago. Mr. de Gruchy is still in a lather about the naughtiness of children; Mr. Hart still warns gravely of unspecified disaster unless we all listen more carefully to head teachers; Mr. Smith still seems to regard everything with mild amusement; Mr. McAvoy's jowls still quiver at any mention of testing, appraisal or standards." [20]

It isn't fair but it is funny, and it's funny because it's half true. The representation of teachers in the media, by themselves as well as by others, is not accurate, positive or interesting, and we've all paid the price of that. It's a tough but important challenge to consider ways in which that might significantly change.

1   TES 15.11.96

2  TES 1.11.96
3  TES 16.10.98
4  Ian Murch, NUT executive member, letter to Guardian 2.11.96
5  TES 16.10.98
6  TES 15.11.96
7  TES 16.10.98
8  Letter to TES 30.10.98
9  TES 15.11.96
10  TES 15.11.96
11  Observer 17.11.96
12  Children's Express, quoted in TES 8.5.98
13  Independent 22.12.97
14  File on Four, Radio 4, 6.2.00
15  TES 25.6.99
16  TES 5.11.99
17  TES 5.11.99
18  Channel 4 News, 10.12.99
19  Philippa Nettleton, TES 23.4.99
20  Peter Wilby, TES, 22.11.96

# Chapter 4:

# WOODHEAD: "the only hope"?

## THE MEDIA STAR

Nobody else in this book has a chapter to themselves, but nobody else has occupied Woodhead's curious position at the heart of the triangle which connects education, politics and the media. There was a gap just waiting to be filled.

"This is a man who will always get a better press than he deserves for the simple reason that he provides good copy. He speaks in short, quotable sentences, at dictation speed; he does not care whom he offends; and he never uses jargon. Education journalists, in my experience, will find someone like that in a prominent position no more than once in ten years." [1]

At the peak of the Woodhead Affair, Libby Purves analysed Woodhead's position and his impact on education. "I rather hope he is not guilty. I like the man, and..." [2] Sorry? What's that got to do with it? Do we appoint people to high-ranking positions on the basis of whether or not they're nice? But you can see where it comes from, if you listen to Woodhead on Purves' radio programme, as the casual, relaxed insertions of "well, Libby" imply that he's talking to a friend.

He was speaking to an education conference of primary head-teachers. One of them complained about having to follow the national literacy strategy, since his results were already above the national targets. Woodhead's immediate reply was as follows:

"If you send me the details of your results, and if they are good enough, I will write you a letter saying you can implement whatever parts of the literacy strategy you think might be useful." [3]

On a personal level, this is terrific. National leader responds to teacher's dilemma – Chris gives you instant response. But will there be other head teachers in this position? Do they miss out, if they weren't at this conference? Or can they write in, and get the same deal? Will Chris deal with all these enquiries personally, or has he set up a system to cope with the demand? It makes him sound direct and friendly, but it can't have been good news for the people who have to do the work.

This is Woodhead, the media star, coping with a crisis on radio. Having mentioned the new numeracy tests for trainee teachers, Liz Barclay sprung a surprise:

"LIZ BARCLAY: What is a half of three quarters?

CHRIS WOODHEAD: A half of three quarters?... I would have to think quite hard about that... No, I'm going to delay... I'm certainly not going to fall into the mistake that one of the ministers fell into and make a mistake on that..."

It's an impressively cautious performance. He repeats the question, in case that will give him enough time to answer. Then, he knows that he doesn't know the answer, but he remembers what happened to his friend Stephen Byers. In a similar trap, Byers was asked to multiply 8 by 7, came up with 54, and was ridiculed. No answer is better than a wrong answer, so Woodhead keeps flannelling until she moves on to something else.

At the end of the programme she asks him again. He replies:

"I still haven't thought about that. I'm a total disgrace, but I'm not going to make a complete fool of myself." [4]

You can sympathise. This isn't what his job is about, it isn't what the interview was about, and it's a silly stunt. Many listeners would accept "Sorry. I can't do it, but I don't think it's that important." But that isn't the way Woodhead works. This was the subsequent statement that was offered by an OFSTED spokesperson:

"Chris did know the answer, but he chose not to give it. He has never claimed to be a maths expert – his background is English."

This makes it so much worse. "Chris" suggests a lovable friend rather than a boss who requires protection. Nobody who listened to the programme could believe that Woodhead knew the answer. To give it would have filled two long embarrassing pauses which left him floundering. But the people who read the statement may not have heard the programme, so they can imagine that Woodhead has the answers.

"He's English, not maths" is the worst defence of all. It dates him, placing him in the sixties, choosing between two cultures, English and Maths. The point of the numeracy tests is that they are for all teachers, including English teachers. This statement separates him still further from the subject of the interview, young teachers today.

The key, though, is the lack of honesty. This statement is total calculation: How will it sound, how will it look, now and later? What should I say, or should I say nothing? What he rejects is the possibility that he might tell the truth.

He thinks on his feet, and the media love him. At key points, they keep him in his job, as Woodhead happily confirmed. When Blair was bounced into keeping him, the Chief Inspector thanked David Frost for performing "his habitual alchen.y." [5]

When he first got the OFSTED job, Woodhead had his own agenda, but "I didn't tell anyone what it was because if I had they wouldn't have appointed me." [6] This is the voice of a politician, calculating appearances and advantage.

Woodhead likes to present himself as a pioneer, the one who got there first. "For years a conspiracy of silence has prevented any public discussion of how the education system fails young people." [7] He said this in 1996, three years after a National Commission, packed with experts, had produced a 400 page report.

And yet he's right. He wasn't the first to do it, but he was the first to gain sensational coverage for attacking the work of schools, with headlines like – "Incompetent teachers to blame for high crime rates." [8] He spoke for anyone who was fed up with schools and teachers. For parents or critics who had been fobbed off, here at last was their revenge.

Why wasn't there such a figurehead before? The leaders of teacher unions, however intelligent and responsible, come across as dull. They have to consider the views of their members, and are also aware of each other. As a result each public statement has to be checked for its potential effect, and the result comes across as grudging.

In the civil service, there was no tradition of grooming figureheads who could produce good headlines. In the education world, adventurous teachers or academics felt that it was their job to get on with the work, and the media's job to report it. Reporters liked simple ideas and dramatic personalities, and weren't keen on complex analysis or long-term developments.

Enter Chris Woodhead, the lean, lone hero, prepared to speak his mind. This was a treat they could not resist. The fact that what he said involved simplification, distortion of evidence and damage to professional work was someone else's problem.


## THE LONE PROPHET

Media awareness is now a part of the job. When Woodhead got a payrise, it was because he had met targets, one of which was "getting good media coverage of the inspection service."

His precious independence let him say what he wanted, and he was answerable to no-one. Occasionally he would concede that he was responsible to David Blunkett "in a sense", guarding an undefined territory in which he was not. Graham Lane once asked Gillian Shephard "Who is Chris Woodhead responsible to?" Her second-in-command beamed and said "That's a very good question", while the Secretary of State settled for "If you find out, please do let us know." [9]

Shephard often found herself undermined, as Woodhead went to Major direct. "There is criticism that Mr. Woodhead does not observe the convention of keeping his department informed of his contacts with No. 10. The informal discussions he has with Dominic Morris, the education adviser at the no. 10 policy unit, are not reported to Education Secretary Gillian Shephard." [10]

Woodhead repeated the trick with Blunkett and Blair, providing the Prime Minister with soundbites to illustrate his speeches. When the Blairs' nanny was considering teacher training, it was to Woodhead's then partner that she turned for advice. During Woodhead's period of power, regular leaks suggested that Blunkett would happily have done without him, and that antagonism became public in November 2000, when Woodhead finally left.

It wasn't always like that. When I first knew Woodhead, in the early eighties, he was a Shropshire English adviser. Roughly the same age, we'd both been heads of English, and had followed different paths on a common fork – adviser or deputy head. We got on fine, but we were very different types. Sixteen years later I was happily living in the same place, in the same job, but Woodhead had moved on.

None of his colleagues then would have picked him as a national leader. He was personally pleasant, sharp and busy, but the keynote was movement. A fast and reckless driver, he knew he took risks. He was restless, socially and professionally. Impatient with adminstration and the status quo, he liked to make things happen and start something new, rather than following a project through. He got new advisers in, edged old headteachers out, and moved himself up the ladder. But while he was deep in the politics of Shire Hall, other advisers were working with teachers, developing materials, analysing how pupils learnt.

It was the Tory raid which made him. They were grabbing education from the producers, to hand it to the consumers, and they needed an interpreter. Woodhead spoke the language. They didn't want analysis, convictions or new ideas; they wanted someone to tell the good news.

There weren't many candidates. Most people in education knew that these ideas would benefit few. If this programme worked, it would break up the system, and wreck some good work. So a fluent spokesman, who had been a teacher, teacher trainer and LEA adviser, and was willing to cover up these changes, was a rare asset.

They appointed committees to decide policy, and then gave them right-wing leaflets. English produced some fierce arguments, because it has always encouraged creative and independent teaching. In that subject, coursework and mixed-ability were popular and achieved better results. John Marks said that "English teaching has become the main ideological weapon for those who want to politicise education in a left wing direction," and John Patten made English teaching an election issue in the 1992 election campaign.

So when they were fixing the National Curriculum they declared war on English. The Cox working party had agreed a flexible framework, but that was not what ministers wanted. Changes were forced through the NCC, and Joan Clanchy, an experienced head teacher, resigned in protest:

"I do not think that a quango of 'plain' men and women with a team of three professional officers whose advice was often ignored was the right body to rewrite their work... I did object to a council member only being given Centre for Policy studies pamphlets to read by way of homework." [11]

And this was where Woodhead came in. English teachers knew where they stood, with Clanchy. But the public must have found it confusing. How reassuring, then, to hear Woodhead, ex-English teacher, saying: "We simply recognise that creativity and self-expression depend upon the mastery of critically important basic skills." [12]

Creativity, plus the basics. What could be wrong with that? It sounds reasonable, but it is a powerful piece of distortion. That "simply" suggests that what we are dealing with here is common sense. "Well, Jimmy, it's a very nice poem, but we do need some full stops..." It isn't like that at all. Joan Clanchy knows about full stops, knows about basic skills, and she has taught many more pupils than Woodhead. She is protesting about a political takeover of education, and Woodhead is providing camouflage.

It's important to notice that Woodhead's value here is not in what he knows or in what he can do, but in how he can make things look. At the same time that Peter Mandelson was developing the Blair project, Woodhead was already busy spinning.

"I see my job as trying to promote a professional debate about what constitutes good teaching," [13] he said, in 1995. I began teaching in 1967, and from then on I've known that one of the distinguishing marks of a good teacher was one who said "Yes, it's good, but what else could we do? Are there ways of making this better?" Teachers have always been communal operators, sparking off each other, and for Woodhead to imagine that he began this process is sheer conceit.

But it is a story that papers were happy to print. "The Chief Inspector poses a stark question: 'What must be done to reduce the number of lessons which, year after year, are judged to be unsatisfactory?' That question is the inescapable starting point if standards are to be raised. His aim is to promote a professional as well as a public debate." [14]

If you want to start a debate, you ask questions, but you also listen to the answers. You use the discussion process to enlighten all concerned. That hasn't been the case with Woodhead, who is concerned with his own, starring role. He is the hero, the lone figure who stands against the tide:

"My mission, in a nutshell, is to challenge vested interests, to change the culture, to defeat those forces that remain committed to ideological beliefs which haven't delivered, to encourage pragmatism. It is framed in my mind as a battle." [15] The "Mail on Sunday" article quoted on p.52-55 does a brisk run through ten educational names, providing a slanted portrait of each. Only one figure is presented in a positive light:

"It is this general conflict within the system which could explain the relentless campaign of vilification against Chris Woodhead, the Chief Inspector who has done so much to expose the under-performance of schools and the intellectual shoddiness of teacher training." [16]

This is how the Daily Mail sees things:

"We have a department of education and, in David Blunkett, an effective minister. There's Chris Woodhead, who has the guts to say what he thinks, and there are qualified educationalists." [17]

It's an interesting contrast, that Woodhead's value is in his outspokenness, not his educational expertise. If he was there to shake people up, like Richard Littlejohn or Graham Norton, then how was he qualified to be in charge of OFSTED?

Newspaper editors granted him a unique status, with the right to speak for pupils and parents. To The Times "Mr. Woodhead is not on the side of any political party: he is on the side of parents, children and the national interest. On whose side are the teachers that criticise him?" [18] The Observer thinks "He is not the representative of the education professionals – his job is to represent the consumer." [19]

But if he is the voice of the people, where does he get the right to comment on class sizes or teaching methods?

This is how the Sun editorial recorded his departure:

"The resignation of OFSTED chief Chris Woodhead is a sad day for us all. The fact that the teacher unions were celebrating says it all. Woodhead is a man who does not suffer fools gladly. The problem for him was that his job was to deal with fools. True radical reformers are rare in English public life. It is depressing that we have lost one of them." [20]

The idea that he is uniquely concerned puts him above criticism: if he says it, in the national interest, then you can't question what he says, because that puts you against the national interest. The argument is close to fascism, and hero-worship is not too strong a phrase.

Melanie Phillips wrote a long piece for "The Observer", which described an imaginary country, where "to make everyone equal, the physicians decided that no-one should be cured of their diseases." The land is overrun with sickness, with the single, dramatic exception of the Chief Inspector, who stands out against this corruption: "Despite the mounting pressure, the Chief Inspector still refused to renounce health and embrace disease." [21]

It's bad enough that his fans see him this way, but Woodhead does it too. Maurice Kogan wrote an article questioning the competence of OFSTED to assess LEAS, and criticising Woodhead's personal role. He included the sentence "It is not for the Chief Inspector to play the role of Ezekiel." [22]

Woodhead's response ended like this:

"I'm still not sure whether or not to be flattered by the comparison with Ezekiel. Prophets were, after all, men with outstanding insight into the affairs of their day. They were not afraid to speak out against the majority view, no matter how unpopular their message. They were also invariably right." [23]

Woodhead asks himself "Am I like Ezekiel?" He decides that he has the necessary independence, vision and clarity. But Kogan was not saying "You're like Ezekiel"; he was warning "Don't try to be Ezekiel", and Woodhead's refusal to grasp that is a sad form of vanity.

Blunkett tried to make Woodhead into a team player, by appointing him to a standards task force, as a joint vice-chair with Tim Brighouse. It didn't work. Woodhead was angry about Brighouse's testimony to the select committee, and threatened resignation:

"If you really think that your comments to the select committee were 'moderate and constructively critical' then you are either speaking a different language to the rest of us or you are deluding yourself... You have taken every opportunity you can to undermine OFSTED. It disappoints me, given your promise to David, and it makes my continued participation in the standards task force difficult." [24]

In fact, it was Brighouse who left, but his absence didn't make it any easier for Woodhead to collaborate. He missed six meetings in succession, and then returned, without enthusiasm:

"He appeared openly contemptuous of Government policy, huffing and puffing his way through the meeting, drumming his fingers and sighing deeply. Twice, he had to be put down by ministers Estelle Morris and Jacqui Smith for interrupting, and when Estelle attempted to sum up by saying that the group seemed to agree on various policies, Woodhead piped up in dissent.

Not even Michael Barber...escaped his withering ridicule. When Barber mentioned a novel concept he'd picked up in the states of, er, praising teachers, Woodhead's despair was complete. 'Oh, pur-leeze' he groaned." [25]


## OFSTED AND THE CHIEF INSPECTOR

Kenneth Clarke wanted to get rid of HMI. He invited teachers to despise them as out of touch, and planned to replace them with people from the real world. The local butcher would be along to check that teachers were doing their job. But it didn't work out that way, and most OFSTED inspectors have an educational background.

Chief Inspectors used to come from HMI, professionals who had been members of inspection teams. Woodhead's appointment changed all that. This was a political decision, where a government committed to a programme of change imposed its own spokesman on an organisation that was generally doubtful and in some cases hostile. More than a dozen senior HMI left within six months, and others kept their heads down.

In July 1996 "16 HM Inspectors on the OFSTED training-team had a furious meeting with Chris Woodhead. The chief inspector apparently confirmed that primary training would be re-inspected because he was unsatisfied with the rosy reports and wanted a tighter focus on reading and numeracy. The HMIs regard this as a slur on their professionalism." [26]

Colin Richards was a senior inspector before Woodhead joined OFSTED, and could have expected promotion. With Woodhead's arrival that was ruled out, and it was soon clear that the two would find it hard to work together. Richards wanted to publish findings about the successes of small rural schools, but Woodhead didn't – perhaps because that might undermine his view that class-size made no difference to the quality of teaching.

Richards attacked Woodhead's approach to primary education, arguing that it would make classrooms drier, duller places, with less artistic activity. He protested against a late change to the OFSTED pattern of assessment. Point 4 on the seven point scale had been neutral middle ground, but for his annual report in 1996, Woodhead changed the definitions attached to grades, so that 4 became unsatisfactory. He did this before writing the report, but after some assessments had been made, which meant that the final report was more critical than it should have been. On the issue of whether or not Woodhead was dealing honestly with the evidence, Richards is therefore a rare expert witness, who was prepared to speak openly.

This was Woodhead's comment: "I'm not saying he has made anything other than an impeccable contribution to the debate, but people should understand the special circumstances of his departure." [27] He left, he didn't get the job, so that's why he's talking this way. In other words, Richards isn't making an impeccable contribution to debate, and you can safely ignore what he says. There's no attention to the details of argument. Woodhead suggests that Richards has a personal grudge, and invites us to ignore his evidence.

It's a regular theme for Woodhead, one of the great job applicants, that other people disagree with him because they are dispossessed, or frustrated in some way. Like Tony Blair, he assumes that he must have got it right – how could anyone who's thinking straight not see things in the way that I do? Therefore, if they disagree with me, there must be something wrong with them.

Woodhead is also like Blair in that he won't just settle for good work. It must be competitively measured. Without supportive evidence, he proclaims "We are the world leaders in inspection." [28] His deputy Mike Tomlinson was dispatched to inform American policy makers that they should consider imitating the English model. "The special measures policy is working because it has enabled us to expose the weaknesses in schools and tackle them." [29] What he didn't advertise was the unease in this country about how OFSTED works.

Now, the pay for inspections has been cut, and inspectors are only paid for the days they inspect. Preparation has to be done in their own time, and travel and accommodation expenses are reduced to a minimum. The job is less attractive than it was, and the proportion of retired inspectors is likely to increase. Jane Hattat, a headteacher whose school was subject to a favourable report, commented on the inspection team:

"Several inspectors lacked first-hand knowledge of teaching the national curriculum since they were already several years into retirement... All but two had no experience of teaching over the past 10 years... Even the one responsible for technology had retired in 1993. The English inspector had started teaching in 1951. That's before I was born." [30]

HMI used to develop work on particular themes, looking at issues, and publishing useful reports. If you were interested on that kind of work today, you wouldn't join OFSTED. Many inspectors are moonlighting advisers, having to inspect because their authorities need the money. Others are lecturers in need of extra cash, or retired headteachers. They don't have the time to meet when they are not inspecting, and do not carry out trials to check that their marking is consistent. As a vehicle for looking honestly at work in schools, it's not a promising model.

It's hard to be definite about OFSTED, since there is fierce control of who comments, and what they are allowed to say. Paul Lashmar made a documentary on the schools inspectorate. "I've been all over the world", he said, "but I've never met people as frightened of talking as Woodhead's staff." [31]

But it is still worth looking at Woodhead's own view of how the system is meant to work. It started life as part of a two-prong attack, whereby the Tory government assured parents that they could test the quality of schools. Together the OFSTED inspections and test results (arranged in league tables), would tell you how well they were doing.This was a political job, hurriedly planned and criticised by many experts, so its development was not smooth.

Woodhead was direct about the problems. When evidence from the two prongs clashed, he was blunt: "Either OFSTED is rubbish or performance tables are rubbish." [32] And later, in case you weren't sure which one was dodgy  – "There are no reliable national curriculum tests." [33]

So, what is "the principle of external inspections, without which we would all be blissfully ignorant of the state that schools are in…?" [34] Note the sarcasm of that "blissfully", with its dismissal that things could be done in any other way. "An outside team brings to any school an awareness of what might be done differently." [35] True, but could that be any outside team? Teachers from another school, perhaps? Or do they have to be using the very particular OFSTED framework?

And what happens next? If the external view finds problems, "Only the head teacher and the school governors can take a school forward." [36] Do the inspectors play any part in making the necessary improvements? "OFSTED should not get involved in helping schools to improve, because this would compromise inspectors' judgements. There were two jobs to be done, inspection, and advice and support, and the two roles are best kept separate." [37] So, the school can't see what's wrong, but when OFSTED have pointed out what's wrong, then the school can see how to put it right. Really?

The early stress on the head and governors passed with the Tory government, and by '99 Woodhead was encouraging schools to learn from each other. But if they could do that, did they still need the external view from OFSTED? Not necessarily. Woodhead told heads of independent schools that if he were a head, faced with an unhelpful OFSTED report, his advice would be "Put it in the bin. I would."

And he means it. The limit of Woodhead's management experience in schools was three years as a head of department, but there is no doubt that if he were a head he would throw away unnecessary paperwork. As a personal approach that's appealing; but where does it leave the work of his organisation?

Woodhead's view of OFSTED, and OFSTED's place in his thinking, varies according to convenience. Sometimes it suits him to present OFSTED as a vast team, producing masses of data from which he can provide advice. At other times, he's just saying what he thinks, with no relation to the experience or views of anyone else.

This was the picture presented to the Select Committee, whose chairman, Malcolm Wicks, perceived two OFSTEDs: "The first is the calm professional inspection of schools and the other, which is about blood and thunder and guts and tears and is about giants stalking the land and sacking people." [38] Wicks was too kind. There aren't two OFSTEDs, there is OFSTED and the HMCI, and the difference between the two was entirely Woodhead's fault. He tried to blame this on "the rather Wagnerian way in which we are reported in the media" but he is hardly a media innocent. The problem, of judging whether he's talking for OFSTED or for himself, was there from the start.

It derives from his personality. When I knew him we were both aware that we were very different people. He was more restless, critical and ambitious. That isn't a crime. But each personality carries with it the risks of its distinctive limitations. Where I might be reluctant to change familiar patterns or force in a new appointment, Woodhead might underestimate the value of established relationships, or the need to involve all staff. But if someone achieves substantial power, and then bases their operation on their personal style without any attempt to include corrective pressures, then those original risks are seriously magnified. This is what has happened with Woodhead and the work of OFSTED.

Back in 1996, Melanie Phillips raised this crucial question: "Was there not a danger that through his confrontational style he was making himself the issue rather than educational standards?" Woodhead's response ran as follows:

"I'd like people to understand that our reports are the result of a collective endeavour within OFSTED. If adopting a lower profile means the world becomes less aware of issues of tremendous importance to the future of our children and of this country, the answer is no." [39]

It's worth following this exchange closely. The question is about him, so he deflects it to the 'we' of OFSTED, in case you thought it was just him being difficult. Then he offers us an unreal choice – "adopting a lower profile" is not the sole alternative to "confrontational style". He follows this with a dose of self-inflation ("tremendous importance to the future of our children and of this country"), and then rises to a defiant climax – "the answer is no." Only a careful reader registers that the original question has still not been answered. Yes, there is a danger that he becomes the issue, and it doesn't worry him at all.

This is from an interview on Radio 4's "Learning Curve":

"LIBBY PURVES: Do you think this is healthy, that school inspection, which is a very complex, very human process, should be this hot emotional issue?

CHRIS WOODHEAD: ...Parents have got huge interest in their children's education... Information is in the public domain. It is going to inspire very strong reactions, reactions about standards in school, and reactions about me. It's simply inevitable."

At which point she needs to ask, so how do they manage the inspection without the reaction, in Scotland and in Wales? Why is England the only country anywhere which thinks you have to attack teachers to make them better?

There are different ways in which this job could be done, and Woodhead cannot take seriously the possibility that he's got it wrong. We don't know who he learns from, how he improves, because he is so dismissive of other views. In a complex business, where improvement means collaboration, he remains a solo operator, polishing his image at a distance from the actual work. When others want to get involved, and offer suggestions about how OFSTED might improve its research, or make its judgements more consistent, he doesn't want to know.

Woodhead didn't refer to useful work by colleagues, or share his spotlight. He was conscious of criticisms that he was not a team player, but his rare attempts to answer them were not convincing:

"At that point his secretary glides in with a tray of coffee. 'Thanks, Barbara,' gushes Woodhead. 'I'm just singing your praises. Do you feel part of a team?' She laughs. There is silence. She laughs again. 'She does, she does. We're a really good team,' Woodhead says. 'I do, I do', she says. But it came a bit late." [40]

In the decisions and the reports, there is no sign that Woodhead is interested in teamwork. When he says OFSTED is a team that comes across as a tactic, a way of camouflaging that he is a lone operator. There is no evidence from other people that Woodhead does anything to encourage, develop or share in their work. And when the time came for him to leave, there were very few thanks, good wishes or acknowledgements. His memorial was to be found, not in the memories of his colleagues, but in newspaper editorials.

As a result of his solitary style, OFSTED's relations with other organisations were often poor. Three witnesses suggest ways in which things could have been better:

(1) Professor Colin Harrison, expert on the teaching of reading, comments on Woodhead's presentation of a report on reading standards in 45 inner London boroughs:

"I felt anger and frustration not only because I regard teaching literacy to inner-city children as one of the most difficult jobs in education, and because such teachers need all the help they can get, but also because the discourse of derision is anti-educational – it does not bring about change or improvement; rather, it causes those who are scolded, threatened and blamed to react negatively, and to shrink towards resignation or apathy." He goes on to outline how more supportive methods have produced tangible results in reading standards in Scotland. [41]

(2) Margaret Maden, in a letter to the Guardian: "As a former

headteacher and chief education officer, I believe OFSTED has made a positive contribution. It depresses me that Chris Woodhead appears to demonise those who express qualified support, and ask for a cooler, properly informed debate." [42]

(3) Harvey Goldstein: "OFSTED does not have a good track record. Its own research is of a rather low standard. OFSTED should be prepared to put some effort into allowing independent people to come in. It isn't accountable at the moment." [43]

Each of these is a serious professional, anxious to contribute to the understanding of education, and higher standards of teaching and learning. These are not knee-jerk reactions, from threatened special interests. They have constructive comments to make about how the job could be approached more constructively, and what part OFSTED could play. Yet their comments are not accepted by Woodhead, and OFSTED does not explore any of these possible avenues towards improvement.

His fans in Medialand thought that Woodhead alone had the courage to face important questions, while others were too lazy, cowardly or complacent to face the rigour of his scrutiny. The real picture was very different. Concerned, intelligent professionals were frustrated that he wouldn't get involved in the thinking, the work and the courtesy of intellectual exchange, but instead rushed off in pursuit of the next negative soundbite.


# INTELLECTUAL ARGUMENT

"An aggrieved mantra that is substituted for rational engagement." [44] "...no more than a knee-jerk reflex from those who want to evade the substantive issue.." [45] ..." time would be better spent if we looked at the substantive issues." [46] "Logically flawed, anecdotal and/or politically motivated evidence" [47] .. "If your critics cannot answer your arguments, they will seek to attack you by other means..." [48]

Through Woodhead's fights runs a common theme – the enemy is stupid. Where they are emotional, biased, defensive, he is clear, consistent, logical. But if you are intellectually superior other people will say so; you don't have to claim it for yourself. And if you brag about lying to get a job and keeping it through the support of David Frost, you suggest that intellectual rigour isn't all that's on your mind.

As an education lecturer, he wrote a book of comprehension exercises, "Reading and Responding", which was orthodox, wordy and very similar to others in the field. Over the last ten years he has given a number of lectures, and published a couple of pamphlets – for Politeia, a rightwing group better known for politics than education. Compared with Ted Wragg, Tim Brighouse or Peter Mortimore, he doesn't have titles to his name, sustained pieces of research or argument which develop a position for others to explore.

He could say "I'm a practitioner, not a writer. I'm too busy to get into that." But he doesn't. He was disappointed not to get into Oxbridge and is still, thirty years later, irritated that he didn't get a first-class degree. [49] He clings to the idea that he is a philosopher king, the man who gets things done but who also has ideas, the one who "wins the argument", as Margaret Thatcher liked to say. In this section I look at two arguments, on incompetent teachers and attainment in reading.

Bad teachers are a problem. They bore or depress their pupils, and create pressures on their colleagues.They take up too much of head-teachers' time and energy. And they cannot be happy in their work. Critics attack the idle incompetent, cheerily picking up a pay packet and lazing in the holidays, but to any teacher the idea of doing this job without enjoying any of it is a grim sentence.

For years, there was no way of defining what a bad teacher was, or how bad they needed to be before they had to give up.There was a line to be drawn between a struggling teacher, who could be helped to get better, and an incompetent, who should pack up. It was reasonable to raise the issue.

It could be done with government and/or the unions. It could be done by setting criteria for incompetence, and then measuring the size of the problem. Woodhead's solution was different. He announced, calmly and confidently, that there were 15,000 incompetent teachers.

This got headlines, and a range of instant responses, from "Sack the lot" to "As a proportion, that isn't so surprising. It means that there are x thousand teachers doing a good job." Within teaching, the reaction was more cautious. Are there? And if so, how does he know?

At no point had OFSTED inspectors been asked to find out how many incompetent teachers there were. Woodhead's calculation was based on the number of poor lessons observed, and beyond that on some deduction from the observation of small schools, where he felt it was possible to identify particular teachers within a school, even though the observing inspectors had not been asked to do that.

Prime Minister Major wanted hard evidence, and asked OFSTED inspectors to report incompetent teachers to their heads. The figures were much lower than Woodhead's estimate, but he put that down to the cowardice of inspectors, who had chickened out of naming names.

Since then, Ted Wragg has led a team investigating incompetence, talking to teachers and their managers, looking at various ways of responding to the problem. [50] LEAs have tried to identify and support struggling staff, but to remove incapable teachers from the classroom. In the first year of this scheme, two thirds of local authorities revealed their results. Between them they looked at 3,000 cases. Of these, 600 are no longer teaching, 200 have significantly improved, and 400 were still waiting to hear. 1,800 did not proceed beyond the early stages, but that might have been through improvement, or through leaving the profession. The definite number of certified incompetents, required to leave teaching, was 30.

What's interesting, though, is the absence of Chris Woodhead. He has not been involved in these developments, and has not commented on them. His own role in highlighting the issue seems to have been forgotten, as he explores more promising territory. He has, as they say, moved on.

In 1996 OFSTED was involved in a study of reading in three London boroughs. This was planned as a joint move, with the local authorities, but was then taken over as an OFSTED report, and linked with a government initiative on the teaching of literacy.

Professors Harvey Goldstein and Peter Mortimore, of the London Institute, criticised the lack of longitudinal data. To measure progress you need to have two points of measurement, separated in time, but this report was based on a single observation, measured on one day.

An anonymous OFSTED spokeswoman gave the immediate riposte:

"I don't know why the Institute is doing this. Perhaps for some reason they don't like OFSTED. Chris Woodhead has taken a very strong stance in criticising various things like teacher training." [51] It's a vague but aggressive response, trying to win the argument by suggesting that the other side simply have a grudge. There is no attempt to look at the criticisms of the research.

Jim Rose, Director of Inspection, wrote a long letter, which failed to answer most of Goldstein and Mortimore's criticisms, but ended: "Why on earth are they trying to undermine what OFSTED is doing to give inner city children a better start in life?" [52]

OFSTED shouldn't try to lecture the co-author of "15,000 Hours" about encouragement for inner-city children. Mortimore and Goldstein tried to make their point again:

"The absence of prior intake data for the same pupils precludes any judgements about progress or about the relative effectiveness of schools or teaching methods... It is in everyone's long-term interests that research conforms to recognised quality standards, especially when it may be used to inform policy. This implies taking expert advice prior to designing a study and subjecting research to peer group review, for example via seminars before publication." [53]

It's the traditional route, but there's a reason for it. If the experts get to see it first, then the difficult, important discussions are out of the way before it goes to the newspapers. This means that research which doesn't meet proper standards never gets published, and things that are published are more reliable. It's in the interests of accurate research, but it doesn't suit a lone operator who wants to decide not only his own agenda, but the timetable of the press.

Woodhead's attitude was flippant: "Perhaps professors of education should be as apolitical as chief inspectors of schools." [54]

It's a teenage joke, delivered with a grin, as the speaker knows it's not true but it's smart. But look at what's really political here. This enquiry started as a joint operation between OFSTED and the LEAs, before Woodhead saw the advantage in taking it over, and linking it with government moves on literacy. That meant ditching the LEAs, and saying they were obstructive and complacent. This was part of a letter from Anne Worsley, chair of education for Southwark:

"If there were a conspiracy of silence over failing schools, as chief inspector Chris Woodhead alleges, then this education authority would not be spending money on an enlarged inspection service, the Reading Recovery programme, in-service training on reading, and courses for language co-ordinators...

More baffling is the chief inspector's assertion that teachers are not asking for help with 'effective, direct teaching of reading' when top of the list of requests from Year 2 teachers is 'teaching early reading skills'...

Can this report start a debate about effective teaching somewhat above the level of ludicrously over-simplified and ill-informed comment about trendy teachers and loony-left LEAs? The omens from the press are not promising, and the report itself provides much assertion from the chief inspector, and rather less in the way of evidence than we had hoped for." [55]

That sounds like a reasonable argument about evidence and concern. For power games you have to look at Woodhead himself, who took over the enquiry, and then timed the report to coincide with a government initiative. Finally, he made Gillian Shephard travel to his base for the launch, to show who was really in charge. Political calculation, every inch of the way.

This isn't an academic dispute, where you can read through the evidence and then be faced with a choice of interpretations. All the evidence leads in one direction – that HMCI is simplifying the argument, distorting the evidence to suit himself, refusing to consider serious logical objections to his case. If you follow that route, the long trail of intellectual enquiry, then Woodhead is a fraud.

But if you want a snappier line, he's good value. He's lively, and you can take in quickly what he's saying – "Reading crisis – LEA doesn't care – teach more phonics." The professors are whinging, but that's what you'd expect. He sounds direct and businesslike: less talk, more action. Give the man more power.

Woodhead is a streetfighter, not a researcher. He likes fast movement, quick impact and then to move on to the next skirmish, but that isn't the way you get lasting results. His refusal to accept the disciplines of research isn't simply a failure of etiquette, a charming challenge to outdated custom. It's a serious failure of vision. While he's looking for the insult and the headline, he can't clearly be examining the evidence, so he can't be involved in the argument, or win the respect he seems to crave.

He had a lot of what he wanted. He enjoyed the freedom to comment on a number of issues. He had government backing, protecting him against the pressures which inhibit politicians and civil servants. He had spokespersons to back him, widespread press approval and admiration from his fans. What he couldn't have, if he wanted to keep all those, was a claim to intellectual integrity.


## ONE-WAY TRAFFIC

Time and again, with Woodhead, there are situations which cry out for constructive dialogue – "Isn't this how it is? How could we work together to make it better?" – which are simplified into mutual aggression: "I'm right, you're wrong, end of story."

In 1997, as the long years of Tory government were coming to an end, it seemed incredible that Woodhead could survive the change. There was simply too much in his past record which made him unsuitable for a fresh challenge. Among many letters arguing for a change was this, from David Fontana:

"The objections to Mr. Woodhead arise not from his desire to raise professional standards but from his lack of qualifications – by scholarship or by classroom expertise – for the task. One can have no confidence either in his understanding of research methods or his familiarity with teacher skills. The resounding vote against him ensures his pronouncements can have no credibility with the profession. If Mr. Blunkett persists in his championing of Mr. Woodhead, his own credibility is equally unlikely to survive." [56]

Woodhead was a passionate advocate of subject teaching in primary schools; Labour were pushing a literacy programme that would diminish the emphasis on subject teaching. He had questioned the value of reducing class sizes, and challenged the Labour party estimates of what smaller classes would cost. While Labour wanted a new partnership with professionals in education, Woodhead had alienated large numbers of teachers, teacher trainers and academics. How did he survive?

It's not a rational argument. On the grounds of philosophy and party policy, Woodhead would have gone. On the grounds of personality, too, it's hard to see that David Blunkett, a dogged, responsible puritan, would have much time for this smooth-talking performer with a colourful personal history. As an MP, before she became a minister, Margaret Hodge was a fierce critic of Woodhead. As a past teacher, Estelle Morris must surely be aware of her ex-colleagues' misgivings. So, once again, how did he survive?

We have to look, with Woodhead, right to the top. Tony Blair wants to be elected. He needs marginal votes, of people who wouldn't normally vote Labour, who would buy the Daily Mail and the Sun, and think that teachers need sorting out. He needs something that will signal to these readers, and these editors, that he will be tough with the teachers. He needs a mascot. "Labour sources say that it is unlikely that we will hear any criticism of OFSTED or Woodhead before the election for fear that this will imply that the party is soft on standards." [57]

Some headteachers suggested that tough scrutiny might work both ways. Maybe OFSTED themselves should be inspected, graded by schools. Some inspectors thought that was reasonable, but not Woodhead: "I feel an appalling sense of deja vu. You have the teaching unions repeatedly, year after year, wanting to try to remove OFSTED. There is nowhere to hide for headteachers, and in my humble opinion, there should be nowhere to hide." [58]

"Humble" isn't the first word that springs to mind. Weary, menacing and smug, maybe, and certainly not sensitive. But that's what is needed, to respond to new demands. The Macpherson report made a lot of people think again about racism. OFSTED revised their framework, but many reports did not take account of the new climate, and the CRE produced a critical report:

"Race equality has yet to become a central part of the corporate culture and discourse within OFSTED. There is... no mention of Ofsted's lead in the prevention of racism through education in the 1998-99 annual report of HMCI." [59]

It would be reasonable to say: "We're working at it. We're not there yet, but we'll take this on board." At first an OFSTED spokesman said that they would await full publication before responding, but then they couldn't resist the urge to get their retaliation in first: "The report was very, very poorly researched, based on a false premise, a false understanding of what OFSTED's powers and duties are. It is fundamentally not our job to prevent and address racism in schools. To base your whole report on that renders it meaningless." [60]

Woodhead was not impressed. "The CRE research was flawed. They looked at 30 out of 30,000 inspections. They talked to six inspectors. I'm not pretending that every report gets to every detail of truth in every school, but I don't accept the accusation that we don't take racism seriously." [61]

It's a shame that the CRE researchers couldn't speak to Woodhead, so that he could put them right. That way, we might get a more accurate picture of how OFSTED operates with regard to racism. They did in fact ask for an interview when they were drawing up their report, but he was "too busy" to see them. [62] And when he did finally engage in a dialogue with the head of CRE, Woodhead's tone was lofty and abusive. He used the word 'ignoramus', and Gurbux Singh wrote to say that he was "amazed and disappointed" by his "personally insulting, patronising, rude and sanctimonoius behaviour." [63]

Woodhead can apologise, but it's rare. Durham education authority complained about an OFSTED inspector, and Woodhead tried to influence the result of the investigation. Keith Mitchell describes the outcome:

"Mr. Woodhead intervened in the complaint before OFSTED's investigation was complete, to express a view in OFSTED's favour and directed the investigator to communicate his view to the complainant. OFSTED's own adjudicator judged this as 'unwarranted' and 'implicitly threatening.' Last month – three years after the original complaint, and when, throughout, OFSTED had found no fault with itself – we received an unreserved written apology from both OFSTED and HMCI." [64]

At no point was Woodhead answerable to anyone. Despite requests from the LEA there was no independent arbitration, and although she supported the complaint OFSTED's own adjudicator was not allowed to interview him. He was a law unto himself, above question and beyond reproach.

## THE WOODHEAD AFFAIR

Early in 1999, Woodhead seemed to have come unstuck. He was talking to a conference at Exeter, and a student teacher asked him about affairs between pupils and teachers. This was topical, since the government was considering laws to make them illegal, up to the age of 18. So the safe reply was to say that you should stay away from such things.

Woodhead does not play safe. He thought that while unwise, such affairs could also be "educative and experiential" for both parties. The report of this comment reached his ex-wife, who had brought up their daughter on her own after Woodhead had left her to live with a girl with whom he had started an affair when she was his sixth-form pupil. Cathy Woodhead, whose silence had protected him for twenty years, decided it was time to tell the truth.

The story had been covered by the News of the World in 1995. At the time, Woodhead had begged a lift with a reporter, to smuggle him away from press attention. He and Amanda Johnston then signed a statement, swearing that their affair only started in December 1976, three months after they had both left the school.

Cathy Woodhead said that she was told about it in April 1976, when it had already been going for some time. In August 1976, Woodhead had suggested that they all live together, and in September Cathy Woodhead went to a solicitor to discuss a possible divorce. Her statement encouraged others to come forward, including Woodhead's former colleagues. When the News of the World story had first appeared, they had been threatened with legal action, but with the publication of Cathy Woodhead's statement, his attitude was more relaxed: "My ex wife can say what she likes".[65]

The press pieced together a story, starting from an obvious affair at an Arvon writing course in October 1975. There was open concern at the school for the rest of that academic year, and some complaints to the head, as a result of which she expressed her concern to Woodhead. A friend of his confirmed that at a camping holiday in the summer of 1976 Woodhead and Amanda Johnston were sharing the same tent.

Woodhead's response to all this was very curious. Somehow, it had to be someone else's fault. Maybe the original question was a plant, or Woodhead was just trying to reassure a worried student, or perhaps there was a conspiracy by ex-teachers connected with the Labour Party. Woodhead pleaded with his wife to desist, as the scandal might reduce their daughter's inheritance. He was reluctant to go to court, because this would cause embarrassment to Amanda Johnston.

There was no sense that he was responsible. When the crisis was at its height he said "There's nothing I can do." But there was. Cathy Woodhead's long article in in the Mail on Sunday [66] makes it clear that there were times when she could reasonably have expected an apology, an admission of selfishness, or even an honest conversation. Despite promises and delays, she got none of these. In March 2000, one of the conditions Woodhead laid down for a detailed interview with the Sunday Times was that they should not speak to Cathy Woodhead. What on earth did he still have to fear?

In a similar situation, Robin Cook had been given an instant ultimatum to resolve the break-up of his marriage. Woodhead got a better deal. He apologised for his original statement about experiential affairs, and that put him back in line with government policy. Nobody forced him to talk with his ex-wife. His evasion was officially backed, and protecting his story became a government priority. There was a sense of the effort involved in David Blunkett's comments after Woodhead had resigned:

"Of course I didn't want Chris Woodhead to hand in his resignation, having spent the most enormous political energy and time defending him and the role of OFSTED over the last three and a half years, including through the terrible trauma of eight weeks of Chris' private life." [67] Now, why would that be such an effort, if Woodhead were telling the truth?

In April 1999, it seemed quite possible that he wasn't. As mounting publicity uncovered more evidence, there were twelve witnesses who backed Cathy Woodhead's version of events, and none supporting Woodhead. In a formal statement David Blunkett claimed to remain aloof from the whole business – "It is not for me as Secretary of State to intervene in the rights and wrongs of a divorce which took place 23 years ago; nor to side with either Mr. or Mrs. Woodhead in a dispute about the facts of the case." [68]

But he found it hard to stay neutral, speaking of Cathy Woodhead's "angry and distraught" comments, which he saw as part of "a vile campaign." But this wasn't about marital disputes 23 years ago; it was about signed statements 4 years ago, as a result of which Woodhead kept his job. If the statement was false, Woodhead had lied to his employer. If he had conspired to sign a false affidavit, he was liable to a maximum sentence of life imprisonment. Even Melanie Phillips agreed that if he had lied, he should resign.

If Woodhead was telling the truth, it was surely in his interests that the press reports be investigated and his name be cleared. But Blunkett refused to look beyond the original statement, so in May 1999 the NAHT asked the police to investigate whether or not a crime had been committed.

On November 25th. 1999 I was working on this book, and realised that I would not be able to comment on the outcome of The Woodhead Affair. I rang Scotland Yard, who told me that the case was still under investigation, by the Organised Crime Group. When asked how long that would take, the cheery guess was that "It could take years".

So I was surprised to read next day a small report in the TES that the Director of Public Prosecutions had decided that there was no case to answer. I wrote to him, asking when this decision had been taken, and got a reply from his department, the Crown Prosecution Service, saying that "the CPS was never presented with a file in relation to any allegations against Mr. Chris Woodhead and the decision not to proceed with any criminal proceedings was not taken by us." [69]

I wrote to the police, asking when the decision had been taken. Det. Supt. Hunt replied, saying that it was "some time ago." This seemed vague, so I asked for a specific date. No reply. I wrote again, and was told that the decision had been taken "in October 1999, following our receipt of written advice in connection with the matter from the CPS." [70]

Since Det. Supt. Hunt's first letter had assured me that the decision "has of course been communicated to the relevant parties", I thought that the NAHT could help. Their office insisted that only David Hart could speak on this matter, and they gave me the number of his mobile. I rang him on Dec. 23rd, apparently two months after the decision had been taken.

"I am not at liberty to comment on the Chris Woodhead enquiry..." Maybe not, I said, but since I have a letter here from Det. Supt. Hunt., saying that this was resolved in October... "I am not at liberty to comment on the Chris Woodhead enquiry."

So, what was going on? You would expect the press files to help, but they don't. There is no coverage, no speculation, nobody reporting the resolution of a story which was front page material in March. There is only a tangled mix-up, where the CPS and the police seem unable to agree on what happened to the file, and when the decision was taken. Is this simply incompetence, or had someone been told that there would be no media interest? And who has the power to ask David Hart to be silent, two months after the conclusion of an enquiry he had every right to request?

Whatever the balance between conspiracy and cock-up, it's clear that strong pressure was exerted to make sure that Chris Woodhead stayed in his job. From the start his fans saw his possible departure as disastrous. John Clare wrote: "The life-chances of tens of thousands of children have been improved by his actions." [71] Polly Toynbee thought "He is set fair to halve the numbers of illiterate and innumerate primary school leavers." [72] Most telling of all, "a close government apologist" told Libby Purves "Look, we can't afford to let something like this bring down Woodhead. He's the only hope for education in this country." [73]

So, when a serious allegation was made, "there was no inquiry, no suspension, no police interview or any attempt to examine evidence that he had lied on oath." [74] Woodhead was the mascot, and there was a powerful campaign to keep him in place. Cathy Woodhead, having taken a difficult decision to tell the truth, could be insulted and dismissed. The BBC had started on a profile of her: "filming for this programme was completed at great expense until it was abruptly pulled on orders from above..." [75]

People working in the police, CPS, the NAHT, were told to be careful what they said. The media is packed with reporters who know this story, but can't or won't be part of telling it. Labour party sources continue to turn interesting somersaults as to how much they know, and when they knew it. In November 2000, "The Sunday Times even suggested that Blunkett had threatened to gag Woodhead by releasing details of his affair in the 1970s with his pupil at Gordano School in Bristol. (This story was immediately denied by the education department, no doubt because it had on numerous occasions denied that it had any new information on the affair.)." [76] But by February 2001, with the prospect of an unleashed Woodhead savaging Blunkett and Blair, the Sunday Times were again reporting that "sources warned that if the assault becomes too personal towards David Blunkett and Blair, ministers will counterattack using information about Woodhead's private life." [77] Somebody needs to get their act together.

The coordinated effort to retain Woodhead implies a deep faith that he was worth it. So, it's interesting to look at what he did while this story was being buried. In June 1999 he defied the select committee. In July he chose not to attend the Teachers' Awards ceremony. In October he first challenged the expansion of higher education, and then urged that pupils should be allowed to leave school early in order to learn a trade. In January 2000 he suggested that Clause 28 had caused no problems for teachers, and in February he wrote an article for the Church Times, saying that it was necessary for schools to uphold moral values. None of these views were supported by evidence from OFSTED, some directly contradicted government policy, and one was immediately overruled by David Blunkett.

For two years running the parliamentary select committee criticised Woodhead for public statements which were not based on OFSTED evidence. He retorted that they had not provided examples of this in their summary, although there were plenty in the verbatim report of the sessions. Estelle Morris tried to ease things with an innocent declaration of faith in tradition: "There is a long-standing convention that HM Inspectors' advice and comment on educational standards is in every case underpinned by inspection evidence." [78]

On September 4th. 2000 The Guardian's front page headline ran "A-LEVELS TOO EASY, SAYS WOODHEAD." A detailed interview inside made it clear that this was a personal view, unrelated to OFSTED work. Woodhead even proposed a new enquiry to determine whether or not standards had declined over time, without acknowledging his own role in ensuring the failure of the previous attempt. Students with good results were angry. Teachers and union leaders waited for Estelle Morris to notice that this comment was not underpinned by evidence. They waited for Tony Blair to say that Woodhead had stepped out of line. They waited in vain.

Chris Woodhead was unique. No other country has found it necessary to develop and reward a devil's advocate on this scale. Scotland and Wales have systems of school inspection which operate without a jester licensed to mock the work of their teachers. His role was not about reality, but about image. And the supreme irony is that the man who made his reputation as a fearless critic, the man they couldn't gag, could only be kept in his post by the forceful backing of a false statement and the brutal suppression of the truth.

1    Peter Wilby, quoted in Guardian 7.4.97
2    Times 13.4.99
3    TES 13.11.98
4    You and Yours, Radio 4, 14.10.99
5    Guardian 16.4.98
6    Daily Telegraph 23.6.98
7    Times 5.7.96
8    Guardian 14.12.95
9    TES 18.9.98
10   TES 5.7.96
11   TES 5.3.93
12   TES 5.3.93

13    Guardian 18.4.95
14    Guardian 1.2.95
15    Sunday Times 19.3.00
16    Mail on Sunday 14.3.99
17    Daily Mail 18.9.00
18    Times 7.5.96
19    Observer 5.5.96
20    Sun 3.11.00
21    Observer 14.4.96
22    TES 22.11.96
23    TES 29.11.96
24    TES 30.4.99
25    TES 21.7.00
26    TES 5.7.96
27    Observer 12.5.96
28    Sunday Times 19.3.00
29    TES 13.10.00
30    Guardian 22.2.00
31    Observer 11.4.99
32    Observer 6.4.97
33    TES 18.12.98
34    Guardian 6.2.96
35    Guardian 6.2.96
36    Guardian 18.4.95
37    Guardian 28.2.96
38    TES 12.2.00
39    Observer 12.5.96
40    Guardian 18.4.98
41    TES 17.5.96
42    Guardian 23.6.98
43    TES 8.5.98
44    TES 5.7.96
45    TES 4.10.96
46    Guardian 12.2.98
47    TES 13.11.98
48    Guardian 23.4.99
49    Sunday Times 19.3.00
50    "Failing Teachers", by E.Wragg et al, published by Routledge
51    TES 10.25.96
52    TES 8.11.96
53    TES 22.11.96
54    TES 25.10.96
55    Letter to TES, 17.5.96
56    Guardian 2.6.97
57    TES 7.5.96
58    Guardian 31.5.00
59    Guardian 17.7.00

60    Guardian 17.7.00
61    Guardian 21.7.00
62    Guardian 20.7.00
63    Observer 29.10.00
64    Letter to the Guardian, 5.7.00
65    Guardian 8.3.99
66    Mail on Sunday 7.3.99
67    Times 4.11.00
68    Statement, 16.4.99
69    Letter 5.1.00
70    Letter 26.1.00
71    Daily Telegraph 13.4.99
72    Guardian 14.4.99
73    Times 13.4.99
74    Sunday Times 19.3.00
75    Private Eye 17.11.00
76    Private Eye 17.11.00
77    Sunday times 25.2.01
78    DfEE response to select committee report, 25.7.00

## Chapter 5:

# HOW DO WE KNOW IF IT WORKS?

## TESTS AND TABLES

"Here we go again. This week's publication of the GCSE league tables has produced the usual reaction from the usual suspects. If it isn't Doug McAvoy it's David Hart. It's a rule of thumb that applies as much to education as any other walk of life: if the received wisdom says one thing, work on the assumption that the opposite is true. League tables are a prime example, and the attitude of the educational establishment remains typically wrong-headed.

When the league tables were first introduced in 1992, there was almost universal opprobrium directed at John Patten, the then education secretary. Labour spokesmen pledged themselves to abolition and the teaching unions threatened strikes and the end of civilisation as we know it. But one small, weak, ignored constituency wondered what all the fuss was about, and what was wrong with knowing how good a school was at getting its children through exams. Parents." [1]

That's Stephen Pollard, putting the case for league tables. He's head of research at the Social Market Foundation, but he doesn't sound like a researcher. This is the voice of an ordinary bloke, cutting through the crap. And as soon as you say "Yes, but..." you are branded. You are part of the education establishment, the conspiracy to cover up the truth.

"Parents". It's a good trick, that punchline at the end, but is it true? Did parents all welcome the publication of test results in league tables? One survey said that 32% thought the tests were of benefit, but 36% thought they were of no benefit. Tests set by classroom teachers, however, were seen as helpful by 86% of parents. So it isn't as simple as Pollard says.

There was a time, he recalls, when Labour's spokesperson for education, Ann Taylor, might have scrapped the league tables.

"And then something terrible happened to Ms. Taylor and the other friends of the NUT. Tony Blair was elected leader of the Labour party. It was inconceivable that Tony Blair would sanction the scrapping of league tables. He has never been in the grip of the educational establishment. He understands that no one is better qualified to push schools and parents upwards than a parent. League tables – and the information they contain – are a prerequisite.

The argument is over. Freedom of information has won. The squeals that we hear this week are the death cries of dinosaurs." [2]

It's very aggressive. Pollard thinks that teachers and union leaders know the truth, but are determined to suppress it. They are stupid and predictable – "the usual suspects", "wrong-headed" "dinosaurs" – and can safely be ignored. Tony Blair has enabled parents to push schools and pupils upward, and "the argument is over."

League tables were launched in that tone of voice. They were a part of the Thatcher raid, giving education back to the consumers. Teachers were producers, not to be trusted, so the league tables would tell the truth about their schools, whether they liked it or not. And there were enough parents who felt confused or angry about their children's education for that to look like a popular move.

Gillian Shephard welcomed the 1996 tables with a confident assertion of their power: "the tables have consistently driven up standards, school by school, college by college." [3] She wasn't put off by the fact that this enthusiasm was not shared by the head teacher at the most successful school:

"The tables are a cancer on the body of education, putting pressure on schools to enter good pupils for an unnecessary number of exams. That's not education – that's cramming." [4]

At the other end of the scale, too, they failed to inspire. Brian Lippitt, head teacher at Ramsgate School in Kent, had worked hard for three years. He saw the proportion of pupils gaining 5 A-G grades at this secondary modern rise from 30 percent to 63 per cent. "The message is that this place is recovering and doing well." But the league tables don't want to know about grades from A-G. The small number of pupils with five grades from A-C put his school at the bottom. "One of the negative effects is that I am going to have to spend a lot of time building them up again." [5]

What teachers think doesn't matter. If the theory is right, parents will look at the league tables and choose the best school for their children. Here are two who don't fit the pattern:

"I am a parent who does not feel I will be making an informed choice by using league tables to decide at which school I should aim my son. Can you not see how unethical is the whole shoddy business of school league tables?"

(Hussain Mohamed, Surrey.) [6]

"I chose my son's secondary school two years ago on the basis of fairly detailed investigations and visits... Had I made the decision based on league tables I would probably have made a different choice. My fear is that in the future that is exactly what will happen. Parents will see the results, see that my son's school has not done well in the league tables, and opt for other schools."

(Angela Phillips, London.) [7]

Intelligent parents try to work out what's in the interests of their children – and the league tables are getting in the way. According to the theory, teachers are lazy cowards shying away from the bright light of assessment. Not this one:

"I always favoured a combination of primary teacher assessment, any year 6 nationally validated test results plus at least one NFER group reading test result. This test was taken a few days after entry to year 7, to check on actual level of functioning after ther summer holiday. If time and funding allowed, a group numeracy test would also prove very useful." [8]

Does this sound like someone who is hostile to measurement? If you spoke to her at a parents' evening, would you think she was hiding the truth? I doubt it. This sounds like a professional, who wants quality assessment. And that's her objection to reliance on national tests, not that they're "too much", but that they're not good enough to be the only measure.

This is a complicated issue, and the simple answer just won't do. Caricatures are easy, because they save us having to think more deeply. They can also stir up powerful feelings. But as a basis for policy they are unreliable, and if we want to see clearly then we have to ditch them.

According to the league table argument there are thousands of lazy teachers, who just need a kick up the backside to boot them into action. But this crude attack picks on schools, teachers and pupils who don't deserve it. Every time tables are published there are new questions: What about appeals against wrong marking, which are announced later? What about independent schools, whose GCSE candidates aren't all in year 11? What about pupils who move from school to school?

The argument is far from over, and Gillian Shephard's simple model of competition driving up standards doesn't work. Yes, standards went up during this period, but they also went up in Scotland, which didn't have league tables. A study by Durham University, which looked at primary schools in both countries, found that "publishing school league tables can narrow the curriculum, force teachers to concentrate on borderline pupils and increase the blame culture." [9]

Maybe the results would have gone up anyway. Maybe paying a lot of attention makes a difference. Maybe teachers get better with practice. There was improvement, sometimes dramatic, but it wasn't always sustained, and the greatest improvement wasn't in the areas of fiercest competition. That's the value of research, that it can tell you if a reasonable hunch is true.

If Gillian Shephard were right, there would be a brief period of fuss and then the tests should have "bedded in". But three years later the fuss was very much alive, sparked off by incidents like this:

- Half the schools in the London borough of Wandsworth were given leaked details of this week's national curriculum tests, in the

biggest exercise in cheating since testing was introduced. [10]
- There were complaints that the KS2 reading test was biased by its choice of content against inner city children, and by its format in favour of boys. A school in Godmanchester made their year 6 pupils do the 1998 test as well as the 1999 one – and results were much better for 1999.
- The KS3 reading test, for 14 year olds, was very hard. A reading test said the passage would suit a reading age of 16.
- The Society of Authors complained about chief examiners making money from 'authorised' textbooks of the courses they examine.
- "Headteachers have condemned national test marking procedures after pupils scripts were lost and scores were added up incorrectly." [11]
- Teacher unions said that specialist schools did better in league tables because they could select their pupils.

Stephen Pollard might think this is "just more teacher whinging". But these are different, serious worries, and they undermine his confidence that tests will simply tell us how well children have learnt. Making the tests important puts pressure on pupils and teachers, encouraging dishonesty and putting at risk the accuracy of the test.

In New York City Edward Stancik, special investigator, commented on the 52 teachers who helped their pupils to cheat in tests. "Their purpose was simply to improve their own reputations and further their own careers by creating the illusion that they were doing a good job. By no means do I think we have caught all the cheaters." [12]

And then there's politics. This government has made test scores the key evidence for deciding whether or not it is doing a good job. If they get to a certain figure Blunkett will stay; if they don't, he'll go. So, will officials calmly sit back to see what happens?

"Ministers yesterday described the organisation of last month's English tests as a 'fiasco' that threatened the achievement of education targets set by Tony Blair as a key test of Labour's performance in government." [13] The QCA had taken out of the tests questions which children had found too easy. This gave them lower scores, so later their scores were put up again. Had the results been fixed?

Mr. Blunkett, reported to be "livid", "is understood to have told colleagues that the QCA were "out of their tiny minds to do what they did. If they had any intelligence, they would have retained the easy questions and increased the pass mark slightly. Nobody would have batted an eyelid."

You have to ask if this is Blunkett the educationist, or Blunkett the manager of news. The pressure comes from the bet, that Blunkett will resign from office if 80% of 11 year olds don't reach level 4 by 2002. Nobody asked him to make this promise, and many see it as foolhardy and irrelevant. He could do a brilliant job, and then find that 79% of pupils had reached that level. Would resignation be a good thing for the country?

A QCA spokesman said "the pass level has gone down very slightly this year because the NFER advised us to keep the level threshold at the same standard of performance that mark should be lowered to 47 rather than 51 as last year. Because test questions must change every year it is impossible to set tests at exactly the same level, which is why we have to make these kinds of adjustment every year." [14]

It sounds like a fiddle, but it isn't. It's a reasonable piece of assessment process, but because it is honest about relative assessment and the need for adjustment, it casts doubt on the idea of tests as a simple measure. It also undermines the dramatic nature of Blunkett's bet. Nobody was surprised when the enquiry announced that the results had not been fixed, but there was still plenty to worry about:

"The keystage 2 English test was weakened by unclear illustrations and ambiguous wording, teachers and markers told the inquiry team. Teachers should be more involved in test development, the panel found. The team was also concerned that QCA officials debating where to draw the pass mark were allowed to consider how many more children would he pushed over the 'pass' threshold. To the surprise of the enquiry team, officials also discussed whether each boost in results would 'seem plausible' compared to previous years' test results." [15]

So the markers aren't just marking. They're thinking about the news significance of possible decisions they might take, and while that's not criminal it is likely to distort their judgement. There's so much pressure on these results that it's hard to get them right, and "the present timetable puts pressure on markers, partly to give schools and others as much time as possible to use the results of the tests. This trade-off threatens the quality of marking and needs to be reviewed." [16]

The closer you get, the less simple it seems. We are not just talking about "how children are doing". We are talking about a £30 million pound industry, still in the development process, where a lot of things can go wrong. Steve Devrell, an experienced teacher of year 6 children, looks at his pupils' SAT results:

"Two years ago, literacy hour was introduced in our schools. Assuming it takes two years to get such an undertaking working efficiently, we should now be seeing the benefits in SATs results and – surprise surprise – they have improved.

Children who I confidently predicted would be solid 3s have come out as solid 4s and those whom I expected to be solid 4s have gained a 5... Conversely, the results of numeracy are generally worse than expected. Consider the facts. Numeracy hour only started this year. Schools are still fine-tuning their numeracy plans, so the results are unlikely to improve considerably until next year... What has clearly happened is that numeracy levels have been kept artificially low to make them look good next year when numeracy hour is funtioning efficiently, vindicating the Government's initiatives. The discrepancies are so apparent this year that a colleague has worked out that it was 10% harder to achieve a level 4 in numeracy than last year." [17]

People setting and marking tests make choices, all the time, and it all depends which choices they make. Chris Whetton defends national tests against Chris Woodhead's view that they are unreliable:

"As with any assessment, the tests could be made more reliable. This could be done by having more questions and covering more ground - but testing would then take more time. The tests could be made more reliable by changing their nature, for example, to multiple choice. But this would produce tests which were less valid. For example, it is more valid to test writing by getting children to write than by asking them multiple choice questions about writing.

Mr. Woodhead needs to say what he is proposing. Does he want to make the tests take longer or does he want to make them less valid ?" [18]

A good test has to be both valid and reliable, and that means bodies, time and cash. It is now likely that future A level assessment will have more multiple choice questions, simply because there are not enough markers qualified to assess essays. That would be a huge change, and it would make a big difference to lessons, but the reasons for it have nothing to do with education.

## PROBLEMS WITH THE TESTS

So the tests aren't just there, as part of the landscape. They are part of the Thatcher raid. They were devised fast, under political pressure, in defiance of expert opinion. They were also trying to do too much. When this started, in 1993, Peter Newsam wrote a clear analysis, which began like this:

"When a muddle develops, it is sometimes wise to take a blank sheet of paper and start again. Why do we test children?" [19]

He then goes on to subdivide that "we", into the five groups that assessment is intended to serve – government, local authorities, the individual school, the parent and the pupil. He is not concerned with the media. Each of these five groups needs different assessment, for various reasons. But they can't all be served by crude central tests, with publicised results.

Newsam also quotes Rev. Edward Thring, headmaster of Uppingham, writing in 1869 about how testing affects teaching. The teacher becomes merely a "clerk of the works":

"There is the prescribed packet to be learnt. If a boy does not learn it, it is no business of the clerk of the works, beyond punishing him for not doing it. This soon passes into a neglect of those who cannot, or will not, pigeonhole the daily quota; this naturally advances to finding them very much in the way; the next step is that in the interests of the better boys (so runs the story) they must be got rid of. So the school failures are turned out, and the great authority quoted to support the practice; and all the energy of the place is expended on the strong and active, who will distinguish themselves in the knowledge scramble." [20]

Critics of teachers accuse them of clinging to the past. But what they are fighting is not modernisation, but an old, familiar enemy. They fight the obsession with tests because they have been there before – they have seen junior schools dominated by the eleven plus, poor readers and early leavers left to fend for themselves, and bright pupils gaining passes at the cost of being bored. Teachers, more than anyone, should be able to learn from history.

It also helps to look beyond England. In Ireland, in January '98, the education minister Michael Martin drafted legislation which would prohibit the use of league tables. In Northern Ireland, after extensive consultation with parents, teachers and governors, league tables have been scrapped. [21] In Scotland, which does not have league tables, the proportion of school leavers gaining five or more passes in Highers went from 4% in 1965 to 18% in 1997. In 1962, 75% of leavers had no recognised qualifications; by 1997, the number had dropped to 7%.

Cynics would say the exams got easier. The research says that the following factors were at work:

(1) the children of better-educated parents do better
(2) comprehensive schools were popular, and tapped into excluded talent
(3) the birthrate in disadvantaged social groups was falling
(4) the demand for education had been stimulated (eg. through the expansion of higher education).
(5) reforms of curriculum and assessment favoured pupil motivation.

Scottish research come up with this information, and has helped the Scottish office, without losing its independence. So, the system works, and maintains public confidence. [22] To an English reader, it's a tantalising vision.

The testing fans say we need to catch up, but they don't say that our competitors do less testing than we do. "Teenagers in England and Wales spend more time on exams than pupils in any other country." Anne West points out that across the channel they are much more prepared to trust assessment by teachers. [23] We do more testing, and then assume that if we don't catch up, it means we have to test even more. So, after KS 3 tests at 14, we may have tests at 12 and 13. But why not every term? Why not every week? There has to be a balance between teaching and testing, and you can't test something until you've taught it.

Alan Smithers has an overview of what we've done. "We were under-testing, in that we only had an exam at the end of compulsory education, and really no national testing in between, so we didn't know what was happening. But since tests were introduced at 7, 11 and 14, things have moved on.

We decided that as the tests we put in were probably benefitting the education system we have just started adding more and more and now it looks as though the whole concept has gone away from tests as an indicator of student progress to becoming the main purpose of education... Education is really about the basic ways of making sense of life in preparation for an uncertain future. You don't develop that individual sense of responsibility for your life if you are constantly being tested." [24]

The main model is America, where the testing industry is forcing big changes to what is taught and how. Bob Schaeffer describes the effect of blanket testing: "Schools devolve into being test-preparation centres focused on the relatively narrow curriculum. The closer you get to tests, the more it's drill-and-kill, meaning it's mind-numbing, it stifles thinking, and it turns kids off." [25]

"Across the country, the intellectual life is being squeezed out of schools in the name of raising standards", says Alfie Kohn, an educational adviser and author. "People without the first idea of how kids learn have adopted a top-down, heavy-handed, test-driven, business-influenced approach to raising standards, which is making great schools worse as the curriculum is hijacked in an effort to raise scores on tests." [26]

In Texas, McNeil and Valenzula found that "white, middle-class children continue to receive an education appropriate for their age and grade level, while poor and minority children are devoting class time to practice test materials." One large Hispanic, low-performing high school with a severe shortage of textbooks spent $20,000 (most of its resources budget) on a set of test-revision packs.

In some schools the curriculum for nine-year olds has been virtually replaced by daily practice of the five-paragraph essay that figures in the test. Each paragraph begins with a topic sentence, has three more sentences, and then ends with a concluding sentence. Keeping to this pattern is more important than having your own ideas. One teacher told McNeil and Valenzula that her children were "writing for someone sitting in a cubicle, counting sentences and indentations." [27]

Other experts, here and in the states, might disagree. But that's the point. This is not a simple area where the tests will tell us the truth and we can stop worrying. We can't stop worrying. We might start by finding answers to the following questions:

Are they properly carried out and accurately marked?
Are their results fairly presented?
Which areas of learning do they leave out?
Are different tests consistent with each other?
What effect do tests have on young people?
Are tests the best way of raising academic standards?
What effect do tests have on the pattern of work?
How do they affect the teacher's work?
Do league tables guarantee parents a choice of school?

Each of the above questions has been stimulated by at least one news cutting. But behind each cutting is a bigger story, maybe a book or research project, where professionals have worked to clarify a particular area. Putting the questions is a start, but to get answers you have to do the work, the reading, the discussion, and get properly involved.

At this point the impatient government spokesman says "Well, what's the alternative? Do you want to go back?" Back is the gloomy past, when education was not a government priority and teachers were less accountable. That is not the only choice. There are plenty of alternatives, but looking at alternatives is not part of the current management style. Here is one, from a letter to the TES:

"First, to record trends over time and to see how far government targets are being met, exactly the same tests should be administered each year in the same way to a nationally representative sample of 11-year olds, not by their class teachers, but confidentially by outside testers... Second, to give parents the information many want, the QCA should commission short, standardised tests related to 'basic' reading, number and oracy skills, and require schools to administer these and report to parents on an annual or less frequent basis." [28]

It's short, reasonable and a lot cheaper than what we have. It's calm and less likely to provide headlines, but it would provide useful information. What's wrong with it? Have the government considered it? We are never told.

I go back to my own experience. Here are three assessment memories of mine.

(1) When the tests started, before league tables, there was talk about teacher assessment and the tests, and how the two could be made equally important. (They never got the same budgets, but that's a different story). The LEA set up a KS 3 assessment session for the English teachers from local schools. We met round small tables, and tried to agree on which levels to award each other's folders.

Many of us were used to this, because we had been involved in marking coursework at GCSE. It brought back the value of mixing with other colleagues, the benefits of literally looking at each other's work. New teachers, teachers who felt isolated in their own schools, teachers who might have worried that they were getting out of touch – all could gain from the communal process. This gets you agreed marking standards, but it does far more than that. It's a way of teachers learning, using each other and the work to get better. And league tables have killed it dead.

(2) In the summer of 1997 I was teaching "Romeo and Juliet." This was one of the set plays for my year 9 group, but I liked it anyway. I'm a lifelong Shakespeare fan, and I write my own plays. I want pupils to do improvised drama to explore situations, and to see how Shakespeare explores them. There's this wonderful scene, Act 3 scene 5, where Juliet becomes isolated from her family, and in turn we see how each of her possible allies turns against her... but I'm getting carried away.

Luckily, the kids were carried away too. Not by me, but by Claire

Danes and Leonardo di Caprio, and Baz Lerman's film. The most unlikely candidates came back from the cinema to accost me in corridors and swear to their mates about how this film just had to be seen. So, there's all sorts of directions in which a creative, talented English teacher might move. And what do I do?

I concentrate on one scene, till they're bored out of their minds. I issue vocab lists, as if this was Spanish or German, because lots of the words don't make sense. And I train them to write an essay about a play, because that is how the government has decided to test their understanding of Shakespeare. I know it could be so much better than this, and I'm not alone:

"All too often, it seems to me that Shakespeare's plays, for instance, are spoilt for children by detailed analysis,when instead they should be experiencing the rounded nature of expression and the natural music of the words."

That's David Blunkett. [29] But if he thinks that, and I think that, and my pupils think that, why are we going through this farce?

(3) Before that, I ran meetings for parents about the introduction of keystage tests, and the information they would provide. We also talked about teacher assessment, and the possibility of getting more specific details at parents' evenings.

When the levels actually started, I can remember one parent impatiently demanding to know her son's level. She really seemed to think that this would give her an extra lever, a chance to get more for her child. We gave her the level. And then what? Was she going to return at weekly intervals to see if it had changed?

My main memory is a sense of anti-climax. Most parents didn't have this anger or impatience. They were interested to know how their children were doing, but if I gave them a number they would say "What does that mean?" In a class where more than half the pupils are at level 5, it's a good question. So I'd go back to talking about writing and reading, talking and listening, pieces of work, ways of tackling problems – the old stuff that I did before, which was also what most parents wanted to hear. We had had a lot of sound and fury, headlines and pamphlets, but nothing really had changed.

## CALLING IN THE EXPERTS

Some people are only happy when they're gloomy. If exam results get worse, then we're in decline. But if exam results get better, then it must be because the exams are getting easier, so we're still in decline. There is no way you can win.

In August 2000 A level results continued to rise, for the eighteenth year in succession. The Tories called for an enquiry, to see if standards have slipped. Where have they been?

There was an enquiry, but most people don't know about it, because it didn't come to a clear conclusion. Setting up an enquiry is fine, but it depends who's doing the enquiring. In some cases, you only have to mention a name for opponents to say "Oh, him! Well you know what he's going to say..." Keeping everybody happy, by including the particular expert they think of as objective, is not a simple matter.

The Standards Over Time committee was set up by Gillian Shephard in 1995. She shared it between two bodies, OFSTED and SCAA, who were invited to come together to agree by March '96 an answer to the question "Have exams got easier?" They had access to past exam papers, and had to take account in changes of syllabus and teaching method.

By June '96 a draft report had been written, but there was still some dispute. Alan Dobson, leader of the OFSTED team, was replaced by Chris Woodhead. In August there were reports that traditionalists on the committee felt that they were being pressured into producing a "whitewash". Eventually, they settled for an exhausted draw, where "Mr Tate insisted there was evidence to show no falling off of A level standards over the past decade", while Mr. Woodhead said "nothing had been proved." So much for government experts, working under political pressure.

But there is such a thing as expertise, and professionals whose job this is come up with findings which help us to think more clearly.

(1) Professor Peter Tymms, reader in Education at the University of Durham, said that children achieving 50 per cent in the key stage 1 reading test could have a true score of anything from 17 to 79 percent.

"This is an extraordinary range of uncertainty to accompany an official reading test. ..Many children are likely to have been misjudged and parents will be unaware of this. It is a problem for schools because they are unable to benefit from high-quality information. The unreliability of this test means that value-aded scores will be suspect and there will inevitably be difficulties with target-setting." [30]

(2) "Peter Robinson, chief economist of the Institute of Public Policy Research, concludes that there is no connection between educational attainment and economic performance. He argues that Sweden, for example, has higher standards of literacy than Britain, but its economy is no stronger. The United States, one of the strongest economies, has some of the lowest standards in maths... David Blunkett and Chris Woodhead have promoted the adoption of traditional teaching methods from South-East Asian tiger economises only to see those economies crash." [31]

(3) Julie Davies and Ivy Brember, of Manchester University, argue expenditure has failed to raise standards of primary maths. "The fact that billions of pounds have been spent on the introduction of the national curriculum for no apparent rise in attainment in a key basic skill might be pause for thought." Julie Davies believes that the official testing regime is at fault:

"Our measure has been the same measure over eight years whereas the national tests have changed. We don't in this country have a proper basis for looking at standards. Relying on such shifting measures it's very difficult to say what's going up and what's going down." [32]

(4) Harvey Goldstein. " League tables are fundamentally flawed and the government is wrong to think they can be reformed to show the value added by schools," a leading educational statistician has warned ministers. Repeated studies have shown that even with value-added weighting, valid comparisons between most schools would still be impossible to make.

"There is no justification in using a procedure because it is simple. Schools are complex systems, with pupils' performance influenced by peer groups, inside and outside, by home life, and by previous schools attended. If we wish to capture such complex relationships, then we need to have tools which are capable of matching that complexity."

A study of results in London schools published last year by Goldstein and Sammons showed that junior schools had three times the influence over pupils GCSE results that secondary schools had." [33]

Some of those results are surprising, but together they move us away from simple judgements. This is complicated, and making things better isn't as easy as it looks. That doesn't mean that you don't try, but it means you have to keep thinking, and stay calm.

A confident government should feel able to explore these issues without feeling threatened. But David Blunkett dismissed Robinson's argument as "claptrap", and the QCA answered Davies and Brember's complex contrast of methods with "We're very confident that any improvement shown on our test data is real." For us to progress we are going to need a more positive approach.

Beneath the national debate, it is at local level that results really bite. Below are two extracts from my local paper:

RAP OVER SCHOOLS' RANKINGS

Headteachers in Bridgnorth have condemned this week's primary school league tables... "We must point out to parents that the statistics are flawed – our rankings could vary enormously from year to year based on the quality of our intake. What is really important is whether, as individuals, pupils in our schools have achieved what they were capable of achieving. It is unhelpful to base league tables on who has the greatest percentage of level fours. This is an imperfect measure of standards." [34]

That was a joint statement, from three headteachers, who the league tables suggest are in competition with each other. Stephen Pollard might say they were afraid of being exposed, and were getting their excuses in first. I don't think that's how it looked to parents. They sound like reasonable, concerned professionals, making the most of a bad job.

The second is the standard victim quote. Every time there's a league table, someone's at the bottom, and those are the people who get the press knocking at the door. Tim Barratt, of Brockton School, said "The tables can be very mean but I have just resigned myself to it. There is nothing we could have done about it." He added that of the 12 pupils listed to take the tests, two were absent. Three had statements, and four had special needs. "We are not doing badly. We always have good results, and we are very well supported by parents." [35]

And that's what it comes down to in the end. Do you trust these people? If you do, you may not be panicked by the tables. If you don't, then you may be happy to go to the numbers, the places, as reliable facts.

I worked in a school which had its highest intake of new pupils in the year in which it was bottom of the LEA league tables. It wasn't that we were bad teachers who dismissed the need for qualifications. It wasn't that parents didn't care about their children's future. But their calculation of what they wanted from a school wasn't confined to exam statistics. Will my child be happy here? Can they get help if they need it? If there's trouble will these teachers listen to me, and then tell me the truth?

If your initial reaction to teachers is Paxman's to his interviewees ("Why is this bastard lying to me?"), then you will be glad of some figures to wave at them. But if you think they are professionals, who could work with you to help children succeed, you will look for more positive means.

## BOTTOM OF THE LEAGUE?

Things are certainly bad:
- the government are under pressure to change an unfair system of funding, which splits schools into winners and losers
- the attempt to decide entry into grammar schools using a lottery has led to utter chaos
- wealthy families are offering bribes to get their children into the schools they want
- thousands of students have dropped out of teacher-training, because they can't be certain of a job

- teachers are being paid less than city dustmen
- teachers are planning strike action in a demand for higher salaries
- many teachers take on other part-time work, as taxi-drivers
- an exam chief says the curriculum and marking system must be changed, to reduce stress on pupils
- police are being posted outside tough schools to combat rising violence
- two thirds of head teachers are rarely in school.

Each of these is a real story, from the past four years, but none of them are from this country. The headlines refer, in order, to New Zealand, Germany, Thailand, Italy, United States, Serbia, Mexico, India, France and Malaysia. That doesn't mean that everything in the UK is rosy, or that we shouldn't look abroad for good ideas. But it does mean we should be wary about negative headlines.

We've had a lot of them. Early on, the Tory raid on English education suggested that we should be more like Western Europe. Then there was a fashion for the tiger economies of the Far East, and now we are more likely to be offered American models. But none of these comparisons is offered as a serious look at how other people do things. They were another way of panicking, running from a complicated present, to the shelter of a nostalgic past, or to some future technological fantasy.

We need to look at schools abroad. But we need to go slowly, look carefully at exactly what is being compared, and work out how it can help us. To begin with, we may not need to travel too far. We waver around within this uneasy blur of England/UK/Great Britain, but our current crisis is English, and we can learn by looking north of the border. This letter comes from a Scottish teacher:

"I was surprised to read about David Blunkett's plans for the future of the education system and of the concerns of teachers on the issues of workload and red tape.

As a teacher working in the state sector in Scotland, I already belong to a General Teaching Council; I was promoted to the position of senior teacher, designed to keep excellent teachers in the classroom; and I work under a contract of employment that states a maximum class size of 33 and limits the amount of non-teaching tasks that I can be asked to do.

Perhaps before Mr. Blunkett goes any further he should speak to his colleagues at Westminster to find out how the teaching profession in the rest of Britain operates." [36]

Most comparisons, however, go further afield, and they usually start from tests. Tests look as though they measure things, tell us the truth. But some things are much easier to test than others, and the way the test is set up is just as important as the result it produces.

In November 1996, the results of the Third International Maths and Science Study (TIMMS) were published. Britain came 19th, and that fact was headlined as proof of our failure. But what was being tested?

To get a test which can be taken by all the children in more than twenty countries, you have to be testing them on something they are all doing. This means that good new work won't be part of the test, but it will concentrate on old familiar routines. TG Crawshaw wrote:

"If the TIMSS had assessed the ability to apply knowledge in unfamiliar situations, the ability to describe, reason and analyse situations using a variety of resources (including computers), perhaps we would be looking at a different set of results." [37]

We might still worry that our pupils were not as good at calculations as pupils who were spending more time on calculations. But that shouldn't mean that we ditch the computers, and all the work we've done on them. That work isn't included in the tests, because not all the other countries have done it. It's still useful work, though, and it would be wrong to do endless calculation, just to do better in these tests.

Margaret Brown looked at the TIMSS results, and showed that the maths test exactly matched what pupils of that age were taught in America, but only 57% of the test items matched what the English pupils had studied. 13 year-olds in Japan have spent twice as much time on maths as 13 year olds in this country.

We move all our pupils up each year, whether or not they have reached certain standards. In Germany, 27% of the lowest attaining 13-year olds had been held back for a further year, and so were missing from the sample. In Holland, 17 per cent of the least able pupils are not taught in mainstream schools, and are left out of this comparison. So a country which integrates its pupils with special needs, and moves everyone up each year, will not do so well by comparison with other countries.

Irish children came in the middle of the TIMSS table, but only four years previously they had been near the bottom of the league. Had they made astonishing progess, or was it simply that the two tables were using different tests? [38]

The Bristol University QUEST team looked at maths and language work by 800 9-11 year olds in Avon, Kent, Calais and Marseilles. The English children did better on investigation and probability, while the French pupils were better at computation and geometry.

Some differences in the results were because pupils in each country were used to different tests, but there were also differences in ideas about education. "The French emphasis on effort, rather than ability, as the explanation of differences in performance, helps to prevent pupils being discouraged at an early stage in their school career... One negative consequence of the English culture is that pupils are more likely to believe they are 'thick' if they fail to make progress." [39]

So we may not be worse than the French, but we have different ideas about being thick. They believe in equality, while we have always stressed differences. Both the French and the German systems have been aimed at educating the whole population together, while in England there have been two powerful forces breaking up that unity.

One is the selective tradition, the public schools, church schools, grammar schools and all sorts of later variations, each marking themselves out as special, choosing children, so that they can be "better than the rest." The other disruptive factor is the Thatcher attack on consensus. Consensus can look safe and dull, settling for agreement at any cost. But it can also be a solid achievement, which keeps a country together, and makes sure that education continues without disruption, whichever party is in power.

Talking to The Observer, Uwe Schulz-Hofen, a Berlin civil servant, said:

"There is a consensus about the value of education and training, so it is not so easy for politicians to influence the debate on a party basis."

Denis Paget, assistant general-secretary of the National Union of Secondary School Teachers in France describes a similar picture;

"There is wide agreement about education. People are broadly satisfied with the sysem and for one overwhelming reason – the progress made in providing the population with schooling." Jon Snow adds the vital conclusion:

"The bottom line is this: almost nowhere in France or Germany does a father or mother lie awake at night wondering about how and where they are going to educate their child. That experience is reserved almost exclusively for Britain." [40]

## LEARNING THE LESSONS

So it helps to look at other countries, to see ourselves more clearly. The things that we take take for granted – like the early labels of "bright" and "thick" – may be English habits, rather than a basic fact of school life. But we also look at other countries to see if we can learn from their mistakes, and benefit from the good things that they do.

In the mid 1990s there was considerable interest in Pacific Rim countries, and particularly in the whole-class teaching of maths. Pupils did less work individually or in groups, but were more involved in the lesson, through asking questions, calling out answers or demonstrating on the blackboard. This keeps the class together, and prevents the weaker pupils from falling behind, losing touch with the subject and seeing themselves as failures.

To many junior schools this was a reminder that whole-class teaching didn't have to be dull. Pupils needn't be frustrated, provided lessons were well run. Many schools and teachers in the UK have learnt from that, and made sure that pupils get a better deal.

But it isn't just technique. Burjar Avari points out that there are other factors at work. In Taiwan there is a general respect for the idea of education, which is not shared in many parts of this country. Taiwanese society is based on Confucian lines, which are much more holistic than the fragmented pattern in this country. There is more willingness to impose and accept discipline, and "Finally, Taiwan has been prepared to learn from the mistakes of the others. The Taiwanese do not have any hang-ups about accepting others' ideas and adapting them." [41]

But the traffic isn't all one way. Just as English critics were looking jealously at the Pacific Rim, Japanese leaders were anxious to learn from the British system. They were worried about the effects of central control, the rise in teenage suicides, and wanted to make it their education more flexible and creative. "Japanese children need more yutori – room to grow – and schools have to do more to nuruture creativity, independent thinking, problem-solving and originality."

Toshimi Kushida, second secretary at the Japanese Embassy in London said: "Before the current curriculum changes, the emphasis was on giving knowledge. In history, for instance, children have had to learn strings of dates and facts." [42]

In January 2000 a panel set up by the Japanese government produced a radical report, arguing for a reduction in the national curriculum. Compulsory subjects should only take up 60% of the teaching week, with the other 40% devoted to advanced lessons, review classes, languages or music. [43]

For years we made fun of the French system, where the government says what will be taught on any one day. But while our government takes more control, the French are travelling in the opposite direction, away from centralisation and towards local initiatives: "Continental education policies increasingly reflect local cultures, religions, languages and economies."

This process means there are some disagreements about what's national and what's local, but these are not disasters. They are resolved, and most people seem happy with the result. "In such a context, England is increasingly viewed as an anomaly." [44]

But we are not a complete disaster. The QUEST team looked at differences between English and French children in the way they worked, and Patricia Broadfoot reported that : "One of the significant differences between English and French children is that English children are a lot more confident when it comes to thinking on their feet. They are very good at knowing what to do when they don't know what to do. Although French children are significantly more positive about school, they are subjected to a much more formal, authoritarian approach to teaching, and this can often be very constricting."

This isn't just an interesting detail. It is a crucial factor in future economic performance. "Whilst other countries have been the envy of the world in the capacity of their students to achieve on conventional tests of achievement, it is these same countries which are now desperate to find ways of encouraging their students to be creative problem-solvers, team-workers and risk-takers. It is these skills which will determine the economic tigers of tomorrow." [45]

So maybe we are better than we think, or better than our press believes. And maybe we should not be in such a hurry to change a pattern which our competitors rate more highly than we do. "Broadfoot and her team believe that this raises questions about the benefits of many of the current educational reforms being introduced by the government. By limiting the role of the teachers to the very narrow boundaries of the classroom, the researchers feel that the system will suffer." [46]

That's a surprising ending, to a complicated journey. The QUEST team did test what pupils could do, but they also observed lessons, interviewed pupils in depth, got them to comment on their own education, and also invited them to cross the channel, observe schools in the other country and then comment on that. That's what serious research involves, and that's how you learn things.

It's not quite " BOTTOM OF THE LEAGUE – GET BACK TO SOME PROPER WORK". That is the more usual form of international comparison that we get, whether from press or politicians. A fuller, more thoughtful analysis will occasionally appear, like the Observer article on England, France and Germany, but most of the best things in this chapter have come from newspaper articles which have themselves been summaries of more full-length research. If we want to know what's happening in other countries, then we have to take the necessary time.

But it is worth it. I have been critical of Michael Barber, but here's an instance of him doing what he should do, making his expertise available to the general reader, so that they can get a taste of teaching in action. He reports on a book by Stigler and Hiebert, who analysed video recordings of maths lessons in Germany, Japan and the US, as part of TIMSS.

"In Germany and Japan, teachers designed lessons so the concepts they introduced were developed and built upon while, in America, concepts were generally simply stated. American lessons were more often interrupted and involved more frequent switches of topics. German and Japanese lessons had greater coherence, covering less ground but much more deeply.

Japanese and German teachers encouraged pupils to develop their thinking rigorously, often using students to present to the whole class. Japanese pupils, especially, spent far less of each lesson practising routines and far more applying or even inventing problems and solutions than the American pupils." [47]

Teachers would love to see the tapes for themselves, but even this simple outline raises key questions – "Do I simply state concepts? Or develop and build them? How could my lessons have more coherence, cover less ground but go deeper?" Continuing Professional Development is a part of Barber's work which is aimed to carry this on, making research available to teachers. The press hardly covered it, but it's still a good move.

And so is self-evaluation. Professor John MacBeath describes an international project called "Evaluating Quality in School Education", in which 101 schools in 18 EU countries worked together on a common pattern of self-appraisal. All schools had a set of guidelines, a critical friend, networking workshops and conferences nationally and internationally, and a self-evaluation profile. They varied enormously, and the work respected their different characters, but at the end of a year – which was the period for which the work was funded – 98 out of the 101 wanted to carry on. [48]

And that is why we should be looking at what happens in other countries. It is not because we're terrible and we need to start again. It is because international contacts can stimulate you to be clearer about yourself, to want to work hard at being better, not to beat the others but because that's what mixing with the others makes you want to do.

## A BETTER WAY?

Tests won't give us "the facts." They will give us some information, but not the whole truth. Looking abroad can be useful, provided we do it properly and not simply as a scare. A government looking for serious improvement will have to look beyond the media to people who know what they are talking about. It won't be enough to settle for the simple appeal, the easy answer, if they are really going to understand.

In 1997 David Hart objected to league tables for primary schools: "I don't think the government believes the tables will give a fair reflection of schools' performance. This exercise is political."

Gillian Shephard replied that his protest would make parents think heads had something to hide. "Sadly this is the sort of reaction is what we have come to expect from some of those who purport to speak for teachers. They are seeking to discredit the biggest information exercise of its kids for parents and the wider public ever undertaken." [49]

Information, parents, biggest ever – press the buttons and you get the bonus. Some of us hoped that a Labour government might welcome a more open debate, and allow more room for precise analysis. So far, we have been disappointed.

A survey of 550 teachers revealed serious concerns:

"Some 90% of English teachers said they felt under pressure to teach to the tests although 67% said they were not a valid assessment of the keystage 3 programmes of study. Fewer than 10 per cent of responses offered any kind of positive comment. A substantial minority added critical comments to their questionnaire, describing the tests as "a farce", "a waste of time", "pointless" and "alarming." Other described the marking and administration as "frightening", "appalling", "disgraceful" and "a disaster." In maths, only 27% of teachers agreed that the tests reflected good mathematics teaching, while nearly 60% said they were under pressure to teach to the tests." [50]

An intelligent employer would be concerned by these results, coming from a moderate union. Even if they're mistaken, those views suggest that there's a problem, which needs to be taken seriously.

David Hart warns the government that the timescale for targets is unrealistic:

"We are doing the government a service by telling them they have got it wrong. Any shortfall does not mean that teachers are teaching badly. The reality is that they are teaching better and better." [51]

This was the response, from a DfEE spokesman: "We are confident that the targets will be met. The targets are challenging – they are meant to be. But the government has put the resources behind them and the targets have the overwhelming support of parents, teachers and headteachers." [52]

The Assessment Reform Group, a powerful combination of professors and researchers, produced a carefully argued report arguing for more analysis of learning. "There is no evidence that testing will enhance learning. Instead, the focus needs to be on helping teachers use assessment, as part of teaching and learning, in ways that will help raise pupils' achievement." [53] A government with ambitions for intellectual growth would leap at such a report, but I know of no response.

One crucial issue is the focus on A-C grades. GCSE gives grades from A-G, but many league tables only bother with the grades from A-C. This leads to a concentration on pupils at the C/D borderline, and a neglect of pupils who are unlikely to achieve a C grade. In August '98, following publication of the results, there was pressure from headteachers and educational academics to drop the A-C measure. Alan Smithers said that if the overall points score and A-C score were put out together, then people would ignore the points score.

"This is not just an accounting operation or a way of expressing data. It has a very important effect on the way schools operate, and we can see that in these results."

John Dunford: "As long as A-C remains in league tables, that will be the measurement people use and that is damaging, because it invites schools to concentrate on one particular group of children. Schools don't want to do this, but those in particularly competitive situations, and those which have had poor inspection reports, feel forced into it."

Researchers David Gillborn and Deborah Youdell report the following comments from teachers:

"I've had to make decisions I know have undermined their self-esteem."

"A school now lives or dies on its results."

"The hard fact is that Cs are worth very much more than anything below a C."

And these were the views of some pupils:

"They say they believe in equal opportunities, but they don't."

"You have to get a C, otherwise it's a fail."

"They don't seem to care about what we want to do for ourselves." [54] Academics, head teachers, teachers and pupils. The evidence argues a consistent case which demands serious consideration. But this is the government view: "We are not going to withdraw information from the tables which parents and employers understand and which they are used to receiving. We are providing more information, not less. The A-C grade measure is well understood and well appreciated. It is a goal for schools to strive at, as well as ensuring that all pupils achieve exam success." [55]

But it doesn't. What it does is raise the motivation of a small group of pupils, and lower that of a larger group, which is already disadvantaged. "More information, not less". It's the argument with which league tables were launched, the boast of quantity without consideration for quality. But the information is misleading, telling the public that only a few kids matter.

And there is depressing evidence that this has a damaging effect on everyone. A-C grades are equivalent to the old 'O' level pass, which used to be gained by between a third and a quarter of pupils. Now, nearly half the teenagers in the country get 5 grades at A-C. That still leaves half who don't, and FOCUS spoke to 1400 pupils at London schools, where only 27% of pupils get 5 A-Cs. Yet 70% of the pupils they spoke to thought that they would reach this magic target. [56] It's sad that two-thirds of them are kidding themselves, because they have been told so often and so loudly that this is the only target that matters. It's sadder still that Blunkett won't get involved in fighting this myth, settling instead for the same, simple Tory faith – "giving parents the information they expect."

That is exactly what Stephen Pollard expects, and he at least should be happy. In his picture, Tony Blair always knew the value of league tables and would never dream of doing without them. The real Tony Blair, however, is not quite so simple. He has, it's true, the childish dream of "world-class tests", which is like wanting to play noughts and crosses for England. The really world-class education systems don't bother with this kind of test.

But Tony Blair is more intelligent than that. He is bright enough to see that there is substantial disquiet about these divisive arrangements that he inherited from his Tory predecessors. He just doesn't feel that he can do anything about it :

"I think people understand how crude tables can be as a guide, but as a government it is difficult not to give out the information." [57]

Difficult, but not impossible. Many other countries do it all the time. And for someone who is so proud of his intolerance of poor standards and conservative values, such a move should not be that daunting, given that "people understand how crude tables can be as a guide."

The evidence is that the tables stimulate short-term improvement for some schools, and that long-term they increase the distance between the top and the bottom. The ideal is a situation where we don't have a league table, because we have consistent excellence, but league tables take us away from that ideal, not towards it. So, if we're going to get rid of them, as Northern Ireland has done, we can't just wait for that to happen. It has to be a deliberate, planned decision, but there are plenty of good reasons why it should be taken, and no reason at all for delay.

1   TES 21.11.97
2   TES 21.11.97
3   Guardian 20.11.96
4   Dr. Martin Stephen, head of Manchester Grammar, Guardian 20.11.96
5   Guardian 20.11.96
6   Guardian 20.11.92
7   Guardian 20.11.92
8   June Izbicki, letter to TES 8.1.99
9   TES 27.10.00
10   TES 14.5.99
11   TES 16.7.99
12   Guardian 19.12.99
13   Guardian 1.6.99
14   TES 4.6.99
15   TES 16.7.99

16  TES 16.7.99
17  TES 28.7.00
18  TES 8.1.99
19  TES 30.4.93
20  TES 30.4.93
21  Guardian 11.1.01
22  Lindsay Paterson, in TES 9.10.98
23  TES 30.7.99
24  Guardian 20.5.00
25  TES 1.10.99
26  TES 1.10.99
27  TES 30.6.00
28  TES 23.10.98
29  "On a Clear Day" p.48
30  TES 2.10.98
31  Observer 1.3.98
32  TES 3.10.97
33  TES 3.7.98
34  Bridgnorth Journal 17.12.99
35  Bridgnorth Journal 17.12.99
36  M.C.Barry, from Renfrewshire, writing to the Guardian ,14.4.98
37  TG Crawshaw, letter to TES, 29.11.96
38  TES 26.5.00
39  QUEST project, reported in TES 17.3.00
40  Observer 5.11.95
41  Guardian 11.6.96
42  Guardian 12.5.98
43  Guardian 19.1.00
44  Margaret Maden, in TES 25.2.00
45  Patricia Broadfoot, in Guardian 2.5.00
46  Helen Mooney, Guardian 2.5.00
47  TES 18.2.00
48  TES 16.4.99
49  Guardian 7.3.97
50  ATL survey, reported in TES 1.1.99
51  Guardian 6.2.99
52  Guardian 6.2.99
53  TES 3.9.99
54  all from TES, 26.11.99
55  Guardian 27.8.98
56  TES 18.8.00
57  TES 28.1.00

Chapter 6:

# THE LOTTERY BOOM

## TAKE YOUR PICK

Sebastian Junger describes how the Air National Guard picks its rescue parachutists. "The dropout rate is often over 90%. In one drill, the team swims their normal 4,000 yard workout, and then the instructor tosses his whistle in the pool. Ten guys fight for it, and whoever manages to blow it at the surface gets to leave the pool. His workout is over for the day. The instructor throws the whistle in again, and the nine remaining guys fight for it. This goes on until there's one man left, and he's thrown out of the course." [1]

That's tough, but they're picking an elite. It's not aways like that. Education, for instance, is meant to be for everybody. Melanie Phillips wrote a book, called "All Must Have Prizes", in which she attacked the idea that every child could be a success. To her, this was like Alice in Wonderland, and the crazy sports day where everybody won. But education isn't a sports day, and if the prize is being educated, then everybody should win it.

Imagine a family, going out for a meal together. They stop outside the restaurant, and mum points through the window. "You see? Nice table, expensive menu, and anything you want from each of five courses. Nothing but the best. But only one of us is going in. Now pick a card…"

You may think that that's silly. Education isn't a meal. But it's not a race either, and when we use images, we need to think why we're picking one picture rather than another. To take a current example, there is great concern over education in the third world. This is a serious, world-wide crisis. It's like starvation, like providing a meal. But it's nothing to do with a race. If education was a race, why would the front runners worry about what's happening at the back?

It matters which images we pick. In this chapter, I'm using the picture of the lottery to describe what's happening to our education. A lottery means lots of players, lots of cash, and a handful of winners. And that is fine for the odd flutter, a bit of a risk to add hope for the future, excitement at the weekend. But it isn't the best way to organise our schools.

It began with the Technical and Vocational Education Initiative (TVEI). This was a scheme for making the work in schools more modern, and better related to adult work. For years many schools had developed their own ideas. If there was a new development, like the introduction of GCSE, everybody did it. But TVEI was different. They were going to develop the teaching of technology, but only in some schools. Some would get a lot of new computers, and some wouldn't.

This was new. For the government, it was cheap (you didn't have to provide computers for everyone), and it could easily be monitored – you could make rules about who got the computers, or the sort of work for which they should be used. If you had simply given them to everyone, there was the risk of inconsistent use, or that some would be wasted. So this pattern of bidding appealed to a Tory government which wanted to look as if it was modernising education without spending too much.

You save money, but you lose consistency and trust. The school which didn't get the computers doesn't see the advantages of the system. They may not agree with your rules, or may think they have been unfairly applied. So you get bitterness between winners and losers, less co-operation. With TVEI there was a lot of bad feeling, but the schools had little choice. One winning head described it like this – "There's this man walking past the door saying, 'Do you want a roomful of computers?' I'd have been daft to say no."

Since then this has become the pattern. Goodies are announced, bids are put in, many are called and few are chosen. Fans of the scheme say that competition sorts out quality, so that money is given to deserving cases who will spend it well.

But it's not just a question of judgement. Businesses like to be associated with parental approval and success, so they are more likely to give extra resources to those schools which already have these things. Handing out resources to struggling schools might look like a waste, so it's safer not to reward the places of greatest need.

And then there's the bid. It needs to look good; money, time and expertise are easier to get hold of if you're already rich and successful. A popular school will be able to make videos, print glossy leaflets, draw on the previous experience of bidding to obtain more cash. In competition with a school which is desperate for more resources, the popular school will win. To them that hath shall be given, and from those that have not it shall be taken away.

In June 1999 the Liberal Democrats researched the results of local authority bids for government money. They found that there was no match between funds granted and pupil poverty, and that only a third of bids were successful. Over two years, there were 16,000 unsuccessful bids. That's a lot of paper, a lot of people's time, thought and hope, with nothing to show for it all. There was little comfort from the government official who dismissed these criticisms, saying that "the differences would even out over the next few years." [2]

A year later, nothing had changed. The Directory of Social Change found that 5% of secondary schools raise less than £1,000 a year, while at the other end 3% annually raise between £250,000 and £500,000. It's not a level playing-field.

One effect of the lottery boom has been to emphasise money. Cash is important, and there are many things which schools need to do which cannot be done without it. On the other hand, it's not the only thing, and it can have a distorting effect on the priorities of a school.

At the height of the argument about SATs and reading scores, John Patten was suggesting that schools that did best in the league tables should also be paid more. In May 2000 Labour took on this idea, offering every school which got out of special measures a share of a

£60 million pound fund. It's like a Victorian mill owner, lashing his men to greater efforts, offering them an extra sixpence if they do well.

But it's based on a crazy picture of failure and success. I have taught in a failing school, and in a very successful school, and I know which is easier. A successful school has its own rewards. There's support from management, a wider agreement between staff about what they're doing, the confidence from parents that although you may make mistakes you're on the right track. All those things make it easier to come into school each day, and to put in more than the minimum of effort. You don't need a bribe as well.

If the school is failing, despite the efforts of its staff, it's much harder to keep going. Parents take their children out of the school, and ambitious staff look for a move elsewhere. Kids pick up the atmosphere of unease, and push harder at the limits of behaviour. Schools don't fail because teachers could do a decent job but decide not to bother. They fail for a mixture of reasons, but the sense of a vicious circle, which drains away confidence, pupils and resources, is made worse by throwing money at those who don't need it, and taking it away from those who are already deprived.

More recent variations include a proposal to pay fourteen year olds to attend extra lessons on a Saturday morning, and an announcement of government announcement of incentives to cut truancy:

"The government will today offer prizes of up to £10,000 to the 50 schools doing the most to cut truancy over the next year." [3] They should be attending school, but how many schools should be working on this? If you bust a gut and end up as school no. 51, do you try so hard next year? If you're way down the bottom of the league, is it a help to know that other schools way above you are getting richer? We have to tackle truancy, to make schools think about it and share good practice with each other. But do we have to make it a lottery?

The City Technology Colleges were set up as models of excellence. They were meant to show co-operation between government and local business, but most firms didn't want to play. Huge amounts of money were poured into setting up these palaces, and at the time Labour objected.

There was plenty to object to. The CTCs were a massive disruption to the pattern of local education. Parents would choose as usual, and their children would be allocated to local schools, but then the CTC would choose who they would take. Selection processes were mysterious, and while the CTC took some with low scores, the level of parent support and pupil motivation was always high. Secondary schools would get lists of their future pupils, and watch as some names – attractive, positive, grade-winning names – were rubbed off their lists.

An individual CTC could be very successful. That's not surprising, if you can choose who you're going to take. If you then find that a pupil doesn't fit in, you can talk with the parents, suggest a change of scene, and a transfer takes place before there is any talk of exclusion. So a disruptive child can leave the CTC, creating a space for a more amenable child from somewhere else. "Somewhere else" is the leftover school, the comprehensive which takes in rejects from the CTC, and loses CTC candidates. It can't pass on its own rejects because the CTC is full.

So while pupils in the building may be doing brilliantly, the impact of such a school on the area is destructive. Parents are given an image – of cost, comfort and containment – which they can't get elsewhere, because it's been set up with special money. Many will apply for it but only a few will be lucky. The demand is maintained, which keeps up quality control, but it means that parents who tried to get in and failed will feel that wherever else they go is second rate.

The original plan was that the CTCs would develop bright new approaches to education which they would then pass on to local schools. "We, with our money and advantages, have developed method x which we think you might find useful – even though you don't have the conditions in which method x was first developed." That was always improbable, and it's even less likely to happen because of the surrounding tension. CTCs had a special atmosphere, with different working conditions and management style, so there was a gulf between CTC teachers and other teachers.

The Thomas Telford School, in Shropshire, has been controversial for most of its life. In 2000 it celebrated its achievement in being the first comprehensive school to record 100% success – which means that all of its pupils in one year passed five subjects at GCSE with grades between A and C. From any school, that's an impressive achievement, but it's also bending definitions to call this school comprehensive.

I have listened to total strangers in shops, comparing strategies for getting their children into Thomas Telford. I have seen entries in the local paper, congratulating pupils on their success in obtaining a place, just as they did on passing the eleven plus. And the school's own description of its admission procedures includes the following: "the headmaster will select pupils from within ability bands and, in exercising his professional judgement, will take into account the following... competence in technology, science and mathematics – attainment and effort will be given a score in each of the subjects. Applicants with the highest score in each band of ability will be given priority." [4] I have worked in four comprehensive schools, and visited a whole lot more, but none of them recruited their pupils like that.

It's not the parents' job to worry about the whole system. They want the best for their children, and if government and newspapers tell them that a particular brand is "better than the rest", then that's what they'll go for. It is the government's job to worry about the whole system, but they don't want to annoy parents, so if some parents are happy with a school they'll leave it alone, even if the way that school is set up damages other schools and parents in the area.

The Labour party used to be concerned for the whole system, for education for all. When New Labour came in, they talked of education "for the many, not the few." That has now become another stale soundbite. John Prescott, better placed than most to know what has been lost in this rebranding, said "voters were tired of constantly repeated messages like 'boom and bust' and 'for the many not the few.'" He said they wanted messages that had substance rather than those that covered a lack of action. [5]

There is one area where targeting would make sense. For years some children have left school with limited ability to read. Labour rightly took literacy as a key aim, and it would have been reasonable to concentrate on those schools and pupils having most difficulty. But this would have been politically risky, directing large amounts of money towards children in poor areas. So the literacy strategy was universal – every child in every school, even if they can read well already.

Once you choose something, you are not choosing something else.

The literacy plan centred on reading, and on short-term activities for all pupils. But that meant less time for writing, fewer chances for pupils to get involved in long-term work, and build up confidence. Many teachers warned that this would happen, but this government doesn't listen to teachers.

As a result we got reports like this. "Chris Woodhead, HMCI, warned yesterday that the government's key education target is threatened by poor teaching of writing..." [6] It suggests that teachers are plodding along on their little track, until a visionary inspector comes to point out what they're missing. They are missing it now, because they've been told to concentrate on the government version of literacy. They weren't missing it before, and some of them had warned from the start that too crude a stress on reading might damage development in writing.

This has become a regular pattern. Will concentration on English and Maths lead to a decline in Science? Are creative activities being sidelined? Do we place enough emphasis on physical education? Are the kinds of thinking encouraged by short-term tests the kinds of thinking we ought to encourage?

Each time such questions are raised we are told that this has been borne in mind, or will soon be the subject of a new short-term initiative. We don't get an honest admission that it had been overlooked. There isn't the necessary pause to ask for other views about what should be done. First we need a calm, balanced look at the overall picture, an overview which recognises that this is a complex business. Then we need a thought out, long-term plan, based on consultation and agreement, which won't need to be revised every few weeks.

The same thing has happened with teachers' pay. New Labour don't want to give pay rises to all teachers, so they make a series of selections – superteachers, superheads, the Fast Track. The main idea is the always the same: it's too crude, too expensive to reward them all, so we'll pick a few and give them quite a lot.

The first attempt at this was the Advanced Skills Teacher status, which the press called "superteachers". There were two models for this. The TTA suggested a broad definition, which could eventually include all teachers. The other, proposed by the DfEE, could only apply to a limited number of teachers. The School Teachers' Review Body preferred the TTA model, but were told they had to accept the DfEE version.

This created problems in a relationship which was already tense, after David Blunkett had made it clear that the extra £2.3 billion money for education could not be spent on teachers' pay. So an independent review body is stopped from taking the decision it wishes to take, and is deprived of money which it thinks will benefit the profession. How independent is that?

Then, before the review body had approved the superteacher grade, Blunkett said that they would be working in action zones, another new government scheme. The plan is clear: "1. Create a few superteachers 2. Put them in action zones 3. Measure the effect, and announce another success."

The review body has a more difficult responsibility – to look at teachers' pay overall, and consider the impact on morale of any changes that are to be introduced. They saw that these changes would create difficulties so far as other teachers were concerned. Might key jobs (deputy head, head of department) remain unfilled, because ambitious teachers could get more money by being superteachers? Were action zones the best place to put superteachers? What about failing schools? And wasn't the speed with which the whole thing was being pushed through making mistakes more likely?

Then the money ran out. The idea had been that superteachers would advise and help other teachers, so as to improve teaching across the system. It might also sweeten the pill of differences in pay. But then the government said they couldn't afford to pay for that, so that LEAs would have to fund it themselves. This was not only incompetent but dangerous, since it said that the scheme wasn't meant to benefit the system as a whole. So teachers get a bit more cynical, and the gap between the unrewarded many and the privileged few grows wider still.

The scheme is now in total disarray. When it was launched in 1998 the government envisaged 5,000 such posts by September 2001. By October 2000 750 teachers had been successfully assessed. The hub of progess was Beauchamp College, Leicester, where 15 teachers had qualified and 7 had taken up AST posts. With the LEA's refusal to fund those posts, the school has given those teachers extra responsibilities to justify the extra pay. As the head, Maureen Cruickshank, observed 'The agenda has moved on.'

The aim of using ASTs to improve the performance of other teachers elsewhere has been severely limited. Cruickshank says "There comes a point where self-interest takes over and you don't want to take your best teachers out of the classroom and send them to other schools." [7] Of course there does, which is why such a scheme cannot be left in the hands of heads, whose responsibility is to their own schools. Government, however, has a responsibility to the system as a whole, and it was intelligent and courageous of them to try to carry that out; sadly, it was not long before they ran out of intelligence, courage and cash.

This pattern of giving large bonuses to a few people is offered as a commonsense solution, as though that was the way everybody else works and teachers were dim not to see the advantages. But there aren't obvious, clear models on which this system is based, and there are good reasons for being cautious. Many areas of the US have tried some form of merit pay, but it isn't a simple solution:

"Murnane and Cohen say that 'most plans fail because they hurt morale and are expensive to administer. In an in-depth study of six school districts they found that most merit pay plans died because administrators could not provide convincing answers to two questions from teachers: Why did my colleague get merit money, and I did not? and What can I do to get merit pay?' " [8]

It can only work if there is enough money to make sure that everyone who meets the criteria gets the pay rise. If the government only fund it for two years then it won't change much. Rich schools with lots of pupils can invest in well-paid jobs which attract staff, while struggling schools with uncertain futures won't be able to take the risk. So their staff who want promotion will look elsewhere, and the chasm between best and worst will widen further still.

The government has tried to raise teacher morale through the National Teacher Awards. These say that teaching matters, but as a competition they are very limited. The teachers who win awards have the support of their heads, in schools where they welcome cameras. Some outstanding teachers are working against the odds, under unsympathetic management, or in schools where it would be too big a risk to let the cameras in.

What's remarkable about the awards, though, is the regular refrain of the winners. A succession of committed professionals, often middle-aged women, testify to the power of working for a long time with a community of teachers, and put their own success down to the support of familiar colleagues with whom they work. This is waved aside by ministers, but it is powerful evidence to which they should listen. Ministers' taste is for the macho values of intervention and rapid response (not necessarily from men), but there is another pattern, of repeated routine, developing relationships and long-term progress which should also be part of the improvement programme – and part of the image of success.

The extreme vision of the future is the Fast Track. This is an attempt to lure bright young graduates into teaching with incentives. On top of the £6,000 signing on fee, they can get a £5,000 bursary, their own laptop, extra training and the opportunity to network with other recruits. They will have access to special jobs, reserved for people on this programme, and will move into headships faster than the normal teacher. Their pay will be above average, and they need not fear that this will limit them to a chalkbound career – the government expect them to prove themselves in education, become headteachers, and then move on to make more money elsewhere.

It's an exciting trailer, with a number of practical snags. This whole rise will be accompanied by considerable pressure – they give up some of their holidays, their pupils get good results, and they won't experience discipline problems. However, they will be given classes and responsibilities which will help them to follow this route, and if they're not up to it then "exit mechanisms" are in place.

Any teacher with whom I've discussed these proposals has smiled at some point, usually with a tinge of sadness. Where they break out laughing, however, is the punch line – "the teacher will be a fully integrated member of the school..." As John McEnroe used to say "You cannot be serious."

Integration into a school staffroom is not something for which you legislate. If you tilt all the key decisions about someone's work – their power, their money, their allocation of classes, the rate of their promotion – then you are at the same time affecting the way they get on with colleagues. In the best staffrooms, teachers are held together by a sense of common pressures: the importance of the job, the need for all children to be educated, the demands of the timetable. Other things may also unite them – admiration for a respected head, resentment of unfair management, the demands of the catchment area. But once you start to draw lines between superteachers and ordinary teachers, fast track and pedestrian, much of that unity will be lost.

You might, as a government, decide that that was a price worth paying for your future gains. As a teacher who's worked in two very different schools which had that unity, and as a result of it achieved impressive results in exams and much besides, I'd advise caution. But even as I write, the adverts are starting to appear. Two parallel escalators, with the slow one crowded by pupils and average teachers, plodding up at standard pace. Next to them, a single candidate has the accelerated staircase to themselves. Then there's the mountain, with an athletic fast track climber sprinting to the top. Power, speed, special status – the appeals are obvious. Yet according to UEA researchers, "friendly colleagues and intellectual challenges are more important than a good starting salary for young people considering a teaching career." [9]

## SELECTION AND PARENTAL CHOICE

The biggest lottery of all is the choice of school. As a parent, which school do you choose for your child, and how do you make sure that they get it?

Our system has a muddled history, which explains why we have different patterns in different parts of the country, and why religion, intelligence and social class produce more options than anyone could reasonably want. The result is fragmentation, and an increasing distance between the best and worst. Could it ever be different?

I came into teaching in the 1960s, when one good reason for that was that you could be part of a national movement – quality education for every child in the country. That may sound naïve now, but it was a powerful cause, which still attracts believers.

There are plenty of obstacles in the way. There are schools which have been set up on a very different principle – public schools, grammar schools, CTCs, where the appeal is that these are "better than the rest." The rest is what the others get, bog standard education, and it has been an English tradition that most of the people in government make sure that their own children don't get "the rest", and therefore don't worry whether or not it's bog-standard.

As it happens, comprehensive schools do as well with their brightest pupils as grammar schools do, but that hasn't got many headlines. Our media live on myths, and their pet myth is that ordinary education isn't good enough for your child, who deserves better than the rest. But you might have to work to get it.

"Last year, two thirtysomething professional couples in Manchester who use the same child minder were both anxious to get their 'rising fives' into a smart, orderly primary school in the inner-city island of affluence on whose fringes they reside. Neither lived within its catchment area, but the household of one was close by and that of the other was more than a mile off. Both put the school down as their first option. The former provided their real address. The latter gave that of the child-minder, who lived a one-minute walk from the school. Their child was accepted, the first couple's was not. Eye-contact has been problematic ever since. The child minder just feels used." [10]

Tony Blair is a parent, and he knows how it feels:

"When I look at some of the inner-city schools, it is no wonder parents feel they have to move their children out, and some feel they have to make other arrangements for their children." [11]

This might annoy some teachers, but it's encouraging for parents facing a difficult choice. They're in a dilemma, and Tony knows how they feel. But he's not just a parent. He's also Prime Minister, and his government should have a view on how this market works. If there's a school that worries him, he can sympathise with a parent who wants to move their child out. But does he sympathise with one parent, or with all of them? If the school's that bad, should anyone go there? Shouldn't all parents move their kids out of such a school? And where do they move them to? Can all parents get their children into the schools they want?

Blair seems reluctant to appreciate that this is a complex argument. In a Guardian interview, he was asked about the impact of parental choice on deprived families:

"QU: For instance, backbenchers like Roy Hattersley have written that you are deserting the underprivileged. Do you worry about this?

ANS: I worry about the lack of comprehension as to what we are doing, but I have no doubt that the policy we are articulating is the right one, because it is the only way of raising standards in schools where the standards are insufficiently high by taking the types of measure that myself and David Blunkett have outlined. I think that people like Roy are just fundamentally wrong about issues like parental choice. They believe it is all meaningless and that it is only exercised by middle class people, not by anybody else." [12]

He plays the leader role, confident in his own judgement and saying that his critics are simply wrong. But he doesn't follow the argument. Hattersley's criticism is not that parental choice is offered only to the middle class. It is that when parental choice is offered to all, it will be the middle class which benefits. So a fair system cannot be achieved simply by offering a choice. That view is backed up by research into choices made and schools allocated, and it needs much more thought than Blair is prepared to give it.

To professionals within the system, the promotion of new types of school is an attack on the whole pattern. Martin Johnson is a head-teacher and a moderate, but there is nothing mild about his description of government policy:

"The promotion of Tory innovations such as beacon schools and specialist schools... threatens to undermine the whole comprehensive secondary school system, a system... now being dismantled. The government causes a quite unequal distribution of available potential, and then lauds the schools which received great potential and converted it, and assaults with complete brutality the schools which received little potential and converted that.

We are back to selection, a more subtle form of selection, a selection which brings in the marvels and mysteries of the middle-class housing market, a selection which may be by the parents, is more likely to be by the school, and certainly is nothing to do with establishing an intake which reflects the whole community served by the school."

Johnson says "this might be the policy of a Tory prime minister; it is certainly the policy of a bourgeois prime minister. A prime minister with absolutely no understanding of how ordinary schools work..." [13]

Blair has protested that he is not just interested in the middle-class, and that parental choice is for all. But first it works for a few, and then another few, and then maybe a few more. And each time the few get favoured, are given something better than the rest, then the rest continue to suffer.

"Demack, Drew and Grimsley analysed the education experiences of 22,000 teenagers in England and Wales. 'The groups that were doing well in 1988 have improved at a much swifter rate,' said Mr. Demack. 'The gap has widened. The system is giving disproportionate help to those people from advantaged backgrounds. The recent concentration on school performance may be making things worse.

...The latest figures show that the only group of pupils whose GCSE performance was worsening were those from unskilled manual families. In 1996, 24% of pupils from those homes gained five-plus good GCSEs. Last year this figure had fallen to 20%' ". [14]

That's a gulf within the state system. Look beyond that, to private education, and the gulf is bigger still: "Private schools spend on average £5,000 per pupil, with pupil-staff ratios below 10 to 1; state secondary schools spend £2,250 per pupil,with pupil-staff ratios double those in fee-paying schools.. Perhaps most important of all, the children move in a peer group in which academic excellence is valued and expectations are of top jobs and careers. If this is to be challenged, the state system has to increase its investment and effort massively. No such attempt is being made...the drift to private schools is becoming a stampede. We are building one of the most unequal and nastiest societies on Earth – and nobody is protesting." [15]

Far from protesting, ministers are looking enviously across the fence, and are asking for help. Stephen Byers hoped that teachers from independent schools would be able to share their superior techniques with their state counterparts, and assured them that they had nothing to fear from a Labour government. "We are drawing a line under the old dogma." [16] Kate Hoey wished that PE teachers in state schools would put in the extra hours dedicated by their independent colleagues. And Phil Collins, director of the Social Market Foundation, is confident that during its second term of office New Labour will be buying places in the independent sector.

Old Labour found it hard to know what to do about private schools. If you believe in social justice, then it can't be right to have a small elite educating their children separately, with better funding. But what can you do about it?

Some historians think that there was a moment in the Attlee government when it would have been possible to move against the private schools, when government courage and public feeling might have combined to produce a fairer system. But if the chance was there, it was not taken.

Harold Wilson was canny, a short-term operator looking for maximum advantage and minimum pain. He was happy to bury the issue of independent schooling in a long, earnest enquiry by the Newsom committee, which changed nothing.

Now New Labour accepts the idea of private schooling with total enthusiasm. Estelle Morris spoke to Conference and Common Room, a magazine for independent headmasters. "As we've got to know the independent sector more, we've been more honest and more open about what we can learn from it. We would always respect the parents' wish to choose an independent school for their son or daughter. New Labour, no matter how many terms we have, will never go back on that."

On a personal level, this is friendly and reassuring, so that neither teachers nor parents involved in the independent system need feel any alarm. They are safe with New Labour.

But the case against private education was never that people involved in it were unpleasant. The case was that it distorted the system as a whole, by directing an unfair portion of resources towards a small and privileged group. That remains true, and the only people who can do anything about it are the government, but Ms. Morris is not even considering the possibility. "As a minister for independent schools I have grown to like a number of them individually and to like the people who work there." [17]

You could like teachers in independent schools and recognise that their pupils were well taught, but still challenge the unjust distribution of resources and deplore the social division created as a result. After years of fudging on this issue, New Labour has decided to solve the problem of social justice, by pretending that it doesn't exist.

There has been a similar retreat over grammar schools. Tony Crosland briefly changed the shape and feel of British education, insisting that we could have a genuinely comprehensive system of education, given government determination and serious investment, but both were in short supply. In opposition, Labour was vaguely sympathetic to comprehensive schooling and education professionals.

But that stance began to look flabby when the Thatcher raid began. Parental choice was a popular mirage, and repeated attacks on state schools forced parents to fight to get their children into the best possible school. If they could afford it, they might go private. If they couldn't, they might look for a grammar school. Always, the lottery implied, some schools are better than the rest.

Many Labour supporters have always rejected that argument. They have looked for, and in many cases worked for, a universal system of education, trying to provide good schools for everyone. To them, selection undermined that principle, and one of the aims of a Labour government should be to provide excellence for all. In 1995, at the Labour Party conference, David Blunkett kept New Labour in control of the party with an Old Labour slogan "Read my lips. No selection…" but it was the funeral of a principle rather than its rebirth. Since then the stand has been diluted, to mean "no further selection". The aim was to attract floating voters, and their possible support was more important than that of Labour voters. There was little concern for people who couldn't afford to go private, who couldn't get into grammar schools, the parents of kids at the local comp.

Instead, New Labour asked why we hadn't been more economically successful:

"The answer must lie in the vested interests who oppose fundamental reform. Who are these vested interests?

The educational system in Britain has always given priority to the interests of an academic elite rather than to high general standards of education and the promotion of vocational qualifications for the broad majority of young people." [18]

That's challenging, but who are the culprits? "The Blair Revolution" goes on to list who is responsible – missionary teachers, blinkered unions, educational egalitarians. Then there's FE colleges desperate for recruitment, and industry's reluctance to invest in training.

And that's it. It's a pathetic list of easy targets, which denies the political realities. What about parental choice? What about the assumption that you can buy privilege for your children? What about the power allowed to churches, to educate separately? What about the universities, and exam syllabuses, and years of entrenched snobbery about Oxbridge, degrees, A levels, O levels, the historic, dated obsession with "the gold standard"? Don't they come into it?

They do, but they're tough to deal with. Politically they're embarrassing, these features of the landscape which block progress but can't easily be dismissed, so the New Labour response is to pretend that they're not there. This is Mandelson and Liddle's recipe for educational advance:

"New Labour believes that, throughout schooling, standards are more important than structures. Each school should be made clearly responsible for its own performance and be subject to a mixture of external pressure and support in order to raise it. Performance must be regularly assessed in objective terms that parents can understand and compare with elsewhere. Heads must be up to the job. Unsatisfactory teachers – particularly teachers with low expectations of their pupils – must be retrained or removed. Bad schools should be closed – to be reopened with new management and staff. There should be zero tolerance of failure." [19]

That's a potent little paragraph, from 1996, fixing the educational history of the next four years. Without qualifications or consultation, two spin doctors get together to concoct a programme, and hundreds of schools suffer as a result. Apart from the macho soundbites ("zero tolerance" again), there is a concentration on extremes (heads, poor teachers, failing schools), backed up with an innocent faith in crude testing: "regularly assessed in objective terms". They trust in league tables to guide parents through the market, and they see no need to ask how that market works.

"Standards not structures" is a neat phrase, but so is "learning not lessons." Short, alliterative and empty. "Standards not structures" is educational gibberish, but politically significant: what it means is that we don't wish to change the way money is spent, or upset the people in power. Therefore schools must be to blame; as a government, they are not interested in the balance of the intake, the strength of parental support, the amount of funding or the degree of deprivation. Just look at the test scores, and blame the teachers.

So, how did New Labour in power respond to the rapidly fragmenting mix of schools, with the triple lotteries of religion, funding and selection?

## BETTER THAN THE REST

Religion in education has always been awkward, and sometimes decisive – the 1944 Education Act was careful not to offend the churches. Since then, the impact of the churches on our society has decreased, but there is still a vocal minority which governments wish to keep happy.

This might not have seemed important, until other religions looked for the privileges which had been given to Christian groups. Their case was logical – either they had to be allowed to form their own schools, or Christian schools had to be closed down. The government settled for a quiet life, and we now have schools specifically for Sikhs, Jews, Muslims and Seventh Day adventists, some of which are popular and highly successful. The government is now looking for ways of helping the Church of England find money to set up 100 new secondary schools – at roughly £2 million pounds a time. Lord Dearing's committee hopes that they will get some help from developers and local authorities.

On the scale of the individual school, and many parents, that may look like good news. In terms of the system, it's a disaster. You don't need to go any further than Northern Ireland to see the damage done by sectarian schooling. We are supposed to be working to ensure that we are a multi-ethnic, multi-faith society, in which racial discrimination is outlawed, and our children to grow up with an appreciation of different traditions within our society. Is this really the time for public money to be spent in setting up sectarian schools?

The private schools can't simply be abolished. There's a lot of power and money there, and any threat to reorganise them would be time consuming and expensive for government. But there are possibilities which could be explored. In opposition, David Blunkett wanted to look at how funding rules worked in favour of private schools – how does our money help their children to get a better deal? For anyone who wants a fairer pattern, it's worth a look. But Tony Blair didn't agree, and Blunkett was stopped from even looking at the options. [20]

The 'solution' to the grammar school problem was the most cowardly of all. New Labour strategists knew that a straight attack would mean angry defence, lots of publicity and tough arguments. So they broke up the fight, and turned it into lots of little fights, where parents for grammar schools fought with parents against grammar schools. Margaret Tulloch describes the rules:

"Some of the inconsistencies are just plain bonkers. A parent in a feeder school ballot area whose children are sent to a nursery unit attached to a primary school will be eligible to vote, but if the children are sent to a separate nursery school they will not be. A parent whose child attends a feeder school of a grammar school is eligible to vote in a feeder school ballot, even if they have no intention of sending their child to the grammar school in question and live many miles away, whereas in an area ballot only the parents living outside the areas whose children actually go to school in the area are eligible." [21]

It's a farce, but it matters, because it comes from muddled thinking. Ms. Tulloch goes on: "The Government justifies these arrangements on the basis that 'parents at feeder schools have the strongest interest because their children might be expected to become pupils at grammar schools.' Does the Government not know that selection affects those rejected as well?" [22]

You would hope so, but you can't be sure. It's so much easier to take the parent view – "I understand, I want the best for my child" – rather than the overall view : what effect does this selection, this division, have on the education of all the children in this area? That's a management decision, about running the country. It's not going to be fairly resolved by contortions like this:

"In Barnet, for example, parents at only 31 of the north London borough's 91 state primary schools will be entitled to vote. The rest have been disenfranchised. Yet parents at around 15 private schools outside the borough will have a vote. Indeed, parents at state and independent schools in eight authorities have a vote on the future of Barnet's grammar schools." [23]

Mike Baker has his doubts about New Labour's motives:

"Without the active involvement of central government, and with local government forced to sit on the sidelines, it is hard to see how volunteer groups of local parents can get over the high hurdles of the ballot arrangements to achieve much change. That, of course, may be exactly what New Labour is banking on." [24]

Margaret Tulloch has followed the change in Labour thinking:

"Labour promised that we could have a comprehensive system if parents voted for it. Then they came to power and told us we would have to climb over an obstacle course before we could get a ballot. Surely, when we have done that, they could give us a level playing field." [25]

But the sharpest sense of betrayal was felt where a ballot was held. Believers in comprehensive education were involved in a fight from which the government had run away. When Debbie Atkins was active in the campaign to end selection in Ripon, she took on a lot of extra work but also received anonymous rude letters, phone-calls and e-mails. [26] She feels angry and betrayed:

"It has been horrendous. I resent the fact that the government is putting us through this. Tony Blair says education is the government's number one priority. It should be the number one responsibility. Instead, he has placed responsibility in the hands of parents like me." [27]

This evasion was resented by parents on both sides of the argument, caused intense local bitterness, and is unlikely to alter the fate of many schools. Its one advantage is that it saves New Labour from attack.When it comes to a crunch, belief is sacrificed to comfort.

So the messy lottery of the Tory market is preserved, and the chance is lost to create a fairer system. What we have is an admission of defeat: there is no system, we care only about individual schools, and the most powerful parents. The talk about education for the many not the few is only talk. When it comes down to it, the lottery will decide.

There is a concern for poverty and social inclusion. Considerable work and money has gone into the Excellence in Cities programme. But here again, selection is involved. It's only some schools, in some cities, and roughly 40% of the lowest achieving secondary schools are in rural areas. What is the programme, and the budget, for making these gains generally available?

Things don't stay the same. New variations are constantly added, so that there's an even more bewildering range of choice. I have watched the impact of specialist schools on the local area, and on two schools in particular. One was hopeful, and excited by the prospect of becoming a specialist school. To do this they had to find £50,000 sponsorship, but "If our bid is successful the Government will match this with a one-off capital grant of £100,000 and recurrent funding for four academic years."

Less than twenty miles away, in a much poorer area, another school was pursuing the same target. The hurdle was reduced, to take account of their catchment area, but they still had little chance. I confidently expected the first school to be chosen in preference to the second. I was wrong. Both were turned down.

But two other schools in the same area were more fortunate. One had already been selected as a technology centre of excellence, and was used to extra funding. The other got help from the county council (£88,000), the district council (£50,000) and the town councils (£14,500), plus external sponsorship (£60,000) and £40,000 of the school's own money. The government will be delighted to see all that extra cash coming in, and will show their gratitude by putting in even more cash of their own. To them that hath shall be given, and God help the suckers that hath not. They will just have to forget the effort of form-filling, the time spent touting for sponsors and the pain of disappointed hopes. They need to buckle down to their appointed role, of being "the rest."

That basic injustice would be bad enough, but we now learn that the idea of 'specialism' is a lie. LSE researchers spoke to 138 heads of specialist schools. More than half of them said that their supposed specialism was not the school's strongest teaching area. The main reason for pursuing specialist status was to get more money for the school. [28] Whatever the title says, it's lottery business as usual. Except that business is limited, since in October 2000 "The Government has put a cap on the number of specialist schools in each local authority even though some hopefuls may have already raised tens of thousands of pounds towards their applications." [29]

And there's more. David Blunkett is adding an extra ingredient to the swirling mix. "City academies" are to be started under the same legal framework as city technology colleges, although the government is keen to change the name. Graham Lane said it was "a half-baked idea, borrowed from the charter school movement in the US." Nigel de Gruchy saw it as "the nail in the coffin of the traditional comprehensive system." Doug McAvoy said "the net consequence of his blizzard of intitiatives is high staff turnover, head-teacher resignation and general dismay and demoralisation." John Dunford said "the proposal for city academies is the sticking plaster over the government's failure to prvide adequate support for schools serving the most disadvantaged communities."

Blunkett, however, is bullish. "My vision is one of excellence and diversity; a vision of transformation. It is already starting to change the way every secondary school operates... But we must go further and faster." [30]

He sounds like the driver of a runaway train. But behind the determined optimism is a refusal to face the disintegration of the system. There has been a failure of honesty, a reluctance to tell the truth about the limitations of parental choice. This isn't a delicate plant which is going to 'bed down', or an infant system which should 'get over its teething problems'. Each year, increasing numbers of parents realise that their choice is limited, and they appeal against the school they are given. In September 2000 Joe Hallgarten reported on research for the IPPR which recorded a 50% rise in appeals since 1995. "There is no doubt that, in certain pockets of neighbourhoods, parental choice is breeding a collective panic, one that uses up irrational amounts of precious school time and resources." [31]

Government has a responsibility to see how this lottery works. Who gains and who loses? How well does it work? Labour's refusal to do that is cowardly. And if they have decided that there can be no system, that they are aiming to save a few lifeboats while the rest of the Titanic goes down, it would be a relief to hear them say so, rather than listening to more boasts about how their efforts will produce a system which will be the envy of the world.

Given New Labour's ideas, their faith in testing and their anxiety about the middle class, it's tempting to offer them some help. Why don't they run a simple exam? Instead of this time-consuming, frustrating illusion of choice, they could make all 10 year olds do a world-class test. Then the brightest ones, as well as those with the most wealthy and influential parents, could go into into specially favoured schools. They could call it something snappy, like the Eleven Plus. What would be wrong with that?

## A SECRET STRATEGY

I started teaching in 1967, in a large comprehensive with a twelve-form entry. They were carefully graded, from 1A1 to 1A6, from 1B1 to 1B5, with 1C bringing up the rear. I had an English group, lower 3B4/5, who were meant to be the triumph of selection. 3B4 and 3B5 were reckoned to be roughly level, but my group was the result of setting the two – I had the weakest pupils out of these two low groups. This was real fine tuning.

As a group, they were certainly trouble, and they probably taught me more than I taught them. But the memory that remains is how mixed a bunch they were – slow kids who tried hard, lazy kids who didn't care, bright kids who were seldom in school, stroppy kids who'd been thrown out of higher groups.

It's not as easy as it looks to put 'kids who are the same' together. There were problems elsewhere in the school. At a parents' evening, I was worried about why Jim didn't seem to be working as hard as he might. He was in 2B2, but he knew other children from his previous junior school, who weren't as bright as him, who were in 2A6. His parents had queried this in the first year, but had been told "If he's bright enough, he'll be moved up." He had worked hard then, but nothing had changed. Maybe the numbers were wrong, or it was disruptive to change classes, or a teacher had forgotten. For whatever reason, Jim stayed where he was, and stopped trying.

In my training and during my early years of teaching I read books like "Downstream", "Streaming" and "Education and the Working Class". They traced what happened when pupils were put in sets and streams, how their self-image and motivation were affected by the structures of selection. Other books looked at the effects of exams, the way pupils' writing could be improved if they had freedom to write at greater length, in more realistic conditions, with more say over what they wrote.

These were some of the roots of mixed-ability teaching, in which I was involved for most of my working life. It wasn't an easy option, and it involved hard thinking and hard work. At an interview I was once asked ""What are the advantages of mixed-ability teaching, for the able child?" which still strikes me as a beautiful question. The beautiful answer, at its best, is that mixed-ability teaching allows for differentiation, and sometimes accepts that pupils in a group will work at different rates and will confront different problems, and can't therefore always follow the same route together, at the same pace. For the very brightest children, the problem is not that they are surrounded by pupils less able than themselves, but that they are kept to the pace of others in their class. If they can be freed from that, some of the time, then the ability level of their classmates is less important.

This differentiation is hard, and does not often happen. But it is possible, and it can produce exciting results. It can also contribute to an atmosphere in which all pupils feel equally valued, and the least able are encouraged to aim at the best they can possibly achieve. I remember an adviser, looking round my mixed-ability class, surprised by the quality of literature which all the pupils would meet. In a low set, there's far more chance that the teacher will play safe, "give them something they can cope with", and that as a result the pupils will miss out.

"What do you expect of a C child?", or "Is that a good book for set five?" aren't criminal questions, but they are lazy, and the laziest teachers I've met have been happiest where setting is applied.

Mixed-ability, on the other hand, is a challenge. It accepts that there will be differences within the class, and that time and thought will be needed. But it also places all the teachers in the same boat, having to cater for a range of talents. In departments committed to mixed-ability teaching you can often find a high level of discussion, awareness of problems and techniques, and a willingness to share strategies and materials. That's demanding but also exciting, and it generates an extra commitment to the business of teaching.

Or it can do. Those things don't follow automatically from the fact of mixed-ability grouping. If it's imposed on teachers or schools, by fanatical heads or enthusiastic politicians, it can be a disaster. It's not a faith, but a series of techniques, and unless the time and thought has been put in then it's unlikely to work.

Does it work? That's the key question, and it would be nice to have a simple experiment which showed the relative merits of streaming/setting and mixed-ability. Such an experiment was set up at Banbury, with parallel groups being taught in different ways, but although the study was intelligent, it could not produce a decisive verdict. Since then, research evidence has been interestingly mixed.

Reson and Hallam found that mixed-ability classes achieved equally good academic results and were better for pupils' morale. [32] Girls would have earned many more A-grade GCSEs in maths if they had been taught in mixed-ability classes, according to a team from King's College, London. [33] Britain uses more ability grouping than almost any country in the world. The highly successful countries in the Pacific Rim teach mainly to mixed-ability classes. [34]

Not all the evidence is on the same side, but this isn't an argument for introducing mixed-ability teaching everywhere, at once. It is an argument for taking it seriously, because it can be successful, here and elsewhere. But mixed-ability teaching has been branded as silly and old-fashioned.

Before the election Tony Blair told his listeners that "Mixed ability teaching is for some people as much of an ideology as the principle of comprehensive admission itself. Not to take account of the obvious common sense that different children move at different speeds and have differing abilities, is to give idealism a bad name." [35]

At one moment, Blair is Everydad, the innocent who is against the eleven plus but supportive of grammar schools. And now he is telling me that what I know is a sophisticated and promising structure, used successfully all over the world, is really an outdated fashion I should ignore. How can he be so sure? Does he really think that this was just a whim, which a lot of stupid teachers fell for, but which he has now exposed? I can list research that shows successful mixed-ability teaching in action. What is it that makes him so sure it's bound to fail?

In an address to a Labour group called Progress, Blair offered his version of educational history. "Too often comprehensives adopted a one-size-fits-all mentality – no setting, uniform provision for all, hostile to the notion of specialisation and centres of excellence within areas of the curriculum... comprehensives should be as dedicated as any private school or old grammar school to high achievement for the most able." [36]

In 1973 I became head of English in a new comprehensive school, which was replacing a grammar school and two secondary moderns. We were going to be teaching mixed-ability classes in an area where pupils and parents were used to a very different pattern. We talked about this, thought about it, held meetings and detailed discussions, and one of our keenest concerns was that the ablest pupils should not suffer from this change.

In 1981 I became deputy head at another school, in a deprived area. We didn't have many bright pupils, and for that reason we were anxious that they should not be forgotten. I chose a small number of 11 year olds, followed them through their lessons and interviewed them about their work. I ran meetings with staff about how we were teaching them, and how we might organise teaching methods and materials so as to teach them better. And I had access to a considerable body of work in which other teachers, other schools, were confronting the same challenge. But we also looked at how we were teaching boys and girls, weak readers, pupils who found it hard to talk.

None of that is surprising. It is what you would expect responsible professionals to do. What is astonishing is that the Prime Minister does not know that such work was going on, and that he thinks he is offering some kind of new, tough thinking when he argues for setting. His picture is crude, appealing to interest groups who like that kind of thing, but a distraction from the serious analysis of teaching. It is unwise of him to claiming expertise in an area where he hasn't worked, and he needs some fresh advice.

Blunkett, too, calls for teachers to abandon "a dogmatic attachment to mixed-ability teaching", as though it were some form of Scientology. There's no sign that this follows from an analysis of how and where it's used. OFSTED is notoriously coy. It praises schools which do good mixed-ability teaching for their skill in responding to the diverse needs of pupils, without actually mentioning the dreaded phrase. So, how do the politcians know what they're talking about?

They don't. This isn't about teaching methods. It's about politics. Middle class parents whose children go into comprehensive schools know that one of the things which might affect their progress is the presence of children who are less able, less motivated. So clear signals have to be given that such pupils will be separated off, whether or not that is the best thing for all concerned.

The government has set up schemes for gifted and talented pupils, as part of the Excellence in Cities programme. As usual when more money and better resources become available, middle class parents see an opportunity and point their children in that direction.

"According to a study by King's College, London, middle-class children are coming under tremendous parental pressure to qualify for the schemes. Interviews with 45 children from eight London schools revealed all the pupils on the programme came from middle-class homes. Children who were not deemed bright enough to be part of the programmes felt a 'painful exclusion' which led to a 'backlash of self-attack." [37]

Meanwhile, outside the magic circle, teachers consider mixed-ability as a possible route to give all children a fair deal. But they are being pressured to overlook a route that can lead to better achievement and higher motivation for many of their pupils, so that New Labour can continue to give the right signals to their chosen constituency. Will it work? If it does, it will work for the few but not the many, and the immediate losers will be those at the bottom of the heap, pupils who feel that school is not for them. Whether it works for the lucky ones, the chosen few in the top sets, only time will tell, but like so much else it's a  gamble, yet one more instance of the lottery at work.

1   The Perfect Storm p.176
2   Guardian 9.9.99
3   Guardian 1.11.99
4   TES 1.12.00
5   Observer 18.6.00
6   Guardian 6.7.99
7   TES 13.10.00
8   Murnane and Cohen, in Guardian 13.4.93
9   TES 22.12.00
10   Observer 23.6.96
11   TES 29.1.99
12   Guardian 17.7.95
13   Martin Johnson, NAS president, Guardian 25.4.00
14   TES 2.4.99
15   Will Hutton, in Observer 9.9.98
16   Guardian 28.11.97
17   Guardian 30.9.00
18   Mandelson and Liddle, "The Blair Revolution" p. 91
19   Mandelson and Liddle, "The Blair Revolution" p. 92
20   Guardian 2.1.95
21   Margaret Tulloch,  TES 25.2.00
22   Margeret Tulloch, TES 25.2.00
23   Mike Baker, TES 12.3.99
24   Mike Baker, TES 12.3.99
25   TES 3.11.98
26   Guardian 3.10.00
27   TES 18.2.00
28   TES 15.9.00
29   TES 13.10.00
30   Guardian 16.3.00
31   Observer 17.9.00
32   Guardian 1.12.99
33   TES 28.8.98
34   Guardian 24.11.98
35   Guardian 8.6.96
36   Guardian 9.9.00
37   Helen Lucey and Diane Reay, TES 15.9.00

# Chapter 7:

# LEADERSHIP AND LIES

## GOVERNMENT AND MANAGEMENT

The drums rise to a climax as the people gather in the clearing. Sudden silence as the beat dies, and one lone figure steps forward, to address the tribe. Take me to your leader, one more time.

It's not always as primitive as that. I have in front of me a glossy brochure, with a soft focus photograph of a field of flowers. At the edges of the picture they merge into each other, and all of them are red, except one. So my eye is drawn to a single isolated flower, clearer than the rest, in bright yellow. And just in case I don't get it, the yellow caption reads "Leadership marks you out as different. Leadership, because of your responsibilities, means your needs are different. That is where we come in..."

This was the from the NAHT. I was a deputy head, and they were a union of head teachers, but they wanted more members. So they appealed to my vanity. As a deputy, I was slightly different; if I became a head, I would be even more different. But how did I get to be that way? Was I always a secret yellow, or did I magically change from being red?

Mrs. Thatcher has a lot to answer for. She changed the way we think about leadership. Before her, a good Prime Minister was a wily man who could balance different factions, inside and outside his cabinet. By wheeling and dealing, by keeping different people happy at different times, he retained control, and created a feeling of agreement.

She changed all that. Her solution to the challenge of a varied cabinet was to sack those who disagreed with her. Consensus was a dream, a mirage which stopped you from getting things done. If you were going to make things happen, you picked people who shared your vision, ignored the doubts and protests of those who didn't, and got on with it.

In some situations that can be the best response, and in any case it has a powerful appeal – you don't need to think about the arguments, or listen to consultation. You just go ahead and do it. Sometimes that leads to disaster (the poll tax), sometimes it means a gamble (the Falklands War), but always it carries a surge of adrenalin – look, we are getting things done.

Tony Blair's personal style was more conciliatory – he was presented as a smiling family man, young by political standards, reasonable and in touch. But as a leader he took over the Thatcher pattern, undiluted and without regret. There was the same concentration on a small circle of close believers, and beyond that others were devalued, regardless of intelligence, experience or loyalty to the party.

The best of the Labour Party tradition was its emphasis on valuing each member, so that a large national organisation looked for ways of involving supporters in the discussion of policy. This produced committees and conferences, which are easy to mock but contain a vital idea – different views and experiences come together, for the same cause. This could lead to fierce debate and the appearance of disunity, media images which implied a lack of control, but it puts across an important truth – nobody knows all the answers. If I collect the reactions and suggestions of others, I will end up with a wiser, fuller view than if I do it all myself.

New Labour has no time for such considerations. They have the answers, and their job is to supply them, fast and with maximum publicity. Previously, when the government appointed a royal commission, there was some suspense as to whether or not they would approve its recommendations. Now, the creation of a commission is a sign that a problem is being shelved, as with long-term care, the reform of the voting system or a rational policy on drugs. Government representatives are put onto the commission to guide it on what's acceptable, and they dissociate themselves from embarrassing conclusions. But even if the report is carefully balanced and conclusive, its recommendations will be ignored.

Tony Blair treats the Labour Party as a rubber stamp. He has scant affection for it, little sense of its history and no clue that it might contribute positively to his thinking. Reports of his handling of cabinet suggest a remote, autocratic pattern. Where a dispute involves differences between minister A and minister B, Blair speaks to each separately, and then they get the Blair decision.

This leaves uncertainty and suspicion hanging in the air ("So, what did he say to the other one, and what did they tell him?") but it also devalues everybody else but him. Is there a chance, that in open discussion, A and B, or A and B and Blair together, might have come up with a solution? The shuttle model, by assuming that only the leader has wisdom and power, rules out that possibility.

Shuttle diplomacy can come unstuck. The Good Friday agreement was an important step towards peace, and the Blair government's concern with Northern Ireland has been more serious and consistent than the approach of his predecessors.

But there was a dangerous moment in the Good Friday negotiations when the loyalists were not convinced by the seriousness of the IRA's commitment to decommissioning. A key opponent was absent from the scene, Blair provided a personal written note of reassurance, and the deal was done.

But which deal? Sinn Fein had signed up to an agreement; the loyalists had signed up to an agreement, plus a note from Tony Blair. So, were Sinn Fein committed to the note from Tony Blair? That was the question which nearly wrecked the whole process, because of the dependence on Blair's risk-taking. It contrasts with the style of George Mitchell, the American senator who made the earlier progress possible. He kept the tone low key, and focussed on the needs of the main parties, rather than his own role.

There is a vivid illustration of Blair's style in a leaked memo:

"It is bizarre that any government I lead should be seen as anti-family.. But all these things lead up to a sense that the government – and this even applies to me – are somehow out of touch with gut British instincts." He then looks for a series of initiatives as a corrective future strategy, and concludes "I should be personally associated with as much of this as possible. TB " [1]

His concern with his own image is worrying. Why should it be so surprising that his government is seen as anti-family? Because he loves his own family? Or because he's allowed that image to be consistently promoted through press photographs? Why should he be more certain that his personal values will be expressed through the workings of his government than previous prime ministers?

He asserts, as if it were a law of nature, that "I should be personally associated with as much of this as possible." But why? Because it would feed his vanity, or it's good for the country, or because it's the best way to get things done? It's been a feature of New Labour that at key points Blair has muscled into departmental areas, to take over the controls and grab the glory in foreign affairs, health, education, law and order. In the short-term that may make him look good, but it devalues the people with whom he's working – and fuels the resentment which produces leaks.

There is an alternative approach. He could be a calmer, more remote figure, who watched with admiration as his varied, trusted team of ministers demonstrated their talents. Because he has established the framework of a shared programme, the trust is mutual. That wouldn't be easy to achieve, and it wouldn't bring immediate tabloid coverage, but it would make more use of his team, improve their morale, and take pressure off him.

Blair extends his concentration on the isolated leader to education policy. Head teachers are promoted as the key figures in a school, sometimes the only figures that matter. And when the government acts tough, they will also act tough with heads:

" 'FAILING HEADS FACE MINISTERS' SUMMONS.

Headteachers of failing schools will be summoned by the Education Secretary for a meeting with ministers if they have not made enough progress after five terms, standards minister Stephen Byers has warned." [2]

This is comic, because it reverses the traditional pattern. "Going to see the head" was the classic carpeting, the ultimate telling off. Now imagine a headteacher, waiting nervously outside the Standards Minister's door, as he waits to be told off.

But it is also silly, in its reliance on fear. Will teachers faced with such threats really do a better job? What exactly in their approach will change, and how will that result in better work by pupils? When challenged to explain why further punitive measures were necessary, Byers responded:

"These schools have been in special measures for a total of 346 months between them; they had had 49 inspections and were responsible for 7,900 pupils... I would have been failing in my responsibility to those pupils if I turned my back on them." [3]

Once more a government minister makes himself the star of the show. The number crunching is pointless. Adding up the months for which different schools have been in special measures is a roundabout way of saying "I've had enough of this", and yet again alternatives are ignored. It's down to a simple choice – does Byers turn his back or not? No, he doesn't. He really cares. So that's all right. Except that within months he was moving off to another department, and the pupils were abandoned to the mercy of teachers.

That aggression was toned down after he left, but the basic pattern did not change. A year later, new head teachers were summoned to a conference on leadership skills, where management guru Ben Zander taught them about one-buttock piano playing, and the importance of confidence. He was preceded by Tony Blair, who promised the new heads that they could expect better rewards if they were successful, but that those who were not up to the job would face the sack.

It's a classic Thatcher pattern. You concentrate on the boss. You give them power, and more money. They bully and threaten the people below them into getting better results, and the head then gets more money still. Some of the sums are astronomical, but they still end up cheap because only a very small number of people are getting the bonus. We are offered a myth of improvement, which says that teachers are the problem, and heads the solution. A tough new head will come in, and turn the school around, and standards will rise.

Maybe they will. There are schools which fit that pattern, but there are also schools where the head is the problem and the teachers are the solution. There are schools which have been turned round that needn't have been, and others which have been turned round, and have then turned back again. It is a complex business, and comparisons with heavy tankers will only get you so far.

We need a more careful analysis of what heads do and what teachers do and how those two kinds of work connect. But we don't get that, because both government and media are happier with cartoons, which are simpler to run. Superheads could easily have been a comic strip, but government seriously offered them as a solution to educational problems. They were given extra pay, extra resources, extra powers, in return for which they are expected to deliver miracles. It's worth looking at what happened when the fantasy was put into practice.


## SEARCHING FOR SUPERHEAD

In April 1995, Hammersmith School was struggling. It had had five heads in three years, exam results were poor and few parents chose it for their children. William Atkinson, successful head of a suburban school, was persuaded to take over. He named it Phoenix School, set a distinctive, charismatic style, and two years later the school came out of special measures.

Atkinson was a media star, invited on to task forces and the subject of drooling reporting: "Morning patrol begins at 8.30 am sharp. William Atkinson tugs at the sleeves of his jacket, straightens his tie and strides purposefully out of the school gates like a predator emerging from his lair." [4] You can see why Lucy Gannon found him a useful model for the star of "Hope and Glory."

Atkinson was used in an advert, to tempt other inspirational messiahs into the profession. There was a large, imposing picture, and the slogan: "This is the Head that raised all the heads at Phoenix School". Notice that the hero is in capitals, and the peasants in ordinary letters. There is no room for doubt; the job description requires self-belief, and the candidate is full of it:

"This wasn't a place to learn the game. You had to have bags of confidence that your prescription was right." There are times when Atkinson himself seems to believe the hype: "I took this job to see if I could climb Everest. This school has become my Everest. It has called for all my energy and commitment and I couldn't resist the challenge. But I still have a mountain to climb." [5]

Then he remembers this is also a team operation, in which other people play their part. Christine Blower insists "the Phoenix experience is a model for others. It has proved beyond doubt that success and improvement are based on partnership with teachers. This partnership has not yet been given the recognition it deserves." [6]

Paul Hampton was one of the new teachers that Atkinson brought in. This is his perspective on the process: "The government's plan for 'Fresh Start' seems to require old teachers to be turfed out and a new bunch come in – but no magic is provided by people like myself coming in fresh. Indeed I have learned a great deal from teachers who have been here a long time: without them the school would have gone down." [7]

As the voices gather, so the picture become more complex, less clear, less sexy. There is no doubt that progress has been made at Phoenix School, and that Atkinson's leadership has been a key part of that progress. He himself insists "the real job is much more difficult than I thought it would be." [8] But when OFSTED visited in June '99 attendance was still low, and the school had failed to attract sufficient good quality staff. By the key government measure, only 11% of pupils had gained five GCSE grades at A-C. So, what went wrong?

Atkinson didn't lose his touch, or lose interest. He and his staff were, as they all maintained throughout, dealing with long-term problems. To expect quick solutions was short-sighted, and the strategy came unstuck. There were plenty of people warning that this would happen, but those people were ignored.

What would really make a difference? Atkinson faces a pressure common to many struggling schools. They have empty places, so they cannot turn pupils away. Many of the pupils they are offered, particularly in the older age groups, are pupils who have been excluded from other schools. His judgement says that he has enough of such problems already, but he's not in charge. This is how he describes the situation:

"Someone like myself needs to say 'Hold on! This system is rotten.' If you start from a low base of ability and behaviour and keep topping it up with children who've been excluded from elsewhere, it's set up to create failing schools. We should either spread these kids around the system, or give failing schools the best accommodation, the best teachers, and pay them accordingly. I have to confront this every day, and I'm getting to the point where I want some honesty." [9]

More generally, he wants funding and planning to be less dependent on quick fixes. "We need less short-termism and more long-term planning and commitment." And on the issue of headship, the unrelenting focus on the figurehead, Atkinson is better placed to than most to comment:

"The view has been that you just need a talented head. But you also need quality at every level – the very best teachers of maths, PE, English, the best middle managers, an experienced senior management team who are not fazed by working overtime every day. The most important single element is highly talented, resilient staff. A superhead with supply teachers cannot do it." [10]

Chapter Three of this book has a section on "Making the Grade", the Fresh Start at Firfield School. That programme followed the usual pattern of most TV documentaries about schools by focussing on the head, partly because they're a convenient central figure, partly because keeping them sweet is the key to the whole business of filming in a school.

Carol McAlpine also came from a background of success, brimming with self-confidence – "I've turned another school round, and I wouldn't mind doing another." Her appointment was a high-risk deal between her and the local education authority – additional resources, freedom to appoint new staff (and to dispose of old ones) and a large salary, in exchange for increased attendance and raised exam passes. To me that sounds like a pact with the devil, but I'm not the stuff of which superheads are made.

McAlpine felt in retrospect that she came over too harshly on the film, as someone whose softer side was ignored but who continually seemed to be in situations of conflict. The TV crew said that they wanted to show the pressures under which she worked. But there was a telling moment when one of her star pupils, in an acceptance speech on prize day, thanked "Mrs. McAlpine, who put pressure on the teachers." She may vary from smiling to stern, but the consistent message is that whatever you're doing, it isn't enough. She is David Blunkett's dream.

But after eighteen months McAlpine was on her way, for a £70,000 job in Norwich. She explained that she could not pass up the opportunity of being head of an education action zone. [11]

She could, actually. It would be quite reasonable to say "this is an interesting challenge but I have already taken up another, and I need to see that through." But it's part of New Labour's view of heads that they should see themselves as ambitious and mobile, not even tied to education, let alone to particular jobs.

But what about the kids and parents at the school? How do they now feel about the promises she made? What about staff, who lost their jobs because they didn't fit into McAlpine's version of the future? What of the teachers who came to work for her, who moved job and house to be part of turning the school round – where do they go from here?

It's tricky to balance personal amibition against the needs of a school, and everybody has to go sometime. But a school in the process of improvement is a delicate structure, and it doesn't help that heads and teachers are seen to occupy such different worlds, not only in salary but in freedom of movement. I can remember a similar case where a head suddenly announced that he was leaving a school which during his headship had improved dramatically. (He had, to be fair, been there more than twice as long as Ms.McAlpine). The staff's reaction was anxious and suspicious, particularly among those who had deliberately come to the school to be part of the improvement – "What does he know that we don't? But I thought things were going all right...."

In the case of Firfield, they weren't. Or they weren't going well enough to meet the terms of the deal. Two months after her departure, the local authority announced that they were planning to close the school. Whether or not McAlpine knew of this prospect, or guessed at it, you can imagine the morale of the colleagues she left behind.

The George Orwell School, near Finsbury Park in London, was

transformed by Fresh Start into the Islington Arts and Media School. The new head, Torsten Friedag, started in September 1999 with a large salary, massive publicity and the personal backing of David Blunkett. By May 2000 he had gone. George Orwell had received a damning OFSTED report, and had only achieved 10% with 5 A-C grades. Estimates for the following year suggested that they would be between 7-8%.

It's hard to be precise about what went wrong. Friedag was popular personally, and may have suffered from his openness to the press. He got some good publicity, but there was also well publicised misbehaviour, and wide reprinting of a false rumour that at one stage he was hiding under his desk. There was manoeuvring by local politicians, and delays in a massive rebuilding programme, which can't have made his job any easier.

His successor Dr. John Hudson said that "the school has had problems with its timetabling, curriculum, disciplinary systems and attendance-monitoring procedures under Mr. Friedag." [12] This was the reason he gave for delaying the start of term for pupils, to allow a ten day period of retraining for staff.

What is certain is that this is complex. There are different ways of tackling this situation, but considerable thought and sustained effort will be required to make any sustained improvement. It is therefore rash to make too much noise about the appointment of superheads, or the timescale in which they should be expected to register results.

This is particularly relevant at the Islington school, because Andrew Adonis, the Prime Minister's education advisor, was one of its governors and was involved in Friedag's appointment. It would be nice to think that he was also involved in the process of picking up the pieces, but he resigned when Friedag left.

This might be an admission that a mistake was made. We can't be sure. Facing failure isn't easy, but in this area we need honesty, for the sake of the teachers who will come into situations like this. Ian Garwood became the third superhead to resign within a week, and when he left the East Brighton Fresh Start School he said:

"During this year we have begun the process of creating a new college aspiring to high standards. It is my judgement that the college will be best served by appointing a new principal whose skills close-ly match the key tasks." [13]

This suggests that there are two jobs – starting the process and keeping it going. He's fine at doing the first, but for the second it needs somebody else, better suited to the job. Was this clear when he was appointed? If they had known he was doing a six month burst would they have given him that salary, or appointed him at all?

We don't have to pillory individuals, but we do have to be clear about what's happening. If the expectations of superheads are too high, then that needs to be said, by them and by government. Otherwise the search for comic strip heroes will continue, and we are doomed to repeated, expensive failure, which can't be good for teachers or pupils.

I'm not asking for gloom and doom. I've worked in a school which was treated as a failure, and was regularly, publicly slandered long after it had made massive improvements. I know the effect of damning pub-licity. This is not about schools, but about thinking. It should be possi-ble for articulate politicians to recognise the failure of their own think-ing without damning the schools that have suffered from their illusions.

When there's a new initiative to be announced, or credit to be gained, ministers are there to claim the glory. But when something goes wrong, we have to make do with "a government source." And their brief is always to be positive – never apologise, never explain. This was the response of a DFEE spokesman to the news that Firfield was threatened with closure:

"Giving schools a fresh start is an important part of the govern-ment's drive to raise standards in inner city areas. There are some good early signs in Fresh Start schools. We expect that investment in these schools will be worthwhile." [14]

It's positive and forward looking, and it gives no hostages to enemy critics. But it also denies the past, and refuses to acknowledge mistakes that have been made. If they're not being honest with us, we wonder, are they being honest with themselves? Can they see clearly enough to know what's going on, and respond to the evidence of their own miscalculation?

Between March 9 and 14 three superheads resigned. An official government source commented:

"The thing to remember is that in these schools, the alternatives have all been tried. There is no alternative, other than to close the school and disperse the children, or see a continued drift into failure." [15]

This simply isn't true. That combination – focus on head, massive money, expectation of short term success, measured in A/C grades at GCSE – is a very particular set of choices. They were criticised at the time, and have been cruelly exposed since. It would have been quite possible to intervene, but in a different way.

The TES talked to four headteachers about Fresh Start. Their responses went as follows: 1. Every school has its challenges and the idea of some superhero taking over is not on our agenda. 2. We mustn't be blinded by our egos. Heads are deluding themselves if they think £100,000 and a short-term contract is going to change the culture of a school. 3. I haven't seen anything that leads me to believe that 'superheads' would actually have any real power as opposed to influence. 4. Extra money does not necessarily solve the problem. [16]

So maybe it doesn't matter. This was always a fantasy, a bubble for the media, and in the real world schools and teachers get on with the job. In the meantime, however, the scheme has been an expensive failure, and it's clouded the necessary thinking about how schools should be run. It's also left a powerful image that what we need is some kind of messiah, a special person who is just that bit more energetic, radical, charismatic. It's important to say, and for the government to accept, that this is just a dream.


## THE HEAD'S JOB


Back in the real world, head teachers have a job to do. That job is now more pressured than it has ever been. There are increasing demands, from a variety of sources, and the direction in which those demands lead is away from lessons and kids. During the 1990s I watched good heads, knowing the vital importance of classroom teaching, who visited lessons, were around the school and aware of the work that was going on.

That was time well spent, because it kept them in touch, and stopped them being marooned by paperwork. But it also signalled to teachers and pupils that this was the real work of the school, where the head's priorities lay, and that fact was appreciated by staff.

As the decade wore on, such heads found that work increasingly hard to carry out. The lessons had not become worse, or less important, but the demands on the head's time had become more insistent – meeting prospective parents, attending LEA meetings, talking to sources of funding, liaising with employers, colleges and higher education. None of these things were evil, but all of them drew heads further and further away from what was happening in the classroom.

One of the sickest jokes in the PRP arrangements was that heads alone were to be responsible for the assessment of teachers. Schools which tried to involve deputies in this role – both to reduce the load of work, and to train them for future responsibility – were told off, and reminded that this was a job for which heads were uniquely qualified. Yet how many teachers, if you asked them to name the three best judges of teaching in their school, would come up with the name of the head?

Head teachers have been paid more, although many of them would say that the increase does not balance the extra work. What the increase does do, though, is sharpen still further the division between chiefs and Indians. The pay rise may not be enough, but it's more than the workers in the staffroom are getting.

Quite as important as money is the lack of clarity in the role. Heads have to work with governors, local authorities and government, but the precise nature of those relationships is very vague. Governors' powers were originally increased for a mixture of motives. These included a concern for local democracy, an urge to counter teacher power, and an attempt to mask national cuts by getting volunteers to administer them a school at a time. Heads who work well with their governors are glad of their support, but when the relationship breaks down the guidance is very vague.

Occasionally governors surface to show their power by sacking a head, but a more common pattern is for heads to control the agenda and flow of information, so that they decide the governors' role. This is often limited, and there are few avenues open for a governor with anxieties about a school which the head does not wish them to raise.

A teacher governor outlines the scenario at their school: "I see it drifting into destructive conflict and realise how powerless a teacher is. Our head has his strong points, but avoids any debate about school policies, panics and becomes secretive over anything controversial, refuses to discuss complaints and handles governors badly. The atmosphere is terrible. An opinionated political governor feels the school could do much better... An overenthusiastic parent governor sees herself as the watchdog for all parents' interests..." [17] So, exactly whose job is it to sort out this mess, and who makes sure that it gets done?

Then there are the LEAs and the government, in tension about the nature of each other's power, but both seeking to influence heads, and anxious to secure the short term results which will provide the proof of success. This urgency produces crises, like the fiasco over exclusions.

We exclude more children from school than we need, and the impact of that is damaging, on them and on us. The Metropolitan police estimate that 40% of robberies, 25% of burglaries and 20% of thefts are committed by school age children during school hours. So it makes sense to try to cut down the number of children excluded from school.

But not at any cost, and not by imposing an arbitrary quota or by assuming that you can do it through bribes and fines. Tony Hardman is a Liverpool head, who gets £380,000 a year to help prevent exclusions. He has two pupils who are determined to get themselves excluded. "But every time I exclude one child I lose money too. I've lost £20,000 from the project through exclusions. That's money that could and should have helped support some of the younger ones now to stop them getting excluded later on." [18]

Three days later, delegates at the ATL conference at Belfast warned the government that its policy of discouraging the exclusion of unruly pupils was causing problems for the obedient majority.

The next month, however, the government were confident that things were going well. "Ministers are taking the credit for a massive drop in exclusion rates, saying it is due to the extra investment and support they have provided for disruptive pupils to remain in schools. But teacher organisations say the reduction has led to increased stress for members, forced to deal with badly behaved children in their classes who would previously have been expelled." [19]

Headteachers threatened to take court action against appeal panels who had forced them to take back disruptive pupils. The government made an exception for violent pupils, but that isn't the main problem. As a teacher, I'm far less worried by the prospect of being attacked, than by a kid who might sit in my lesson saying "This is fucking boring. I'm not doing this."

David Hart pointed out that drug dealing and bullying could also cause serious disruption. He said "We simply think the government ought to back off on this ridiculous target. The exclusions process is falling into disrepute." [20] The NAHT view was that "ministerial guidance on exclusions is designed simply to meet their target rather than sort out difficult situations." [21]

By August 2000, a succession of disputes between schools and appeal panels led the government to retreat, ordering local authorities not to override headteachers' decisions on exclusion. A government source said "the minister will make it clear the appeals panel have no right to interfere in schools' disciplinary policies. This is all about justice and fair play." [22] It didn't seem that way to Chris Gale, chairwoman of the National Governors' council. "Headteachers do not have the last word. Governors have to uphold their decisions. I'm fed up with ministers undervaluing governors." [23]

This was not just a personal view, as a NAGM survey discovered in a survey published in September 2000.

Heads warned that as a result exclusions would rise, but Jacqui Smith, the schools minister, insisted that "The targets stand and we expect to hit them." [24] So as a head, you're told you mustn't exclude. Some pupils you exclude are sent back to you by the local authority, but you appeal and a judge backs you. You seem to have a right to exclude, but the government says it will still force you to exclude fewer pupils than you did. You could be forgiven for not knowing where you stand.

It's a minefield, and it has to be controlled at the school level, taking account of the pupil's situation, and the needs of other pupils, as well as of teachers. It is interesting that Peter Clark, the head who was put in to turn The Ridings around, came very close to resignation over precisely this issue. He felt that if he wasn't free to decide that a particular pupil needed to be excluded, for the sake of others, then he could not carry out the improvements which the school required. [25]

Exclusion has to be discussed, by heads, teachers and governors. But ministers' attempt at a pre-emptive strike by remote control – sound-bites followed by the confident prediction of reduced percentages – has made the situation worse. Meanwhile, the head is at the point of contact, between the school and the governors and the LEA, and beyond them government regulations, and that's a wearing place to be.

Where does that pressure go? In one direction, it leads to a more autocratic way of running schools. When I was an acting head, in 1988, I went to a head teachers' conference, where it was fashionable to talk about team management, as follows: 'The job of running the school is now so complicated that no one person can carry all the expertise in their head. Areas of responsibility have to be shared out between team members, so that between them they can cover the whole territory, and combine their insights for the good of the school.'

That's what they said, and it can work. But I knew, because I knew the deputies in the schools that they ran, that some of the heads paying lip service to this doctrine were not putting it into practice. It's not easy, and if you haven't had previous experience of it you can't be sure how team management would work. For a new head who's anxious not to make mistakes, it's reasonable to play safe, and to treat your deputies in the same way that your head treated you.

That argument has been strengthened by increasing government pressures, which have led to a more autocratic pattern. In a study of primary school management, Mike Wallace found that heads, facing a whirlwind of change, have been retreating into hierarchical styles of management. "Senior staff find themselves becoming mere underlings doing their master's bidding. If you have strong accountability, then heads are going to play things close to their chest." [26]

If that is true in primary schools, it's going to be even truer in secondary schools, whose size makes management a much more obvious challenge. Heads have always wielded power, being able to control timetable decisions, the allocation of classes to staff, and the movement of staff through references. It may seem short-sighted for a head-teacher to prevent a member of their staff from getting promotion: if they don't like them or don't think much of them, surely they're better off letting them go? But in power games it isn't always logic that wins.

To that old power is now added a new set of weapons. The head as judge of threshold payments can visit lessons, and decide who gets a pay rise. The head as figurehead responsible for continuous improvement can demand that teachers produce endless schemes of work or lesson plans, much as old-style teachers would set their pupils lines.

"A deputy head who had been a teacher for 25 years suffered a breakdown after his head persistently criticised him and plagued him with demands for work. She would sit in his lessons and take notes on his performance. 'I was told my teaching plans were not good enough. I had to repeatedly do new ones and write endless reports.. In the end I couldn't bear to look in my pigeonhole because it was invariably stuffed with memos from her criticising me.' " [27]

This kind of persecution isn't reasonable or useful, but in the present climate it's not preventable either. Unions, governors, OFSTED and local authorities may all know about headteacher bullying, but only the severest cases are tackled, since the government gospel is that each head must be free to pursue excellence in their own way.

The pressure can also turn inwards, and persuade head teachers that they have had enough. "HEADS CITE OVERLOAD AS REASON TO GO EARLY Almost half the London heads and deputies who have quite or are leaving their posts this year will go early – with more than a quarter of them taking ill-health retirement..." [28]

"In the first three months of the new millennium, more than 1,100 schools have advertised for a new head. Normally, 800-900 advertise for a new head in this period." [29]

This looks like a worrying situation, but our leaders are not worried. "The government yesterday denied there was a continuing recruitment crisis among headteachers, despite the publication of research saying that one in five schools in England and Wales was last year unable to fill an advertised vacancy for their senior post vacancy." David Blunkett's spokesman had been here before, and wasn't going to be thrown: "We have these surveys every year and we do not believe they are accurate. Our findings show that there is not the evidence to support these claims." [30]

It depends what you mean by evidence. There are plenty of case studies, and they are not just weary, exhausted by the demands of the job. One head is leaving to be a lorry driver [31], another would rather run a pub. [32] "Sally Carr, 50, is taking early retirement... only two terms after arriving at the school... She chose to leave after plans were announced to relaunch the school this September under the government's controversial Fresh Start programme." [33] Clare Short's brother had been a head for five years, when he decided to leave teaching at the age of 52.: "You have so many initiatives pouring in from everywhere – from the government, from your local authority, and ideas you'd like to pursue yourself – but there's no conduit to control how much arrives..." [34] "Government threats to close schools with poor exam results have cost an inner-city comprehensive its new headteacher.. the prospective candidate – described as 'outstanding' by the man he would have succeeded – said he could not face the prospect of year of government criticism. His predecessor said 'He told me the last thing he needed was to be told that he was no good, It is understandable.' " [35]

It's sad that we are losing good people who could do a useful job. But the scary part is that they say that their main reason for going is government policy. The job is strenuous and taxing, and has always been, but it is the added layer of official pressure – initiatives, revised targets, public judgement and closure – which is decisive. In a properly run system, that should be ringing alarm bells.

All the signs are that we are heading for a serious shortage of head teachers. In secondary schools, this isn't surprising. In the old days, schools had two or three deputies, most of whom hoped one day to become head teachers. But the number of deputy jobs has been reduced, and within that number there are more deputies who have decided that headship isn't for them.

I became a deputy in 1981, assuming that at some point I would be applying for headships. Between 1986-7 I applied for four headships without success. My experience of the selection procedures over those four attempts suggested that I was wasting my time. I therefore gave myself six months without making any applications. This was so restful that I stopped applying altogether, and eventually worked for 17 years in one school as a deputy, and loved it. While my original decision was due to an eccentric appointment process, there were long-term advantages in staying put. I have always had an interest in developing new resources and teaching methods, and it was much easier to do that work as a deputy than as a head. I had much more control over my time and what it was spent on, and more of my evenings were free.

I went to meetings with other deputies, and saw what was once an eccentric position ("I'm a deputy but I'm not going to be a head") become increasingly common. Some good friends of mine did become heads, and good heads, and I'm delighted that they did. Whatever the dangers of government thinking, heads need to be intelligent, imaginative people, and the more good teachers become heads the better. But it was noticeable that during this period the reasons for not becoming a head became increasingly persuasive.

Despite the lack of applicants, the journey into headship is increasingly tough. The old pattern was haphazard, and many started their first headships with inadequate training, so preparation for heads is a good idea. On the other hand, it's yet one more area to be subject to frantic short-termism. Students for the NPQH, who a year ago were told that this was an indispensible requirement to be a head, now find that a newer, shorter course is to be introduced, and some of them will be abandoned in midstream.

Similar problems afflict the establishment of the National College for School Leadership, where there is a clear difference of opinion within the government. "As a prime minister whose success is founded on his own charisma, Mr. Blair has attached great importance to school leadership" [36] reports the editor of the TES, who learnt from an exclusive interview that Blair wanted the project to be headed by someone with the practical experience of running a school. The DfEE were either not convinced by this argument, or disappointed with the calibre of actual heads that they looked at, and decided to appoint a local authority official. It's hardly a vote of confidence.

My worry is a more long-term one, that people lower down the teaching ladder will look up at heads, and at the image of heads in the media, and decide that this isn't for them. Two profiles from the TES suggest the flavour:

"Monica Cross says "At my current school I've written a lot of bids, learned to read plans and so on. I won't have to worry about that but I will need a relationship with our PFI partners. It's a new ball-game for both of us – we'll be pioneers on both sides. I'm anxious to meet them, because if we don't share a vision I'm going to find it very difficult." [37]

If you're an ambitious entrepreneur then you'll recognise the sentiments and won't mind about the language. There's nothing here, though, to suggest that this job is related to intellectual activity, or that it involves students. Here's another:

"Gill Eatough doesn't like lingering in the foothills – she's been in the profession for less than a decade but is already a headteacher." The breathless excitement is the responsibility of the reporter rather than the teacher, but the two work together to provide an image of ceaseless, solitary activity:

"Mrs. Eatough was seconded by her local authority to a special measures team and spent two terms turning round an urban comprehensive. 'Failing schools get a lot of negative publicity but I could see there were some very good things happening there. Creating new structures and management systems, motivating the pupils and rebuilding staff morale was hard work and the clock was ticking all the time, but I found it enormously rewarding and the experience has made me a more effective head.' " [38]

Phew. It's tiring just reading it. But how much, exactly, was achieved in those two terms, and how does this read to the teachers who were there before she came, and stayed after she left? Do student teachers reading this long to emulate her, or do they consider that there might be room for a different kind of contribution, less driven and hectic, but equally valuable?

## THERE IS AN ALTERNATIVE

"There is no alternative" was a favourite Thatcher saying, which has been made part of the New Labour pattern. In the case of headship, it is just plain wrong.

The model of headship – dynamic, fast and uncompromising – has to be more varied. There are good heads like this, but there are also good heads who are thoughtful, reflective, and quiet. Pat Collarbone quotes the American guru Max de Pree. "Leadership, like jazz, is a public performance, dependent on so many things: the environment, the volunteers in the band, the need for everybody to perform as individuals and as a group, the absolute dependence of the leader on the members of the band." [39]

That is the opposite of New Labour hype and most media reporting. John Benington and Chris Husbands quote Ron Heifetz, who says that good leaders are those who "give work back to the people." An old Chinese proverb summarises it well. "As for the best leaders, the people do not notice their presence." [40] Collarbone, Benington and Husbands all currently work in education management. Is it too much to hope that this calm, considered approach can be adopted in the training of future heads?

In this chapter, many of the heads have themselves provided antidotes to the sillier excesses of head-worship. One of my favourite texts is an article by Bernard Barker, entitled "SUPERMAN IS OUT." In it, he describes his own developing approach to headship:

"My life as a head seems in retrospect to have been an eventually self-defeating pretence that I possessed superhuman powers. Naughty children, upset parents, jaded teachers, unsafe buildings, league tables, OFSTED inspections, discipline cases and redundancies were all the same to me. I believed that my duty was to soak up the punishment without complaint. Eighty hours a week and no absence in 27 years...

When I started as a head my energy seemed unlimited. I had the youthful confidence that life's misfortunes happened to other people. Divorce, disabling disease, debt, violence, mental illness, stagnant careers and bitter disappointments seemed alien afflictions, brought into my busy room by colleagues, parents and children built from inferior stuff. My scheme of improvement did not allow for suffering humanity nor my place in it. Two winters ago, when I found myself in tears for no reason, when I saw myself as broken if not defeated, I had a richly deserved lesson. I was human too." [41]

This is a stunning piece of honesty, a powerful expose from the inside of unreal expectations and the cost they exact. I have twice shown it to headteachers, because I thought they might be interested. In neither case did they comment in any way. Did they disagree, or disapprove of a colleague letting down his guard? Or did they feel that such openness was simply too threatening to face? We urgently need such honesty as this, among heads and between heads and others, if we are to end up with a view of headteachers which makes sense.

There are plenty of models outside teaching, to remind headteachers that this myth of their infallibility is an illusion. Nelson Mandela, on a trip to Scandinavia, would call his three secretaries to his room each evening. Then he would say "Now tell me what I have done wrong today, because I don't want to make the same mistakes tomorrow." [42] That is intelligent leadership.

Such honesty in education would give us a more realistic awareness of where heads come from and how they are made. After the Ridings excitement, Peter Clark was hailed as the superhead who would sort it out. He had no time for such nonsense, and it was clear from the start that he was doing a necessary short-term job, which he did. He went back to his original school, and Anna White, the deputy who had come to the Ridings with him, took over as head. So far as one can tell from a distance, this was a smooth, professional transition, totally unworthy of headlines.

But it's worth thinking about. What did she do as a deputy? What did he do to help her become a head? How was she able to make that move between the two jobs? If there's going to be public attention to the business of headship, why not direct it to that careful, long-term development, rather than the headlines about macho gestures and astronomic pay?

There are always alternatives, possible ways of approaching the same target by another route, and in other countries they do it very differently. The research about school improvement is agreed on the importance of heads – in the UK and the US. But not in Holland, which has a much less autocratic pattern. In France heads are recruited for their business and organisational skills, without any claim to teaching expertise. And in Switzerland they have primary schools without any heads at all.

This, you might think, is worth a look. So it was encouraging that members of the select committee on education should go and see what was involved. Select committees are not valued by this government, but it was still a hopeful sign that they went, and there was a fascinating TV programme about their response.

Nobody expected them to come running back with a confident proclamation that "We don't need headteachers after all!" It was better than that. During the programme you could watch someone changing their mind, gradually forming a new idea. This is one of the joys of teaching, but you don't catch adults at it very often, and politicians least of all. But Margaret Hodge said that she went on the trip thinking that what mattered was the quality of the headteacher, and came back thinking that it might be just as important to concentrate on the role and status of the class teacher. The Swiss had managed to give their teachers a freedom, power and respect which made their work both valued and effective. Ms. Hodge, rightly, wanted us to have some of that.

But she couldn't follow that line up in the select committee, because she left it to become a minister. In one sense that's a cause for rejoicing. This intelligent piece of research, this valuable insight, can pass direct to government. But what happens to it there? Has Margaret Hodge raised the possibility of a campaign to raise the status of the ordinary teacher? Has she been told to wait a couple of years? Or has she decided that that was then and this is now, and actual government doesn't need the stimulus of new ideas? I would be delighted to be proved wrong, but my fear is that this precious piece of learning has vanished without trace.

We shall not get real improvements, until those in power develop the honesty to welcome such insights, and look at the business of leadership rationally, without the tribal drums.

1   Leaked memo of 29.4.00, in Times 16.7.00
2   TES 21.11.97
3   TES 21.11.97
4   Guardian 23.2.98
5   Guardian 23.2.98
6   The Teacher July/August '97

7   The Teacher July/August '97
8   TES 16.1.98
9   TES 16.1.98
10  TES 16.1.98
11  Guardian 14.3.00
12  TES 5.5.00
13  TES 17.3.00
14  Guardian 9.5.00
15  Guardian 14.3.00
16  TES 3.1.00
17  TES 11.8.00
18  Guardian 14.4.00
19  TES 12.5.00
20  Guardian 31.5.00
21  TES 2.6.00
22  Guardian 1.8.00
23  TES 11.8.00
24  Guardian 2.8.00
25  TES 23.10.98
26  TES 8.10.99
27  TES 11.8.00
28  TES 25.4.97
29  TES 4.14.00
30  Guardian 20.10.99
31  Guardian 6.7.00
32  TES 30.6.00
33  TES 14.4.00
34  Guardian 25.5.00
35  TES 10.3.00
36  TES 21.1.00
37  TES 2.7.99
38  TES 4.2.00
39  TES 23.10.98
40  TES 4.2.00
41  TES 23.1.98
42  Guardian Weekend 22.5.99

Chapter 8:

# TEACHERS AND THE TRUTH

## TEACHERS UNDER PRESSURE

Recognise anyone ?

(a) "Bad teachers are to blame for illiteracy and high crime rates [1] ... Primary schools are wasting children's time with colouring-in and sticking [2] ... A friend said to me a month ago 'If I hear another teacher whining on about how stressed they are, I shall scream.' " [3]

(b) "They had expected soft words and what I have given them is hard action [4].... however important they think they are, they will not stand in the way of me and my colleagues delivering the changes to improve the education system [5] ...a miserable bunch of sneering cynics." [6]

(c) "The language of opportunity too often went hand in hand with an acceptance of poor standards [7] ..the culture of excuses... small c conservatives, left and right, who are suspicious of change and who resist change." [8]

Woodhead, Blunkett and Blair, showing why there is some doubt about whether they want partnership. The aggressive tone, aimed at the media rather than the teachers, is familiar. But what I don't recognise are the people I worked with for thirty years. There was the occasional moaner and cynic, but not this vast, dreary band of oppressive skivers. By contrast, listen to four voices from the real world.

(1) "In the last week I have heard from six teachers. All are in their 40s. Five have a track record of excellent classroom work; the sixth is a graduate trainee. All regard the new term with gloom. Two will have abandoned teaching by August. Between them they have around 30 years' experience of senior management. They are the age group on whom our schools will depend when the babyboomers retire and we should ask why they are so disillusioned." [9]

(2) "Five years ago, 30 year-old Wilfred Matos became a teacher. Two weeks ago, he handed his notice in at Redbridge community school in Southampton. He has a mortgage, has just become engaged and has no job to go to. His salary is just £18,303.. At the NAS/UWT conference David Blunkett urged him to reconsider the decision, and this was part of Matos' reply: 'I do love teaching. It's being a teacher that I have come to hate. Why do all society's ills have to fall on my shoulders? What has the government ever done for me? Well, there's OFSTED, the Green Paper, class size, Woodhead, appraisal, target setting, longer days, the five-term year, open-ended contract – open to abuse, anyway. I am tired, stressed. I am exhausted. I have realised that I cannot make a difference.' [10]

(3) "I really think that we, the reviled schools with less than 25% of 5 A-Cs at GCSE, need to start shouting back. I can't believe how my colleagues, working heroically and creatively with radically disadvantaged youngsters, can be treated with such contempt and disdain. And I'm damned if I can see how the Secretary of State's denunciation will now help us to recruit a music teacher of the quality that our youngsters so desperately need." [11]

(4) "I am an experienced, dedicated, forward-thinking teacher, who is now a deputy head of an infant school. Yesterday, I was saddened and disheartened to find out that I now join three other members of staff in our school who are taking anti-depressants. With 20 years successful and enjoyable years of service in the profession I once loved, I am now in the position of considering that my health is more important than the career to which I was once so dedicated...

Isn't it about time the government, teachers and unions recognised what is happening to our good teachers and the very low morale of staff in so many schools around the country?" [12]

This is a selection from a large pile of cuttings, which chart the rise of teacher anger. They do not simply reflect weariness with a demanding job. They express rage, very precisely aimed at politicians who refuse to understand what is involved in the job, and who add to the pressures on those that try to do it.

And it is not only teachers who have noticed this. Dr. Richard House wrote in a letter to The Guardian:

"The details in your report on Muriel Benson's stressful experience in her prematurely curtailed teaching career were tragically all too familiar to me. I am losing count of the number of despairing teachers referred to me in my work as a GP counsellor in recent years....

Perhaps the government should start asking itself why a third of trained teachers decide not to enter the profession. They're in for a rude awakening if they really believe that merely tinkering with the symptoms via stress help-lines is going to solve this profound malaise." [13]

The stress helplines are not the answer, but they indicate the size of the problem. Teacherline had over 12,000 calls in its first year of operation, and 27% of those were already suffering from high levels of stress, anxiety or depression. In 1999 more than half the teachers in England took sick leave, with over 2.5 million working days being lost, at a cost of £300 million. David Blunkett's response was to set a target for reducing this rate by 30% before 2002, and by 20% in 2001.

Nigel de Gruchy sees the government as the disease rather than the cure: "This scandalously high figure cannot be put down simply to teachers fiddling the system. It is a savage indictment of the stress and workload teachers have been placed under by successive governments." [14]

One way of tackling teacher absence is through medical support, but it matters how that is done. Denis D'Auria is a director of occupational health: "I would hate to think that any of my colleagues were into policing absence, but managers frequently see it in precisely those terms." The government want teachers back at work, but from an occupational health viewpoint the non-stop teaching day is not 'back to work' but a key part of the problem. "Teachers too often give all their free time to school. They are putting their health on the line." [15]

ICM carried out a poll of teacher attitudes. 32% thought their job was about the same as it was two years ago, while 52% thought that it had got worse. 91% thought that bureaucracy had got worse, and 88% identified the source of that bureaucracy as being the government (compared with the school 3%, the LEA 6% or don't know 4%). 69% thought that the government were too hard on teachers.

31% of primary teachers planned to leave the profession within the next five years. 56% expected to go within the next ten years, and of those under 35 more than a third planned to leave teaching within the next ten years. Offered various reasons for leaving, percentages were as follows: heavy workload 91%, bureaucracy 88%, stress 86% and pay 53%. [16] A reduction in bureaucracy might therefore not only be popular, but also cost effective.

Tony Blair appointed a task force to get rid of unnecessary red tape, and in April 2000 they reported on the results of a three month enquiry. The chairman, Lord Haskins, said "Everything must be done to make sure that the management job of the headteacher is as relevant as possible – not spent on form-filling... Over-elaborate processes are being used to achieve straightforward objectives."

The DfEE "admitted that more could be done to cut bureaucracy and said that by 2002, when all schools were connected to the Internet, it aimed to have phased out most paper-based communications." [17] That's nice to know, but it isn't quite the point. If there's a massive overload of messages, then sending them by e-mail changes the format without reducing the pressure. What's needed is not just high tech, but a change in thinking.

"Since Labour took power in May 1997, a total of 4,585 targets has been set for schools, colleges and local education authorities, according to Lib. Dem. research. Targets are in turn broken down into 306,480,472 separate measures to be monitored." [18]

Haskins reported in April 2000. By July, little had changed. Between January and July 2000, the DfEE sent every secondary school 75 separate documents, totalling 2,063 pages and covering everything from the national curriculum to guidance on exclusions and performance management. " David Prior MP, attacked the avalanche of paperwork flowing into schools. Jacqui Smith, education minister, admitted that they had added to workloads, but said that they also raised standards." [19]

So that's all right, then. The workload problem doesn't matter, because standards are rising. The only things government will take seriously are those which they think matter. Other issues, which are serious to other people, don't matter, because ministers are meeting the targets they have set. It's a blinkered approach, and it helps to account for the resentment among teachers. Ministers think they have to do all the thinking, take the decisions, care about the standards – and then pass it on. Teachers get the paperwork, the flak, the suggestion that they have no active role, and they get fed up.

Gardner and Oswald carried out interviews with 7,000 workers annually during the 1990s. While generally they found that public sector workers were happier than those in the private sector, teachers were an exception, with lower levels of job stisfaction than any other group of workers. "We believe it is something to do with conditions of work. There have been repeated attempts to assess teachers and make their life tougher in lots of ways." [20]

Teachers in an NUT survey picked out two factors as exerting the most pressure – OFSTED inspections and "constant criticism." One experienced teacher said: "Good teachers never make a child feel inadequate, but good teachers are made to feel inadequate every day of their teaching lives, with 'must try harder' on every end of term report." [21]

And it's unlikely to improve. Since September 2000, heads and teachers have faced performance management systems, with targets set by governors, under pressure from the government. Guidelines include a target of improving staff morale, thus reducing absenteeism by 3%. [22] So, will they start by asking teachers what will improve their morale, or by checking on the absentees?

There will also be new academic targets for junior schools, but the teachers will have no say in deciding what these targets should be. "Ministers are not planning to consult schools or the teacher unions on new national targets for 11-year olds in literacy and numeracy." [23]

Teachers have expressed anxiety about the effects of tests (because they focus on some activities at the expense of others), and the impact on staff morale (because they are pressured into making their children achieve targets in which they have had no say). None of this is seen as important. It is what ministers think that matters, and that is all that matters.

To good, caring teachers this is an intolerable situation. That was how it felt for Carole Clayson, a primary head from Norwich.. On Nov. 9th. she wrote to David Blunkett to outline a variety of issues which she felt were putting teachers under pressure. Shrewdly, she wrote in braille, hoping to attract David Blunkett's personal attention. On February 10th, she got a pre-prepared response from a DfEE official, which failed to answer her points, but offered the consolation that morale would improve once standards rose. Clayson sent her original letter to the TES, which published it on February 18th., 2000.

The response was tidal. In the first week after half-term she received nearly sixty letters and a large number of phone calls, all expressing support. Many offered examples from their own experience of similar pressure on teachers, and frustration with government. The TES published four pages of the letters Clayson had received, and reading through them is a moving, depressing experience. These are not whingers and skivers, but hard-working idealists driven to the edge of despair. And what is driving them is not the difficulty of the work, but the refusal of government to listen to the people who know about that work, and who are measuring its current costs.

One lone voice stood out against the tide. Ciaran Clerkin, head of a London primary school, felt that she had got it wrong:

"Leadership style appears to be the key issue that separates Carole and myself. I believe in an entrepreneurial approach, accentuating the positive to achieve success. There is, in my experience, a danger that if you do nothing but complain you can poison the atmosphere in a school.

Even when the odds are against you, an enthusiastic, cheerful head is more likely to find such an attitude reflected not only in the staffroom but in the classroom. We live in a changing world. There is no point in simply moaning about change. Change is a fact of life.

Successful leaders in every walk of life have to accept change and manage it effectively. Why should headteachers be different?" [24]

Letters from Carole Clayson and from one of her staff made it clear that theirs was a positive, enthusiastic staff. The difference between Clayson and Clerkin is not management style, but honesty. He is arguing for unquestioning acceptance of any change, and blind optimism as the way to bluff teachers and pupils into success. If in doubt, whistle a happy tune. She is questioning the way in which this particular change is being carried out. She is identifying obstacles which are getting in the way of her and her teachers doing their job properly. The passionate response to her original article suggests that there is a deep need for such protests to be voiced, even if there is no response.

## GETTING MORE TEACHERS

224,000 teachers left the profession between 1993 and 1998, but only 77,000 of them retired. A large number of people within teaching plan to leave it over the next ten years. The recruitment of new teachers has fallen every year that New Labour have been in power. Does this amount to a crisis?

Just as the government talked of "standards not structures", looking for better test scores rather than an even playing field, so with teachers they looked for quality rather than quantity. They threatened teachers they regarded as incompetent, and looked for elaborate ways of encouraging the high-flying heads of the future. But such figureheads will achieve little unless they can staff all their classrooms, and the fewer kids in each classroom the better.

The government accepts that this is true, but they think it only applies between the ages of 5 and 7. It made sense to start the reduction of class size there, but that isn't where it should stop. Developed nations, and our own private schools, see the advantage of small teaching groups. All successful countries manage, over time, to reduce the size of their classes, yet between 1997 and 2000 "Tony Blair conceded yesterday that the pupil-teacher ratio had increased since Labour came to power." [25] The average class size in English secondary schools went from 18.5 in 1990 to 20.3 in 1999. In the private school sector over the same period, it went from 10.9 to 10.00. [26] Could this be connected with examination success?

In June '97, a Guardian headline reported RECORD SLUMP IN TEACHER TRAINING. Anthea Millett said she had warned ministers about the problem several months ago, and was planning a recruitment campaign in the autumn to convince more young people to consider teaching." [27]

In November 1997, the education select committee (chaired by Margaret Hodge) looked at the supply of teachers: "We conclude there is a crisis in teacher recruitment. We have grave concerns that if this crisis is not tackled then the government's drive to raise standards may not be realised." [28]

In December 1997 John Howson warned, on the basis of a careful statistical analysis, that: "A successful, knowledge-based society cannot flourish if the teaching profession is headed for its third staffing crisis in as many decades." He also quoted the view of the DfEE, reporting to the Pay Review Body that "there is no need at present for a large general pay award on recruitment and retention grounds." [29] Not all the unions were so confident, and the NAHT suggested that trainee teachers ought to be paid.

In February '98 there was a 77% increase in applications from British teachers who wanted to work abroad. Speaking for VSO, Jill Stainton said "A lot of the teachers contacting us say they feel demoralised in their current jobs and want to go somewhere where they will be valued more highly." [30]

In July '98 "the crisis in teacher recruitment has moved into the once-buyant primary sector, with new figures showing the first drop for five years in the number of graduates applying to train." David Hart said "I'm very concerned indeed. Optimism about primary numbers has always been misplaced because it has been on the basis that we should allow primary class sizes to go through the roof." [31]

By August, "A collapse in the number of graduates signing up to train as secondary school teachers is playing havoc with ministers' plans for raising standards of education, head teachers' leaders warned last night." [32] The government admitted concern about numbers in Maths and Science, but also promised that their green paper would recognise recruitment problems.

In December '98 the government shocked teacher unions by reducing their targets for teacher recruitment. DfEE officials said the lower targets reflected "new data on wastage rates and teacher-pupil ratios." John Dunford said that this was not credible, and attacked ministers for releasing these figures just before Christmas. "There is a crisis situation which is being dealt with at the highest level of the DfEE and the TTA. I'm absolutely amazed the targets should be reduced at a time when secondary-school teacher problems are so great. The fact that they failed to meet their targets this year means they should be higher next year. It will particularly affect those areas where schools find it hardest to recruit already – disadvantaged schools in disadvantaged areas." [33]

In April '99 Dunford tried again. "The crisis in secondary school recruitment cannot be underestimated. What has the government done about it? They reduced the targets for secondary recruitment." Other heads reported on the difficulties they already had in appointing suitable staff. [34]

By September '99 £5,000 sweeteners for language teachers were having little effect, and recruitment for Maths and Science was down on the previous year. The number of unfilled teaching jobs had risen to 2,660, and Howson said that ministers should worry. The TTA and the DfEE said it was too early in the recruitment year to draw any conclusions. Figures could change weekly. [35]

In November 1999, Howson suggested that tuition fees and student loans were deterring possible teacher trainees from doing a fourth year of study. A senior government source, however, was happy with their progress: "The reality is that we've started to turn around what was a very serious problem." [36]

In January 2000 maths vacancies were higher than for ten years. Teacher education faced its own recruitment problem, with four times as many education lecturers over 50 as there were under 35. In March teacher recruitment was 20% down on 1998, and a third of newly qualified teachers were thinking of leaving.

On March 15th Chris Woodhead was asked about a reference in

the previous year's OFSTED report that "we are not experiencing the crisis in teacher supply that some commentators predicted." He said that he was aware of problems in maths, physics and foreign languages, and in some areas, particularly in London. "At the time of writing the report we were not facing the crisis, or the meltdown that some commentators suggest we are facing." But he did not revise that view, in the light of current evidence, and he repeated his well-publicised opinion that the quality of teaching was more important than the quantity of teachers. [37]

Two weeks later, The Guardian's front page announced: TRAINEES TO BE PAID TO AVERT TEACHER CRISIS. The government is to intervene to avert a looming teacher recruitment crisis by paying salaries ranging from £6,000 to £13,000 a year to graduates embarking on training for the profession in September." [38] Those already in training would not get it. Nor would those who had decided that they wished to prepare for teaching thoroughly, by following a four year B.Ed course, rather than a three year degree followed by a PGCE. What would happen about the money if new students dropped out of their courses? Could you collect the £6,000, be trained, and then not get a teaching job? Nobody knew the answers, because this was a crisis and they were making it up as they went along.

There was a brief rise in interest, but there was also a decline in B.Ed applications. Overall, by June 2000, applications were still below the 1999 levels. But the key questions remain: (1) How many of those who start training will actually work in schools? and (2) For how long? In April 2000 Estelle Morris responded to a question from James Clappison, regarding drop-out rates. At least 1 in 8 trainee teachers fails to get to the classroom, and 1 in 5 of maths teachers. [39]

Teacher recruitment is not easy, and it may not be entirely the government's fault if we haven't got enough teachers. But they should know that we haven't got enough teachers, and not be so scornful of professionals who suggest that there is a problem. Over time, it's clear that they should have been more worried than they were, and that the unions were right to be concerned. But that is never formally accepted. Only the last-minute botched attempt at a rescue plan confirms that they failed to see things clearly, they weren't listening to anyone else, and when they told us it was all under control that was just a bluff.

It doesn't stop there. The damage limitation continues, as Baroness Blackstone assures the House of Lords that talk of a teacher recruitment crisis is exaggerated. It is confined to a few regions, in certain subjects. [40] David Blunkett admitted to the GTC that the government faced a challenge to improve recruitment, particularly in London, and particularly in the shortage subjects of maths and science. [41] In fact, the only subjects in which there is not a shortage are art, history and PE. Blunkett told the Labour Party conference that applications for teacher training had increased by 50% because of the new training salaries, yet admissions to one-year courses (the beneficiaries of this strategy) only went up by 3.8%. [42] Surely, now we know they got it wrong, it is time to tell the truth.

Recruitment is only the start. The loss of teachers is a concern, but the loss of young teachers, within five years of starting their careers, is a national scandal. This is not a new problem, and New Labour have tried to address it. Since September 1999, each newly qualified teacher (NQT) should have an induction tutor, a teacher in their school who supports, monitors and assesses them. The tutor has to devise a programme that will help the NQT to develop knowledge and improve their skill as a teacher, and they also have to assess how well the NQT is doing.

That is a huge responsibility, and most induction tutors have not had the training they need. The TTA produced booklets, but these were not published until after Christmas and were not sent to all schools. Above all, this job needs time; mentors have many other roles within the school, and aren't given extra time in which to do this job.

In turn, NQTs are supposed to have a timetable which is 10% lighter than other teachers, so that they have half a day a week for their induction. Sometimes this is cancelled because teachers are ill, sometimes its use has not been properly planned. NQTs should be observed at least once every half-term, but that too takes time and may not happen.

Here are two case studies, one from primary, one from secondary. Laura Mannering had a Cambridge first and a glowing report from her training. But a term of teaching was enough for her:

"In my final weeks I became like a child myself, inventing ill-nesses so I did not have to go to school. I was an entirely different person from the confident new teacher who had started in September.

My errors of judgement over behaviour and time management, as well as fatigue, contributed to the crisis in my class. However, I feel that the damage both to myself and my pupils' education would have been lessened if I had been supported by a regular, timetabled monitoring and mentoring system. Although I had a mentor, we met only once during the first half-term as meetings had to take place after school when both of us had work to do. The head's oft-repeated refrain "there's no such thing as a bad class, only a bad teacher," made me afraid to admit problems... by Christmas I hated the job, had failed at it and had resigned. At the same time, another newly -qualified teacher left and we were followed at Easter by the last remaining new teacher, who had faced similar difficulties to mine." [43]

The secondary teacher felt she was coping, although "my predecessor had failed to mark any of the year 11 coursework and the moderation date was fast approaching. I knew other NQTs had been approached by their schools about becoming a permanent member of staff while I had heard nothing. Meanwhile, the headmistress started to open and close the classroom door with alarming frequency...

The bombshell came when I was suddenly told I would have to reapply for my job..I was devastated. My mentor had not even been consulted. My head of department couldn't explain how and why the situation had arisen...

I know my main mistake was in trying to cope on my own, but I find it frightening to think that if it had been the new probationary year..I might have been failed for good and would not be teaching today." [44]

According to an ATL survey of new teachers, one in five were not getting the support that they needed. The NUT said that the funding of the programme was inadequate, with schools getting barely enough to cover NQT's reduced timetables, let alone the costs of tutoring. The thoroughness with which schools tackled induction varied enormously, as did the funding – ranging from £420 to £1200. There is a further long-term problem, that new teachers can only become qualified when they have completed an induction year, but many are finding it hard to get the job that will give them that induction. This is partly because heads are unwilling to take on the work and expense of training teachers who may not stay to make that investment worthwhile.

It was still a good idea. Maybe there are wrinkles that need ironing out, but it's better to try something worthwhile than not to try it at all. And you can't blame them for not getting it right first time, can you? Maybe you can. This extract is from a letter written by Mark Bindley, a teacher angered by the TES leader's comment that when the induction year was announced "Everybody thought it was a good thing." [45]

"Within days of the procedure arriving in school, I had prepared a briefing paper for our governors identifying all the problems that are now emerging. The induction year is typical of the way complex and important policy is developed, in isolation, with no overall view of the management of a school...

Experienced teachers are the legion of the lost. When we dare raise our timorous voices to question idiotic and transparently unworkable legislation, we are immediately labelled by the great and the good as cynical and burnt out, a disgrace to the profession. When the legislation predictably fails, somehow nobody is ever held accountable or named and shamed." [46]

The problem is not whinging teachers. The problem is ministers who think that they have to have all the answers, on their own. So they blunder on to territory where professionals know more than they do; they refuse to ask for advice, and ignore it when it is offered; they bluster and bluff about things that they don't know. And when the whole thing, publicly and predictably, becomes unstuck, they cannot find the honesty to admit it.


## THINGS CAN ONLY GET BETTER?


It would be nice to think that this was exceptional, but there are other examples of good opportunities wasted by ignorant pride. One small instance is the Computers for Teachers scheme, in which the govern-

the problems outlined above. But because there was no consultation, huge expectations have not been met, and large numbers of professionals feel yet again they have been lied to and betrayed. It's a recurrent, and expensive, pattern.

We are now promised an advertising campaign to support the new pay arrangements, but again you wonder about their capacity to learn. The 1997 cinema campaign was devised by Delaney Lund Knox Warren, whose work won a string of awards. Unfortunately, it cost ten million pounds and didn't attract a string of teachers. One recent brainwave is to have a bus touring country fairs, gospel concerts and supermarket car parks, trying to tempt likely candidates into teaching. [49]

There are dramatic efforts by agencies of supply teachers to attract custom. Teaching Personnel ran a £50,000 prize draw, whereby ten of the teachers signed up before October 20th will win £5,000 pounds each. Or you can earn £100 by introducing another teacher who signs on. Another firm offers a salary to new recruits, whether or not they work continuously. Supply teaching, which used to be an occasional resort in times of crisis, has become a large, thriving business, dealing with a rare commodity.

There was a brief lull in the government complacency over recruitment, when they admitted a crisis – in order to boast that they had solved it. "Ministers are drawing up plans to solve the recruitment crisis once and for all with a radical restructuring of the profession." That was the green paper – 'TEACHERS: facing the challenge of change'. The dream was that ambitious young high flyers would zoom in to replace large numbers of middle-aged drones coming out. Estelle Morris claimed that "It is impossible to underestimate the importance of this document." [50]

It was certainly possible to overestimate it. Historians of the future will not trace a sudden leap upwards in recruitment, as young people responded to a new vision of commitment and excellence. The evidence is already gathering that this confident prediction was based on a bad guess. "A survey of undergraduates at the University of York found that performance pay was viewed the least favourably of any of the government's recent or proposed reforms... Some 29 percent said performance pay would put them off teaching. It was the only one of

13 reforms the students disliked." [51] Heads don't want it, teachers don't want it and prospective teachers don't want it. So, why is it still there?

A more fruitful approach might be for someone to take a close look at why we lose so many of the young people who start to train as teachers, but then don't stay to teach. Maguire found that 43% of 241 teacher trainees at King's College, London, felt that they were bullied in school. [52] It may be that some of their expectations or some of their preparation could be better, but that looks like a serious problem worth further investigation.

Taverner and Baumfield analysed questionnaires from 100 former trainees. Some had been deterred by money and poor discipline, others by the range of subjects that they would be required to teach. Many were put off by the atmosphere of the schools in which they worked, or the sense that staff were not willing or able to support their work. But they were not casual cynics who had drifted in and out, and in many cases the remedial action needed to keep them would not have to be drastic or expensive. [53]

What do young teachers need? They don't need to be patronised, preached at or threatened. They do need to feel that there's a useful job to be done, but one in which their talents and ideas are welcomed. They need access to help and advice, but also the space and time in which to develop their own approach to teaching. They do not need the suggestion that all the thinking has been done, and that all they have to do is deliver an approved programme. They do not need repeated doubts about whether they are good enough, and have the relevant competencies in literacy, numeracy and ICT. None of the young teachers I've known have been seeking to be head teachers in ten years, but quite a lot of them liked to have a say, to be involved in discussions and decisions which involved the school as a whole. And in today's pressured schools, how many of them get that?

That's my subjective view, based on reading and personal experience. Nationally, we need a clearer, more detailed picture, based on research, and then consistent action, efficiently carried out in every school. That would be a suitable assignment for a government which likes to present itself as tough and ambitous for success.

There have been attempts to promote a more positive view of

teachers through the teaching awards, and the new General Teaching Council might raise the status of the profession. David Puttnam has worked hard for both projects, while encouraging teachers to develop a better public image. "As a profession you have to develop a more enlightened attitude to the manner in which you are seen by the public. Once that broad confidence has happened I am convinced that dealing with the government will be a lot easier." [54]

I'd love to see that happen, but it will need to be part of a much more radical shift, to which Puttnam also looks forward. 'Teachers should be allowed to be the architects of wide-ranging change in schools and not the victims,' the government education adviser, Lord Puttnam, will tell ministers today. 'The challenge is to avoid seeing oneself and being seen as a figure on whom change is imposed and, instead, to take on a pro-active role as architect of that change.' " [55]

Stirring stuff, but it sounds like the script of a fantasy. For this is not simply a question of faith, of walking tall to make it happen. It is also about power. We are waiting for those in control, the people who make the rules and allocate the cash, to recognise that there is a place for expertise. Genuine consultation can save them from embarrassing mistakes, and give them a more efficient result as well as a more benevolent atmosphere. When and if they are able to see that, then at last – and not before time – teachers can expect their world to change.

1    Guardian 14.12.95
2    Guardian 28.6.96
3    Guardian 16.4.98
4    TES 1.5.98
5    Guardian 1.4.97
6    Guardian 29.9.98
7    TES 4.6.99
8    TES 29.10.99
9    Richard Kemp, TES 12.5.00
10   TES 5.5.00
11   Gill Bryan, TES 10.3.00
12   anonymous letter to TES, 19.10.99
13   Dr. Richard House, letter to Guardian 4.10.99
14   TES 19.5.00
15   TES 2.6.00
16   Guardian 7.3.00

17   TES 7.4.00
18   Guardian 27.6.00
19   TES 28.7.00
20   Guardian 13.3.99
21   Guardian 3.1.00
22   TES 30.6.00
23   TES 28.7.00
24   Letter to TES 31.3.00
25   Guardian 23.11.00
26   Guardian 18.4.00
27   Guardian 24.6.97
28   Guardian 4.11.97
29   TES 5.12.97
30   Guardian 25.2.98
31   TES 31.7.98
32   Guardian 26.8.98
33   TES 25.12.98
34   Guardian 26.4.99
35   TES 19.9.99
36   Guardian 19.11.99
37   Minutes of Select committee, 15.3.00, para.s 2-7
38   Guardian 30.3.00
39   TES 7.4.00
40   TES 21.10.00
41   Guardian 22.9.00
42   TES 13.10.00
43   TES 23.10.98
44   TES 24.9.99
45   TES 5.5.0
46   TES 19.5.00
47   TES 28.4.00
48   TES 23.6.00
49   TES 14.7.00
50   TES 11.9.98
51   TES 25.08.00
52   TES 15.9.00
53   TES 12.9.97
54   Guardian 26.4.00
55   Guardian 22.5.00

# Chapter 9:

# HONESTY IN SCHOOL

One theme of this book is that teachers have had a rough deal. There have been caricatures in newspapers, criticisms from Chris Woodhead, and government decisions which failed to take them into account. That is important, not only because it's unfair, but also because it makes it harder for teachers to get on with teaching. The pressures on them now – to meet targets, obey guidelines and reach quotas – are greater than ever before.

But they're not perfect. Schools may be in a mess, but teachers have contributed to that mess. There have been failures of honesty from teachers, in what they have said to pupils, to parents and to the public at large, which created a crisis in morale. If teachers were all efficient, objective and honest, would we have as many anxious parents and critical reporters as we do?

Confession time. In the past some teachers took advantage of their status. The worries of parents – about reading, behaviour, academic progress – were sometimes waved away, because this was work for professionals, and could safely be left to them. So for years there was little in the papers, on radio, or on television, to explain how schools were changing. Many people outside education had an interest in what was going on, but no access to reliable information, no chance to get involved in a proper dialogue.

The first school I taught at was a huge, purpose-built comprehensive in the middle of a town in north Nottinghamshire. It was the only school for the immediate area, with a genuine mix of ability and no creaming off, and that created a marvellous opportunity for a school to be rooted in the community. But the head was anxious about teacher-parent contacts which he might not be able to control. I remember one boring, aloof address, to a hall-full of parents, and a miner getting up, wearily, announcing "I'm not staying for this."

At another school, where the intake was heavily skewed towards the bottom end, I remember parents looking at their child's exam results in disbelief. "But he got 'A's for all his essays", they said, looking at the slip where their son's GCSE board had awarded an E. Some teachers, wanting to provide encouragement, had invented their own ladder of assessment. For two years pupils were allowed to think they were successful candidates, without any warning that the final exam would be working on a very different scale.

Other schools, worried about the publicity which might follow from an admission of weakness, would pronounce "We don't have bullying here" or "None of our pupils take drugs." Parents who had been told different would be patronised, lectured at or simply waved away.

And then came competition. To the market theorists of the Tory right, making schools compete for pupils looked like a good idea. The consumer would seize power from the producer, and instead of officials deciding where children went to school, parents could choose for themselves. Some, however, had more choice than others, and many ended up with less control than they had had before. The losers, as usual, were the poorest, the least mobile, the least articulate.

But competition was also a problem for schools. Yes, it made them think about how they were doing and what they could offer, but it also inhibited how freely they could speak. How exactly does your school vary from the one down the road? If I am worried about my daughter's progress, what can I do? What exam grades will he end up with if he comes here? We would frame answers on the spot, drawing wavy lines between what we believed in, what we knew was true, and what might persuade this parent to send their child to our school. Some of the lines were a lot more wavy than others. Still, it's a jungle out there, and in a jungle, dare you tell the truth?

## SCHOOLS AND PARENTS

The jungle is just another image. In the real world, good teachers have always kept in touch with their pupils' parents. They knew that was a courtesy to which parents were entitled, but they also knew it would give them a fuller picture of the pupil, and that a sense of positive contact between home and school would give the pupil confidence, and help them to succeed.

In the short-term, that may not always seem true. Teenagers often want to keep school and home apart, cringing at the embarrassment of the contact and desperate to avoid attending parents' evenings. But beyond that cringe is a deeper hunger for support, the reassurance that all these adults actually want them to succeed. If they are smart, the adults can negotiate that in the child's interest. I remember one parent, asking me to recommend an author to her daughter, because she thought there'd be a better chance of success that way than if she did it herself.

The Tory raid offered parents a guarantee of regular reports, as though teachers had been shiftily hiding test scores for years, skulking in the corridors to avoid having to talk to parents. I've been to many parents' evenings, and many post-mortems afterwards, and the most constant refrain was the lament of teachers who hadn't been able to speak to the parents they really wanted to see.

The myth built on some genuine grievances, but it exaggerated the amount of discontent. I went to a meeting in the late 1980s, where Chris Woodhead was explaining to a group of Shropshire heads why tough changes were necessary to meet the demands of parents. And then I thought, "Hang on a minute. I probably meet as many parents as he does. Are they like this?"

And they weren't. Some had complaints, some were curious, and many were very sympathetic to teachers and grateful for all that they had done. They had particular worries and occasional complaints, but they weren't possessed by this general sense of grievance. We were the local school, they wanted their kids to be happy and do well, so if we talked there was a better chance of that. It was a natural, reasonable deal, not a war.

Good schools worry about whether they are giving parents the right information about their children's work in schools. There have been many attempts to find the ideal form or letter, the best pattern of meetings and consultations, which inform parents without exhausting teachers. ICT can help in this process, but it can also be a diversion, allowing teachers with very little effort to produce a string of pre-packaged sausages which fill up the page but sound like an overloaded computer. That effort needs to go on, with schools looking to each other for suggestions, and local authorities making good models available. But a key part of that process is simple dialogue, asking parents: What do you think? What would you like? What else do you want to know?

We have been told that all parents are hawkish critics, angry that their children's academic achievements were so low. OFSTED analysed the returns from parents' questionnaires, and came up with some surprising results. "Parents do not share ministers' high level of concern about academic achievement... what does concern parents, it finds, is homework, assessment and the curriculum, and – in secondary schools – behaviour."

Where there was concern about progress, this was not related to OFSTED's assessment of teaching quality at the school. "High levels of parental dissatisfaction are unrelated to school quality as judged by inspectors' grades." [1] OFSTED, however, decided not to publish this report.

Ted Wragg once interviewed more than 100 parents as part of a research project. All had been invited into school to see their child's primary teacher at work. In reply to the question "what did you think about your child's class teacher?" most said "I don't know how she does it. I can barely cope with my two children and she has 30." [2] I used to get similar comments from parents and cleaners.

This optimism is supported by an ICM random survey of parents, which asked "How happy are you with the quality of your child's schooling?" Among parents of primary school children, 47%were fairly happy, and another 44% very happy. Of secondary school parents, the proportions were fairly happy 51%, very happy 40%. Parents were asked to supply one word to describe teachers, and their suggestions included "brave.. impressive… capable.. heroes.. underestimated.. martyrs." [3] It's not exactly a chorus of rage.

There are, though, real concerns. The charity Parentline says that 20% of its calls are related to school, covering such issues as uniform and exclusion, bullying and special needs. The Advisory Centre for Education takes over 6,000 calls a year from concerned parents, and Susan Rees says "A sign of a very good school is one where complaints are listened to. Too many teachers go straight onto the defensive."

"If they do that to their parents," says Margaret Tulloch, "they are turning away the people who are their biggest supporters. The glib market forces argument was always nonsense. Parents don't want to vote with their feet – they want local schools to respond to their children's needs. People want to be listened to, it's something schools need to address." [3]

There are parents who won't settle for that, but express their anger through physical attacks or verbal abuse. One headteacher described what happened after a boy had been accused of stealing something belonging to a teacher, and his mother came up to school: "I let her into the school because I thought she wanted to talk to me. She made all sorts of demands and then turned rough. She hit me about the head and punched me in the eye. In nearly 40 years in teaching, 23 as a head, I had never been physically assaulted before. It was right to make a stand and prosecute. It hasn't put me off teaching but it does make you sad." [4]

It's also sad that there are many more court cases and compensation claims following such incidents. They often stem from family or friends of pupils, looking for a simple answer to frustration, guilt or rage. I was never attacked by a parent or relative, but many times I've been sworn at or threatened, by people telling me that they knew their child, that the school was useless, and that if we couldn't manage to 'sort it out' then they would do so for themselves.

Despite the wear and tear it involves, I remain convinced that honesty is still the solution. In many cases, this noise is just bluster, and is seen to be within days, as tearful fathers go from aggressive threats to confessions of inadequacy – "I just don't know what she's doing… I can't do anything with her." The more each side in the exchange feels free to admit limitations and confess weakness, the more chance there is of resolving the problem.

If a parent comes to the door mouthing threats and threatening to go to the papers, I am less likely to concede that the teacher who told off their child might have got it wrong. On the other hand, to a parent who says "I know he can be a pain, but he is really upset about this", I am more likely to say that maybe a teacher went too far. But I have to run a careful series of balances, between me and the parent, me and the child, me and the teacher, all the time knowing that further relationships will be affected by what I say. And what I say to the parent about the teacher mustn't come back via the child as a threat - so it's honesty, but with a lot of calculation thrown in.

For example, consider the scenario where a parent comes in to complain about a teacher. As deputy head I am on duty, ready to field such enquiries – and also to ensure that most teachers and pupils are free to get on with their proper work. I could say "Don't be ridiculous – our staff are competent, experienced professionals, and if your son told you that he's a liar." I could say "Mr. Jones? Oh, well, I'm afraid we have a lot of complaints about him. I'm really sorry, but I promise he'll be on his way soon."

Both of these responses would resolve the immediate situation – and lead to damage later. So there is no alternative to the longer, diplomatic route: "Come in, sit down, what exactly did he say? What do you think is going on? Has there been any problem between them before this? Now I must ask you to allow me to look into this, but I will get back to you when I've spoken to the teacher, and the pupil, and anyone else who will help me to get a clearer picture." Then I thank them, having made a note of what they said, and make sure that I do everything I promised, get back to them soon, and monitor what happens later.

That's very time-consuming, and such cases don't come one at a time. However, if a school organises itself so that that is what happens when any parent raises an issue of concern, the long-term gains are enormous. It's easier to filter out the silly ones, the trivial ones, misunderstandings or inventions. And every parent who's received that kind of attention has two consolations: (1) if something happens in the future, their concerns will be taken seriously (2) if they don't hear from the school, it's more likely to be because things are OK, than because there's a problem which the school is trying to hide. Parents are less concerned that their children should be totting up massive scores than that they should be happy, busy and safe. And the best guarantee of that is that the teachers are telling the truth.

## THE HEAD IN THE SCHOOL

In "Leadership and Lies" I traced the damage done to our thinking about leadership by the insistence on isolating the role of the head. This did specific damage to particular schools on whom superheads were imposed, but it also has effects way beyond that. Imagine a new head, not very confident about what they're doing. They look at the papers and TV, listen to education ministers, and assume "I have to turn it round.. sort out the staff... zero tolerance of underperformance."

Maybe there are problems with governors, or teachers resist some of the changes they propose. They go to meetings with other heads where they are assured "Oh, mine used to be terrible... don't weaken... you have to show them who's in charge."

This helps to explain the rise in professional bullying. Cary Cooper found that one in three teachers had been bullied over the past five years. This is expensive in salaries and compensation payments as well as the harm it does to working effectiveness and morale.

"In my view there are two types of bully," says Cooper. "The psychopathic bully has low self-esteem and may not be particularly good at their job. He or she bullies to enhance their status. It's a personality dysfunction and the numbers are relatively small and stable. The other type is the overloaded bully who has too much to do themselves and dumps on others. This sort of bullying is increasing." [6]

And there are different ways of passing on the pressure. Cardinal Hinsley School, in Brent, had trouble getting a head teacher, and George Benham, a former director of education, agreed to take over. He inherited falling rolls, many older, expensive staff, and a deficit of £154,000.

His plan was to merge departments, force staff to reapply for their jobs, and make six teachers redundant. He was also going to recruit more pupils, including pupils who had been excluded by other schools. By the end of the year 26 out of 50 teachers were leaving. Liz Milton, a food technology teacher, says pupils quickly decided Mr.Benham was a soft touch. " 'I was assaulted this year, which has never happened before'... Benham was totally unsympathetic. He said 'the boys don't lie'. She adds 'I have never seen so many women crying in the ladies as in the last year.' "

Another experienced teacher added "There was a lot more graffiti, a lot more challenging behaviour, a lot more aggressiveness towards teachers. They told you to eff off to your face, whereas before that just wasn't the case." In April, Benham told the staff that he was concerned that the school might fail its next OFSTED inspection and be put under special measures, and following that meeting many staff decided to leave.

On the last day of the summer term, Benham asked that there should be no collection or presentations, because so many were leaving. He stayed for twenty minutes, but after he went his deputy said a word of thanks to those who were leaving, some of whom had worked there for more than twenty years.

Benham saw staff complaints as "strategic game playing", because of anxieties about the changes he was pushing through. "You are dealing with a side issue, as tactically how you approach a debate. They didn't want to deal with such a large scale change." He was confident about his own forceful image – "they have all known me since I was director of education, they know that if I said it was going to happen, it was going to happen." He was less confident about the reaction of his teachers: "It surprised me on May 31 when I got a raft of resignations which I didn't have a handle on at all. I thought I'd done my numbers." [7]

It's a classic case of the tough, solitary leader, shut up in his box. He knows about recruiting, inclusion, the management of change. He develops a plan, and has the nerve to force it through, regardless of opposition. But somewhere along the line he doesn't notice that staff can't do their jobs, criticisms are not being faced, and people are ment set out to support ICT awareness by helping teachers to buy their own computers.

But it was not properly thought out. The adverts didn't say that this support was taxable, so that teachers who expected to get £500 towards their computer actually got £380. Also, computers had to be bought from accredited suppliers and not all models were eligible. Existing computer owners who wished to add budget notebooks to a desktop computer weren't able to do so, and – as with the late decision on grants for teacher training – there was some resentment from people who had just bought their own computers, without knowing that this scheme was on the way.

Then, without warning, the scheme was stopped. The DfEE was overwhelmed by 27,000 applications, and there were delays. Some teachers had bought computers, and were still waiting for rebates three months later. The original announcement had said that the scheme would run for three years, but that was now changed to mean for four months a year, in each of the three years. Deadlines were rearranged, and websites failed to carry clear information, making things very difficult for teachers without computer experience, and they were the key targets of this scheme. Then in 2001 the whole principle was undermined, when the scheme was restricted to a limited group of maths teachers. This was not about changing the style of education, but about boosting a few results.

Louise Neve, an ICT co-ordinator who was trying to help colleagues take advantage of the original offer, wrote a long catalogue of complaints in a letter to the TES, and concluded "My verdict on the Computers for Teachers scheme – another great idea which has turned into a bureaucratic farce and will not help those it was meant for. What a shambles!" [47]

They assumed that all training would be carried out in the teachers' own time. Peter Scott told the NAS/UWT conference: "The Computers for Teachers scheme could have provided an excellent opportunity to support the professional development of school staff. Instead, the Government's penny-pinching and greedy approach will seriously undermine it." [48]

A working party of six ICT teachers could have foreseen each of going to leave. So he's left, dominant and on message, with a wreck of a school. It's a sad story, but it's not by any means unique.

"A teacher who suffered a nervous breakdown triggered by a headteacher who shouted at him, criticised him to pupils and allowed discipline in school to collapse has been awarded £300,000 in a record settlement." [8]

This is a tragic case for a deputy head, a man of 45 who was pushed down stairs by a pupil. "I repeatedly warned the headteacher that the school environment was too stressful because of the violently charged atmosphere... Professionally, I was always stepping in between her and the children, because she was at risk." [9]

He had passed on his concerns to the LEA "There was no scale of sanctions which made any sense to me. I said things were so bad that the school was a disaster, staff were demoralised and stressed, and children were very much out of control. I said that I was at breaking point. I was in such a terrible state that I began to cry." [10] The authority assured him that they were aware of the problems and that they would get back to him, but they never did.

It is equally tragic, though, for the head. "According to the NUT, she promoted divide and rule, was inconsistent in disciplining pupils, and told experienced staff to look for new jobs." [11] Her own deputy tells her that the atmosphere has got out of hand as a result of her management style. What is she supposed to do next?

The answer is – get help. From him, from other staff, from fellow heads, and from the authority. But in the present climate, that may not be clear. The head has been presented as the solution to all problems, the one who turns the ship around, regardless of fuddy duddy teachers. So she battles on alone, turning the ship around and leaving casualties in her wake.

Not all the stories are horror stories. "Talking Cure" a BBC 2 programme, told one which was heartbreaking but ultimately positive. Roger Brind had for 19 years been head of Trelair Primary School, in Cardiff. 90% of its pupils have free school meals, 40% have special needs, and the commitment and quality of its staff have been praised by successive inspections.

Brind agreed to collaborate with Anton Obholzer, a psychologist from the Tavistock Clinic with an interest in how organisations manage stress and change. Obholzer visited the school, and attended staff meetings. He recognised the dedication of staff, and the various pressures they face:

"Is the unspoken agenda that nothing can be done? That it's an impossible situation that teachers can't do anything about, that the head can't do anything about, the Government doesn't do anything about, the consultant from the Tavistock can't do anything about, so we can go home and be reassured that there's nothing to be done and we can all carry on as before?"

The nervous laughter confirmed his diagnosis, but they couldn't carry on as before. There was a traumatic staff meeting, which started without Brind, and discussed the impact that his attendance at LEA meetings had on the school. He returned towards the end of the meeting, when Obholzer fed back to him staff anxieties about the impact of his absence. Next day, Brind was absent, and he had six months off school.

It wasn't just pique, or a reaction to the man from the Tavistock. Brind had high blood pressure, and had already confided worries about whether or not he could continue, and if so for how long. He is now back at school, but working in a very different way. "I've told myself I've got to have a work pattern, and work hours, and stick with them. I'm far more effective and more efficient."

His deputy agrees. "We're very loyal to each other, and although we feel that we're very open, the film brought out that we need to be more open. Professionally, it's been very good for us. We try to make sure that there's never any secrecy and that nobody's left out."

The previous dishonesty had been for admirable reasons – staff inspired by a charismatic head, affectionate towards a colleague they'd known for years, hadn't been able to seriously convey criticisms about one aspect of his work. But their silence had still been damaging, and Brind pinpoints the solution:

"There is a desperate need for honesty in the education system. The problems I've had and we've had in this school have been solved." [12]

There is a staff meeting in the programme where Sheila O'Brien, a hard-working, committed teacher, says "I can't give any more." She's talking about demands on her time and energy, and the pressures facing the school. Within the meeting, she's arguing for brutal decisions about what they can and can't do. Maybe their school shouldn't take part in a particular initiative, even if it's good. Maybe Roger Brind shouldn't go to a meeting, even though the school may lose out as a result.

This is now a common dilemma for teachers. When I first became a deputy, in 1981, the job of management was to help the school be as good as possible. Then the job meant interpreting government guidelines so that the school should be as good as possible. And then it came to mean choosing which government guidelines to follow, and which to ignore. I can remember regular conversations with the head, in which we would reassure each other that ignoring regulation x, while it might get us into trouble, was in the best interests of the staff. Some of them would come back from courses and say "This school are doing x, why aren't we?" "and I'd say, "Do you want to?" "Of course not," they'd say. "So what's the problem?" And we'd smile and move on, plotting in a good cause, teacher sanity. If what you are doing is harming the health of your staff, then what you are doing is wrong.

For months Kate Myers reported a series of interviews with head teachers, asking them about their approach to their work. She didn't ask for the views of their staff, who were sometimes very surprised by what they read. Eventually, she talked to some deputy heads, although here she also included the views of their head-teachers, and this dual perspective helps to give more sense of the interaction between professionals. She asked Heather Daulphin, deputy at Hampstead School, Camden, about working with the head, Tamsyn Imison.

"MYERS: What is your relationship with your headteacher?

DAULPHIN: Only when I became deputy did I see she has a naughty streak, which I like.. She is a crafty and radical woman who has been successful without emulating men. We think alike and we are both finishers. I think she thinks I'm scampish, but she respects what I do and I have a healthy respect for her. I've seen her chop heads and she's given me a few slaps in the past." [13]

Daulphin describes herself as a "working class black woman", which helps to explain the vitality of the language, but it isn't just that.

There's an honesty here, about the two of them and how they work together, through conflict and agreement, which suggests that when difficult problems come up these two, with their colleagues, will cope.

Imison, like many heads, sees headship as the goal and criterion for good teachers. "She will make an outstanding headteacher", she says of Daulphin, who is less certain:

MYERS: What sort of head would you like to be?

DAULPHIN: I'm not sure I want to be one."

But it doesn't matter whether or not she becomes a head. What matters is that these two work well together, and for the school, because there is honest interchange between them. If Imison isn't sure about what should happen, or Daulphin has doubts about a future policy, those will be discussed, and the result will be a better decision.

Decisions matter, and good heads are clear about where and when they are being made, and by whom. The head is lucky, because if they want to they can ensure that they agree with all the key decisions, by making them themselves. Other staff have to live with that, but if there is a decision you don't like then at least you want to know how it came about.

One head was considering a change in the allocation of time to particular departments, from History to Science. Meetings were held, in which all departments were warned about possible changes, and various possibilities were put forward, but no decision was taken. Months later, the head decides this move should be made, and issues a document to all staff, outlining the change. "When was this decided?" asks the head of history. The real answer is "Last week, in the bath", but heads don't talk like that. "It was discussed months ago," she says. The Head of History asks deputies, other heads of department, and the dispute simmers for weeks, not because of the decision (which the head could have made at any time), but because of the uncertainty about how and when it was made.

Another head wanted to propose a change in the school calendar. Maybe event X should happen in March rather than October? The senior management team discuss it, and are in favour, by roughly 4-2, although no vote is taken. The head says that he'll consult more widely, and take it to a meeting of middle management. At that meeting there is a majority against, and the head is angry that two senior management members also speak against it. But he decided that he would go ahead with the change anyway.

The fuel for resentment is endless. The head is angry because he feels SMT members are opposing him in public. The critical SMT members, who could have accepted an SMT decision which went against them, feel that they were justified in opposing it in middle management. The decision had not yet been made, and they felt that they were entitled to make a case. Middle management members feel angry, because they have been consulted and then ignored.

Both these examples show head teachers abusing the power of decision. Heads are fond of saying that they carry the can, but this is not about responsibility. It's about honesty, and saying clearly how each decision is being made. Most staff won't quarrel with "I am head, I feel strongly about this issue, so I am deciding A, even though I know many of you are against it." As a daily management style it isn't ideal, but the blurring of who's deciding and when is much more damaging.

This section is critical of heads, and I don't pretend that headship is an easy job. But it is vital that heads and others have a realistic notion of what heads can do and what they can't, and that they accept those limits. In some cases it may be better for a head to settle for a limited role, rather than trying to match a superhead image for which they are obviously unsuited.

The best heads know that they can't do it all on their own, and work out clearly what kind of help they are going to need, and from whom. Other heads, LEA officers, governors, their secretary, partner – it will vary from head to head who performs which function. But the head who thinks that they need no-one will create the most trouble. I remember discussing the rigours of the deputy's job with a colleague, and him saying "That's when it's tough. The days you have to go into his office and say, boss, you're losing it with the staff."

I was a deputy in one school for seventeen years, while a succession of six different heads were in charge. The complexion and size of the management team varied considerably over that time, but I remember the atmosphere at its best, when the head wanted us all to be clear and honest about what was happening in the school, and everyone gained as a result.

## TEACHERS TOGETHER

At the King's School, Wolverhampton, Tim Gallagher is part of the Fresh Start programme. He didn't start by clearing out the staff. He did cut the time spent on meetings, and introduce 'return-to-work' interviews for staff who had been off. "This was partly courtesy, partly checking on the absence. But these interviews have picked up on at least two cases of stress."

There is also a regular staff development review, which "should celebrate staff strengths and identify their needs. We've instituted a 'no-blame culture'. Anyone can make a mistake, the key question is how the situation is dealt with." [14]

Cynics will shake their heads at this softness, but it's actually more efficient. If staff know that the head won't go mad when they've made a mistake they'll be more likely to admit it, and the problem is sorted quicker. I once circulated heads of department with a sheet, on which I wanted particular returns. After the deadline was passed, I went to chase up one that was missing. The head of department grinned. "Sorry, I've lost it. Can you give me another?" I did think about going ballistic, and sharing with him the pressures of my working week. But then I thought again. If he's lost it, I need to know. I want him to have another, so he can do it as soon as possible. "Sure," I said. The zero tolerance merchants breed a climate of fear in which you survive by lying, so it takes longer to find out what has gone wrong.

There's also a huge bonus in the inclusiveness of this approach. All teachers are valued, not simply high-flyers or superteachers. When I started teaching the more traditional schools graded their teachers by uniform – the academics wore gowns, while the peasants in craft and PE could easily be spotted by their dress. It's easy to joke about it now, but those on the receiving end of that kind of prejudice could easily suffer. In the same way, the current stress on test results, on English, Maths and Science, drives wedges between different types of teacher.

213

Huntington School, in York, got rave reviews for its success in ensuring that "children of an unusually wide range of ability achieve their potential to a remarkable degree." Keith Wragg, the head at the time, described the school's policy on recruitment: "There is no element of selection. We follow local authority policy of siblings first, then distance between home and school." When they put a bid in for specialist technology status, it was on condition that the new resources should benefit all subjects." [15]

This isn't just a gimmick. In such a school all the adults who work there are valued, and not just the teachers. One head I worked for insisted that his caretaker was the best appointment he'd ever made. All the staff working on the site need treating with respect. Just as each subject is valued, whether or not they feature in keystage tests, so all pupils are important, whether or not they are capable of grades A-C. That removes the distortion and resentment which follow from such distinctions, but it also gives the community of the school an identity, a positive momentum which gets results.

Teachers need to get better, and most of them know that. They need to build up a clear picture of what they can do, and what they need to work on. When I had been a head of English for five years I had the chance to appoint a second-in-department. We were a good department, with a lot of talents between us, but we didn't know much about children's fiction. So the appointment was a good chance to get in someone who knew more than we did, and could teach us, make us better at that part of the job. When I was younger that might have scared me. I'd have been worried that I'd be shown up by somebody better than me, rather than trying to meet a need. Sometimes people are appointed just because they're safe, and they won't change what's going on.

It can be hard, though, to admit that there's something you're not good at, particularly if your image of a teacher is someone one who knows all the answers. Tamara Bibby reports on research into maths teaching in primary schools:

"Teachers suffered from childhood memories of being ridiculed for showing little maths ability at school. They tended to hide their lack of confidence rather than admit they needed help to improve their numeracy skills. The pressures of time, surveillance from OFSTED, and other demands on teachers may not give them the space to deal with the causes of their shame. They are caught up in a conflict between a desire to change and the need to protect their professional image as being infallible." [16]

Well-run schools encourage their staff to be clear about what they can't do, and what they need to learn. At Howard School, in Kent, they encourage all staff to keep learning. Teachers are encouraged to apply for courses, and the school will support them if they can show how it will help them do their jobs better, or develop in the direction in which they want to go. Over a year most of the school's 108 staff went away for training at some time. [17]

That is a large school, whose support of staff development had at first been boosted by GM status. But even in smaller schools, with limited budgets, its possible to make this kind of commitment. One head I worked for introduced an Individual Neeeds Survey, which all staff filled in at a staff meeting. They wrote down kinds of experience or training which they felt would help them. These were discussed by senior staff, and prioritised. Not everybody got what they wanted every year, but they knew the next year it would happen again, and records were kept of who got what. It was a practical way of taking people seriously, of saying "we know you're good and you want to get better, and we shall use limited resources to help you do that."

It's particularly important that all staff feel valued, as there are pressures working against that. There are fewer deputy jobs, and the nature of school management has changed, so that teachers are less likely to move up the ladder just because it's there. Middle-aged teachers can feel blocked or stranded, facing a long period of work in which there may not be new challenges or fresh stimulus. This calls out for imaginative management – secondments, job swaps, further training – but the fragmented nature of the system makes that much harder to arrange.

And the propaganda doesn't help. A recent Guardian leader praised the PRP proposals, contrasting younger recruits who "bring fresh vigour" with "clapped out, clock-watching uncreative time-servers." [18] They were rightly flooded with angry letters from middle-aged teachers who had worked hard, been criticised and endured mounting pressure from successive government. But this isn't just about fairness; it's also about the efficiency of schools.

An effective school will combine teachers of different subjects, but also teachers of different styles, ages and experience. It needs people who know the area well, teachers who have taught the parents of some of the pupils. The government dream of bright young things sweeping in to make instant changes is a dangerous, short-sighted myth.

We are not looking for one model teacher, and arguing about their age. We are looking for a combination of teachers to work together, and even the most enthusiastic prophet of change can't pretend that we have a whole generation of young teachers ready to do it all. We have some very good recruits, but if we can't find ways of ensuring that they work well with older teachers, then we don't have a future.

It's on that kind of collaboration that our leaders are very vague. Blair and Woodhead seem happiest with dynamic, solitary leaders, autocratic types who function very much as they do. They look faintly embarrassed when winners of teachers' awards talk about the value of teamwork, or the strength that comes from spending more than five or ten years in the same school. Yes, I was a bright young teacher once, and I brought in fresh ideas, and I questioned what was going on. But I also learnt from older, wiser teachers, and many times I was glad of their support.

Good schools know that they have a mix, of subjects, of ages, of talents, and of teaching approaches. They value that diversity, but they also make sure that it works together, feeding off each other's strengths while sharing key assumptions and routines which enable them to work together. It's that kind of interaction that the crudest models of leadership leave out.

The new fast-track teachers, apparently, will be good at discipline. They will partly be helped by the fact that head teachers will protect them when allocating classes, but if they fail to meet the disciplinary requirements than they will be steered towards the "exit mechanism." To me, this sounds disastrous. Of course we want senior staff to be able to control children, but how will they acquire the knowledge to do that?

Some teachers have that naturally, so they don't have to think about it (and they often don't know how they manage it). I had a disastrous first year in teaching, when I nearly failed my probationary year, but it made me think very hard about discipline. I wrote a book about it, gave lectures, and worked hard as a head of department and deputy head to support the discipline of others. This means talking honestly about problems, being prepared to share areas of weakness, and discouraging experienced teachers from belittling colleagues under pressure – "7G ? They're a doddle. I never have any trouble with them."

But a pattern which is testing young teachers for their disciplinary competence works in the opposite direction. If they talk about difficulties, managers may think that they're weak, and not promote them so rapidly. So maybe they should say nothing and hope that no-one notices? It's a dangerous kind of silence, and a lot of pupils will suffer as a result.

Discipline in a school has to be shared. If you know that teachers will look out for each other and will help you in a crisis, then you are more prepared to do the same for them. If together you get pupils to see misbehaviour as an offence against the school as a whole, rather than the teacher as a person, then you share the effort of ensuring that the school is a good place in which to work. If, on the other hand, senior management dismiss your problems, or fail to act against pupils who have disrupted your lesson, you are more likely to ignore offences which don't concern you personally, and to take time off when things are bad.

Pupils are very alert to gaps in the network. Like the children of separated parents who are hostile to each other, they sense areas of weakness and indecision. "Miss J lets us do that... you don't like Mr. K, do you?... I'll tell the head about you, and he'll sort you out..." Such gambits can be laughed away in schools where teachers talk to each other about what they're doing, and know clearly the lines that can't be crossed - refusing instructions, defying teachers, interfering with other pupils' work. But where teachers can't be sure if they'll be supported, or undermined, or ignored, these casual little barbs can be deadly.

Clear collaboration is not just a way of dealing with crises. It's a basic principle, because so much in a school is shared. In secondary schools that sharing is spelt out in the timetable, the grid or booklet

217

which says who has which class when, and where. But how those decisions are made, how the timetable is constructed, is crucial. There are timetablers who elevate it into a cult. They retire from the world for weeks, even months, periodically announcing "Sorry, it can't be done," or "The computer wouldn't wear it."

I was lucky. I learnt about timetabling when I was a head of department. The deputy responsible would show me a board, with pins and coloured card. "At the moment you've got X, which I know you don't want." When I complained, he would walk towards the door. "Try and shift it if you can. Let me know how you get on."

This was a magical piece of trust. Apart from the obvious sit-com disasters – I knock the board over and all the pins fall out – there is the risk that I will make huge mistakes, or muck up what he's done. But that's worth it to him, because I'm learning how it works. I'm understanding that the things I want clash with the things that other people want, and I see that much more clearly if I try to alter things for myself, instead of simply taking his word for it.

In my own timetabling, I carried that on. I stayed with pins and card, and was laughed at by a visiting head, who observed "I can set the computer off, and go and have a cup of tea while it sorts it all out." I'm sure computers can help timetabling, but I'm also sure that I don't want to be somewhere else, having a cup of tea, when crucial choices are being made. It's easier to take the pin board home to work on, and it dramatises more clearly for other teachers what is going on.

At various stages I would issue progress drafts to heads of department. This isn't the final version, but what do you think so far? However much time I spent, they would always check it better than I would. They only had their own area to think about, they knew it better than I did, and they were another pair of eyes. An author shouldn't proof-read their own book.

If they saw something worrying, they'd come to talk about it, look for alternatives, see what contrasting pressures were involved. They might not always get what they wanted, but if they didn't they understood why they hadn't got it, and I would try to make sure that they got it next time – or got something else. All of which was much more time consuming, but much better, than handing out a printed booklet on the last day of term – "That's it: like it or lump it."

What teachers should be talking about is their teaching. Which books or videos should you use? How might you introduce this particular topic? What exactly are you going to ask them to do? Those are the kinds of questions going through teachers' heads, and while a lot of the useful work will be solitary, it's also good to air the questions out loud, and to listen to other people's answers.

A lot of this will happen informally, but in a well run school it will also be part of the meetings. Meetings are much misunderstood. In one school I got flak for running a meeting about meetings, but I have no regrets. For a meeting should be what it says, not a moan or a lecture, but a coming together of minds. They might be sharing experiences, preparing a programme of work, or tackling a common problem – and coming up with a solution that no one of them could have contrived on their own. But a good meeting dramatises the fact that these skilled solo operators, in their separate classrooms, are actually together. So it's worth trying to make sure, together, that meetings do their job.

Sometimes the solo operators are not so skilled. It's pleasant, and not too difficult, to encourage good teachers and recognise their talents. The difficult part of management, at any level, is delivering bad news. Two brief examples, from outside education, illustrate this fact. Jeffrey Archer, when charges of perjury were being considered, was dumped by the Tory Party, and had his membership cancelled. Worse still, they did not directly inform him of that, but he gathered it from a press release. By contrast, when David Young, the Welsh prop forward, was being approached in connection with the captaincy of the Welsh rugby team, he refused to take part in discussions until the previous captain had been informed. Those are the two extremes, cowardice and sensitivity, between which most of us operate most of the time.

Now consider a hypothetical teacher, whom we shall call Susanna. She is frightened of children, which makes her discipline erratic, so that she makes unrealistic demands and over-reacts when pupils fail to meet them.

Mel Myers, a former psychologist who now works as a consultant, suggests ways in which Susanna's head of department might help her. "We have more chance of modifying our own behaviour than of changing someone else's," he says, and the skill lies in helping someone like Susanna to do just that. Unfortunately, it is a skill in short supply.

"People can be frightened of telling others what they are doing wrong," says Mr. Myers. "They start by telling the person how wonderful they are, what talent they have. But most of us are smart enough to see through that." What is needed, he says, is a person who can tell it straight, who isn't vengeful, isn't bound by received wisdom about what you can and cannot say in a situation like this. They can then establish a dialogue and involve the problem teacher in finding a way forward." [19]

I can remember two instances, in which I agonised how to deliver bad news. Both decisions had been made by other people, and should have been delivered by them. One involved a redundancy, and another involved a member of staff being denied resources they had expected to be able to use. In each case I anticipated resentment, partly because I felt that it was justified, both by the decision and by the delay in announcing it. In both cases, though the news was unpleasant, the person receiving it was relieved to have been told. They would much rather know than not know, and would rather be told face to face than on paper. Honesty, daunting in prospect, turned out to be the best policy, yet again.

The same applies to what actually happens in lessons. School architecture varies, and teachers have varying views about being observed in lessons. Some may feel threatened, but there are enormous gains if mutual observation can be established, as a regular positive pattern. One teacher watches another. They don't help out, they don't wander round the class offering comments, but sit still at the back and take notes. That's one way of getting closer to the business of teaching, to compare notes about the different ways in which it can be done.

Another is video. I got into this through a courageous student teacher, who wanted a lesson of hers filmed. I set up the camera, gave nearby kids some unconvincing excuse, and left her to it. Later on, I went through the tape and took notes. She watched it on her own. Then we went through it together.

It wasn't brilliant and it wasn't terrible. To a non-teacher, it would be very dull. But as a way of looking at the details of the teaching job it was terrific. Where should you stand? Why didn't he understand that instruction? How else could you have got their attention there?

I moved on from that to filming teachers, with their permission, to provide material for a staff meeting. It wasn't – aren't these people brilliant? But it was offering examples, different ways of doing the job, and it helped teachers to look very closely at how they operate.

There are problems. Many teachers don't want to be filmed, and some may feel happy about it but then wish they hadn't. You can imagine nightmare scenarios in which heads want to use footage as material for deciding threshold payments, or enlightening the governors. But although it needs handling carefully, and takes a lot of time if you do it properly, I think video has tremendous possibilities for stimulating a more precise analysis of this complicated, challenging job.

But it will not be enough to do that within the school. The best LEA work puts schools together, encourages them to share, makes education less of a race and more of a celebration. Some of them still manage this, and they are not alone. At Sheffield Hallam University, the Centre for Science Education  aims to put science teachers in touch with each other, to stimulate discussion and promote understanding of good science teaching. That is the kind of support needed by teachers, of all ages and all levels of experience.


## TEACHERS AND PUPILS

Sean: You've got an answer for everything, haven't you?
Ashok: He's got to. He's a teacher.

I remember the conversation well, but I'm still not sure how to take it. This could be a tribute to my skill as a sure-footed professional, or an indictment of my two-faced fluency. There's a sense in which a teacher, simply because they're responsible, has to be detached from pupils, and that means that there are some things we don't tell them, some questions we don't answer. Does that make us a bunch of liars?

There is a difference between what you can say to a whole class (work time, many sets of ears, and friends and parents beyond them), and what you might say to an individual in an office (less pressure of time, and the conversation more precisely geared to their situation). On the other hand, as a member of a teaching team there are a lot of things you are not going to say about your colleagues – even if some of them are true.

Many teeenagers feign total distaste for the adult world, and the sad losers who are unfortunate enough to have lived beyond the age of 20. They expect us to have no dress sense or taste in music, and are quick to dismiss the educational party line. But there is still an appetite for honesty there, and a sharp nose for injustice and inconsistency. If you said the deadline for coursework was last Friday, and then accepted a piece of work this Tuesday, there'll be a chorus of "That's not right, sir". And they'd be right.

It's a mirage to pretend that any teacher can be totally open with their pupils, but we still need honesty as a goal, for us and for them, and there's no chance of them buying that unless they see us practising it.

Take, for instance, the busy senior teacher who is delayed on the way to a lesson. He comes into his bottom set of 15 year olds breathless and busy, anxious to start. Perry says "You ought to apologise." The teacher, burdened and gobsmacked, stares in disbelief at this reversal. Perry, often late, seldom apologetic, says "If we're late, we have to apologise. So should you." The teacher, delayed as it is, refuses to back down to this transparent ploy, and pays for his determination with prolonged disruption.

Perry, sadly, is right. If you want pupils to apologise then you have to teach them by the only effective method, which is apologising yourself. The teacher may well have a good reason for being late, and if it's confidential he doesn't have to explain the details, but the fastest way to get to where he wants to be is to say "I'm sorry I'm late. Now we need to make up for lost time." Perry hasn't got a leg to stand on, and the lesson proceeds.

I remember the psychologist David Fontana telling a lecture-hall full of powerful teachers that "Many senior staff underestimate the power of an apology." Power? Apology? Surely an apology makes you weak, vulnerable to attack? Not at all. Once you have apologised, what else can they do? It's before you apologise, when you're uncertain, and they've got a grudge, that there's damaging friction and suspense. Once the apology's made, it's done.

It doesn't have to be a melodramatic grovel, but an acceptance that yes, I got that wrong, and as a result that's made a problem for you. Many teachers find that hard, with pupils and each other. Many pupils find it hard, because noone has ever apologised to them. So it may be that the school has to deliberately teach the business of apology, the routine of what you do when you've mucked something up.

I once had to deal with a nasty incident, when a dinner lady had been sworn at by a pupil, whom she had then hit. Both pupil and dinner lady were notorious characters, better known for loud gestures than diplomacy. From talking separately to the dinner lady, the girl, and her mother, I realised that the only way to resolve this was a mutual apology, almost simultaneous. "You'll never get her to do that!" said various colleagues, some meaning the girl, some the dinner lady. But once they both knew the deal, it wasn't hard. For both of them the hunger to receive an apology, something to put things right, was much stronger than the barriers of pride against giving one.

So an honest school is one where people aren't always blaming each other, are admitting mistakes, and are saying that they're sorry if they got something wrong. Many pupils will tell occasional fibs, and some will be serial liars, but even they recognise that things work better if other people tell the truth. I can still remember the shudders of disbelief that ran through my fifth year tutor group twenty five years ago, when a gentle, intelligent head had told them he would cane anyone not wearing a tie. They knew he wouldn't do it.

Not all honesty will come as good news. Jimmy is lively and pleasant, and wants to be an airline pilot. In your opinion he will never get a grade C in any GCSE subject. At what point in his school career should you tell him this? Head teachers press for exam estimates earlier and earlier each year, but teachers want to give pupils the maximum time to improve their chances, and not seem to damn them with a premature judgement. Should they give a secret estimate, and hope it will never be revealed?

And then there's the kid who comes up quietly to say, "Can I have a word ?" Being a sensitive professional, I nod and usher them into my office. "Can I tell you something in confidence?" They know me, they're serious, they'll obviously feel better if they tell me, but the answer's no. Or it's yes, with a lot of no's attached – no if it's pregnancy, or child abuse, or drug-dealing, or threats of physical violence which ought to be reported to the police. That's the possible context for every child-teacher conversation, and while you don't want to be gloomy it must always be borne in mind.

But it's the work that matters most, and that's where you have to be clear. There's a lot of research to show that pupils learn better when they understand the pattern of the work, the way the exam operates. Critics mock "thinking skills" but there are different ways of thinking, and pupils who understand what kind of operation they are carrying out are more likely to be successful.

So, obviously, I show them past papers, marking schemes, examiners' reports. This, I tell them, is what a marker is looking for. But now, with political intrusion into the curriculum, I also have to explain what's going on. Why can't I do the coursework folder that my older sister did? Why do we have to do these tests? Why do we write about Shakespeare rather than act it?

"Because I say so" was never an adequate reply. Now and again, faced with a less than innocent enquiry, I might resort to "I'll tell you at the end of the lesson." But recent assaults on the curriculum have to be explained to the customers, pupils and parents, and that leaves teachers with a serious dilemma. Just how fully should I trace the educational hijack of the Thatcher raid?

Working with young people should make you look forward. When the politicians and the paperwork get you down, it can often be the energy and wit of youngsters which picks you up. Their curiosity won't be satisfied by "Well, we're very experienced, so we know best." If we're educating them, then we're encouraging them to ask questions, examine evidence, follow where the trail leads, and if that exposes a shambles of short-sighted incompetence, so be it. Our main commitment is not to supporting the government, improved statistics or a rosy view of life, but to clarity of vision and rigorous thought.

1   TES 9.10.98
2   Guardian 11.1.00
3   Guardian 29.2.00
4   Guardian 18.7.00
5   TES 7.4.00
6   Observer 2.4.00
7   Guardian 31.7.00
8   Guardian 11.5.00
9   TES 12.5.00
10  TES 26.5.00
11  Guardian 11.5.00
12  TES 12.11.99
13  TES 2.6.00
14  TES 26.5.00
15  Guardian 5.2.97
16  Tamara Bibby, School of Ed., King's College, London guardian 2.9.99
17  TES 12.5.00
18  Guardian 22.4.00
19  Stephanie Northen, in TES 14.1.00

# Chapter 10:

# FREE AT LAST?

## FACING THE FACTS

"A lie has to expand. It cannot contract." (Jim Crace).

When I became a teacher I learnt about lying. As a nice middle-class boy I had been brought up that lying was wrong, and although it could be occasionally necessary or fun, it was a diversion. Normally, you spoke the truth.

It was a shock to meet youngsters who worked differently. There were kids who often lied, who said what they thought I wanted to hear, or what would get them through the next five minutes.Later, as a deputy head, I would trail down corridors to interview yet again a boy whose story did not tally with the evidence of four witnesses. I would marvel at the next layer of elaboration, the lies told to cover the original lie, and would wonder why it was so difficult to tell the truth.

For dishonesty is hard work. The first fib slips out easily enough, but then you have to adjust what you say later, try to remember who's been told what, and how that will sound to someone else who might know a bit of the truth. Serial adulterers and professional bullshitters may look as if they're getting away with something, but I don't envy them a bit.

This sounds a bit moral for a book on educational politics, but I don't apologise. I think ethical values are related to practical effectiveness, and Tony Blair seems to agree. He invites us to trust him about Ecclestone's money and Formula 1, because he wouldn't get involved in anything dishonest. His leaked memo voices disbelief that anyone should think a government led by him could be anti-family, so I think it's fair to make that link between personal faith and the practical ethics of the workplace. It's also interesting to trace the parallels between leadership in politics and in education.

As head of government, his role is similar to that of a head running a secondary school. He has his cabinet, of experienced professionals in charge of different departments. The head of a school has heads of department, team leaders, heads of year, who may also sit round a table and put their heads together.

Accounts of the current cabinet suggest that that doesn't happen often, it doesn't last long, and it doesn't work well. The real business is done elsewhere, by Blair's small group of advisers, or by Blair in serial negotiation with individual ministers. I've seen schools run that way, with the head tightly guarding information and resources like a precious poker hand. He or she may feel in charge, but it's a waste. There's no common ground where information and insights can be shared, the head misses out on what the others know, and they feel devalued. Autocracy is the illusion that the leader can do it all, and like all lies it has its costs.

There are occasional signs that Blair sees some danger in the notion of the leader who always gets it right:

"CHASTENED BLAIR ADMITS WELSH LEADERSHIP BLUNDER Tony Blair has been forced to admit he made a spectatcular blunder by blocking Rhodri Morgan from standing as leader of the Welsh Labour party." [1] That suggests a one-off error, a moment when Blair thought "Mm – Morgan? No, I don't think so." What actually happened was a careful campaign, sustained over a long period, to bend, break or alter rules so that Morgan was blocked at any cost. [2] Either Blair authorised that, or he allowed the people working for him to do it, or they did it without his knowledge or permission. That is what the apology should addresss, but it doesn't get near.

In education, there is no one campaign which is as corrupt as that, but there are many instances of deception. This book details a series

227

of illusions from which education policy has suffered over the past five years, namely that:
- education ministers are the key figures in education
- solutions to education problems are simple
- everything is getting worse, and is worse than other countries
- most teachers have been misguided in their thinking
- blame and criticism improves performance
- the quality of teachers matters; the quantity doesn't
- head teachers can turn schools round on their own
- the effects of poverty can be overcome by expectation and effort
- simple tests will tell us what standards our children have achieved
- selection and competition benefit the whole system
- only GCSE grades A-C really matter
- top-down pressure will secure lasting change.

Some of these contain half-truths, but in this form they are untrue, and damaging. The reasons for deception vary, from laziness to calculation, embarrassment to ignorance. But the effect is the same – unworkable policy, confused perceptions, damage to morale. There has been some positive action, but too much of it, and too quickly. Patricia Rowan, as ex-editor of the TES, is an experienced observer:

"From Sure Start to Fresh Start, and taking in too many city initiatives to keep track of along the way, this government's impatience for results is fast running out of control. The projects themselves are not the problem – there is virtue in every one. It is initiative overload that is threatening their credibility. That, and the constant threat to discard them if they don't hit targets within 18 months." [15] The purpose of this book is to warn against the distortions which have both inspired and undermined this hectic programme.

Lies have their costs, and as a result of the above we have:
- no confidence in long-term development
- a crisis in teacher morale
- a crisis in teacher supply
- failure to support new teachers
- much school management which does not have the confidence of staff

- a pattern of school work which is increasingly dull and mechanical
- mounting stress on school pupils
- inequality within the schools, and between schools
- disaffection among pupils who know that they cannot succeed
- further fragmentation of an already divided system.

And they don't seem able to learn. The problem of overload has been recognised, examined by a task force, and recommendations made in an attempt to reduce it. But still the announcements hammer out:

"Teachers are fed up with the perpetual reorganisation of education. Has the Government thought through its latest wheeze – 'children taking lessons in different institutions.' How much time will children spend trailing between different sites ? Will transport be provided – increasing traffic congestion – or will they walk, with potential risks to their safety and temptations to truant? How would this work in rural areas?" [3]

Or on a timetable? I used to write a timetable for a school which shared its sixth form teaching with two others. For schools with limited resources and small numbers of sixth-formers it was a brave gesture of commitment and collaboration. It was also a pain, as the joint arrangements had to be fixed first. Because of problems with travel, they involved large chunks of time, which could then not be moved, at the cost of possible benefits elsewhere in the school.

This idea hasn't had any work put into it, and can't have been explored in consultation with any teachers. The only reason for it appearing in the news is because somebody wants regular stories, to show that the government is working hard. And then there's the new vocational courses, which are a nice idea, but a sick joke to anyone who knows the history of English attempts to create an equal status for such work. For such a scheme to work, there is a minimum of thought, consultation and preparation which have to be carried out, before you even think of an announcement.

Part of the problem is coverage like this:

"BLUNKETT RIGHT TO IGNORE CRITICS

If the government has clarity of purpose and single-mindedness on a few issues, it can do great deeds. What the Americans call "a small agenda" has been exemplified here by David Blunkett's determination – at all hazards – to raise basic standards in Britain's schools. He has refused to be sidetracked by Roy Hattersley and the selection debate, to be knocked off course by the "let our children play" complaints of middle-class critics. The result is that more children can read, write and calculate properly than ever before. But you don't get many Blunketts to the pound." [4]

David Aaronovitch has no qualifications or expertise in education. He is a friend of Peter Mandelson, and an opinionated commentator. But he has access to column inches and screen time, and that makes him a voice to which Labour want to listen.

Notice that he's not just indifferent to the anxieties of education professionals. It's positively in Blunkett's favour that he's ignoring concerns about imaginative development or social justice. There's powerful encouragement there, for Blunkett to carry on as he is, deliberately shutting out what other people are trying to tell him.

The leaders of teacher unions are not charismatic, lively or new. But they are often right. This isn't surprising, as their members are teachers, who know about what happens in schools. I have traced a series of stories, where the unions have warned government ministers that they have got it wrong - on naming and shaming, on superheads, on exclusions and on teacher supply. In the end, facts have supported the unions, and the government, with little honesty or grace, has backed down.

But that hasn't bothered the media. The job I've done, of following these stories through, date by date, could be done in any pressroom or television studio. Long-term review gives you a perspective you don't get any other way, yet it's one we seldom get in education coverage. If you just went by the daily newsflash, you could assume that they know what they're doing, and it will all be all right. On a long-term view, they don't know what they're doing, and a lot is going wrong. But nothing like enough of that story has been reported.

Blunkett reads Aaronovitch's column and thinks he's doing alright. In Medialand the image of the hero is the one who stands alone. He doesn't just ignore the others, he defies them, and charges on, looking at the image, regardless of the facts. Education ministers learn that so long as they keep their distance from teachers, unions, intellectuals, the media will approve. They don't have to look back at what they've done and what they've said, and the wasteful pattern of bragging, bluster and deceit goes on.

Between 1997-2001 New Labour was busy, serious and – eventually – spent money. They raised important issues which needed facing. But they could have achieved so much more, and so much more that would have lasted, if they had been prepared to worry less about short-term media impact, and more about long-term working relationships. One example stands for many. In October 2000, the government announced that "Every secondary school will be expected to introduce the new literacy strategies for 11-14 year olds next September, although the controversial pilot scheme is only six weeks old." [5]

Why is there a pilot scheme? Because it's complex, and controversial, and you don't get it right first time. You can learn from mistakes, and from the constructive comments of professionals. Why won't they let the pilot scheme run its course, and do the job properly? Because they think it's more important to feed announcements to the media, and score political points. But that too carries a cost, as Anne Barnes points out: "The general feeling is that the training is rushed and dictatorial and it will be difficult to introduce nationally. There is a sense of frustration from teachers that they have been dragooned into this." [6]

Money continues to be a problem. For years we have become accustomed to schools having to get involved in fund-raising. For their first two years in power Labour were spending less on education than the Conservatives. When money did come, much of it was swallowed up by government initiatives. Those bits that dribbled out to schools were repeatedly trumpeted, and often weren't enough to cover existing deficits. And now, finally, that substantial money is being put into the system it is on terms which favour certain pupils.

"There will be two key pledges on school standards: to raise the percentage of children obtaining five or more GCSEs at grades A-C, and to ensure the number of children obtaining KS2, level 4, at the age of 11 does not fall below 78%." [7]

It's business as usual. O level lives, we're only really interested in those on the C/D borderline, and work with kids below E, or at levels 1 and 2, doesn't deserve any cash. Those bottom grades include many of the children for whom the Social Exclusion Unit is concerned, but this extra bonanza depends on them being ignored yet again. To take a small but significant minority, 70% of children in care get no exam passes at all [8] – no Fs, no Gs. Just how will they benefit from a focussed campaign to drive up grades from D to C? This is from a government which makes cocky noises about "joined up thinking."

Thinking is in short supply. The same announcement expressed concern that "between 6-8% of all children leave school without a single GCSE. The Government will now look at more vocational qualifications to encourage pupils to attempt some form of exam." [9] Really? I've lost count of the number of promises I've heard about catering for this group, devising something special for them, which is immediately seen as low status and of no interest to employers.

But I can remember them working hard, being motivated and getting low GCSE grades of which they were proud. That was when we had substantial GCSE coursework, which valued what they did, without regular reminders which sat them in silence for an hour and a half to tell them they weren't very good. Coursework didn't give away cheap grades, and was not abandoned because it didn't work. It was abandoned because Tory ministers took against it, without evidence or justification. There were problems with it, but nothing that couldn't be solved with ten per cent of the time and money devoted to conventional exams.

One of the myths is that we have a watertight assessment system which will continue to tell us the truth. What we have is "an examinations industry, like the railways, shorn of old systems and values, but required to serve increasing numbers of demanding customers. It is hardly surprising that accidents happen... We have heard of chief examiners exploiting their positions for personal financial gain: markers have been accused of bias, and there have been revelations that exam boards are receiving royalties for books marked with their 'official'stamp. Added to these are stories of missing scripts, computer systems failing to award correct marks and the startling rise in remarks, suggesting disenchantment with the entire process."

Dr. David Lines sees a future in which exam boards compete by approving textbooks and cutting corners. "This might be fine if the end result was unambiguously positive, but with even less time available for formative classroom activities, all it will do is encourage 'teaching to the test', encourage surface learning at the expense of deeper understanding and further de-professionalise teachers." [10]

If you designed education to equip children for the 2000s you would not end up with what we've got. In the process of writing this book, I've compiled a library of news cuttings. They are hoarded in filing cabinets, spread out on the kitchen table, and occasionally lost. But if I can't find a particular date or reference, I don't scrabble around the floor or work through every file. I look it up on the Net. Our ideas about knowledge, memory, original thinking have to take account of how things are changing around us, and less and less of what our pupils need can be found in a simple test.

"At its simplest, students who can beat teachers to information through the Internet will take a dim view of a curriculum which prioritises memory skills at the expense of most others. We continue at our peril to neglect the development of competence in thinking and reflection, in evaluation and application of criticial judgement; of true self-understanding; of understanding how the world works, of how to contribute to society." [11]

That comes from Valerie Bayliss, who is director of the Opening Minds project. Such work has been dismissed by William Hague and Chris Woodhead, but thinking does need to be thought about.

And that's less likely to happen as the government try to do it all. The IPPR is one of Labour's favourite think tanks, from which government ministers and advisers have come. But two of their researchers report that "ministers' top-down approach is stifling innovation and risks, creating a generation of teachers who are unable to plan their own lessons." The dominance of tests, influence of OFSTED and the undermining of LEAs also contribute to this pressure. [12]

All of which is passed on to the customers. There is gathering evidence that this pattern of work, insulting and unattractive to many teachers, is also damaging to pupils. The original idea of SATs tests was that they would be "on the spot", quickly checking where pupils happened to be at the time. Not any more. Now we have –

"…parent meetings organised to warn of oncoming tests; SAT predictions allegedly raised artificially year on year to satisfy OFSTED; rivalry between some teachers for best SAT scores, since noone exactly knows how else performance pay will be worked out; extra coaching to improve statistics; classwork, sometimes a year early, consisting mainly of SAT papers, and priority given to English, Maths and Science…" [13]

This worries parents. They want their children to do well, but not at any price, and some fear that the current concentration is narrowing in one direction, cutting down children's opportunity to do more varied, interesting things. This was a father of a seven year old boy, talking on Radio 4:

"It seems a lot of time is being used in school, because there is so much pressure on the teachers to get good scores in the tests, simply preparing children for the tests, and that this is time that could be better used in other ways." [14]

Andrew Marr describes what happened next:

"Some of the most eloquent moments in politics are the silences, those single-beat hesitations when a powerful person is struck by the possibility that he's wrong; when you can hear a mind turning. At about 8.15 on Wednesday David Blunkett… paused. Then, sounding troubled, he said if that if it was really a national problem 'I would very seriously consider changing it.' " [15]

It was eloquent, but it was only a moment, and it didn't last. Either Blunkett thought better of it, or he was persuaded to file his human impulse somewhere else. Chris Woodhead was less concerned. Pupils would only feel stress if that was communicated by teachers. So long as they behaved professionally, there was nothing to worry about.

But there was. A PAT survey found that the brightest youngsters face more than 75 external tests and exams during their time at school. [12] "Last year, Childline received almost 800 calls about exam stress. Nineteen children said that they were so stressed they had attempted suicide. Half the calls were from GCSE students, but more than 100 came from children under 14." [16] A survey of 1,600 young people asked them about the threats to their health. "Time and again, young people talked of the stresses involved as they worked in school towards their 16+ examinations." Whatever their background, "the vast majority of young people were caught up with this pressure". [17]

This testing regime, and the drive for numeracy and literacy, are based on a false model of learning. "David Blunkett and Chris Woodhead both speak as though literacy and numeracy are preconditions of creativity and imagination. First, they imply, children must learn to read and write and count; later they will be able to apply their hard-won skills to creative effect. They are mistaken. Unless the imagination is ciritically engaged from the outset in the business of acquiring literacy and numeracy, literature and mathematics lose their value no less than their charm. Imagination is central, whatever the subject matter, however young the child." [18]

Michael Armstrong is an experienced teacher, but these ideas are dismissed, as nostalgic and impractical. Education, we are told, is woolly and unrealistic, and should make itself more businesslike. Business measures things, drives forward changes, ratchets up the grades. But Woodhead, a teacher and administrator, and Blair, a former lawyer, have a very simple view of business.

Modern business is nothing like so crude. When Greg Dyke took over the BBC, he recruited Gareth Jones' help. In 1996, Jones wrote a report entitled "What Holds The Modern Company Together." There is no one model for all businesses, but for the BBC Jones proposed the "communal" approach, balancing sociability and solidarity. Birt's drive towards efficiency and productivity had had the effect of dividing people; a more positive strategy would involve the sharing of ideas, more casual gatherings, a reduction in formality and fewer hierarchical differences. That's a management expert giving advice to a large organisation, and it seems very relevant to schools. [19]

The business aspects of education which have flourished are the management consultants, PR experts and lobbyists, who have made millions but not taught a single child. OFSTED, the great token of toughness, now costs us over £100 million a year. Meanwhile, there is confusion at grasssroots level about exactly what part will be played by LEAS, less glossy organisations but more concerned with what goes on in schools.

Certainly government place a high value on private sector expertise. Estelle Morris outlines what consultants bring to the table: "They're slightly distant than us, they've not got a vested interest, they've got experience of managing elsewhere, they know management models that work. They've got a skill in analysing a problem, they've got a skill in designing a solution."

As a plea for flexible thinking this would be fine. Yes, educational leaders should look beyond education, read widely, listen to the views of other professionals. But Ms. Morris is looking further than that. She's not talking about learning, but about the deliberate expansion of a market:

"I can't see that all the expertise happens to currently lie within the public sector. I think there are skills out there in the private sector... that we could harness to the cause of efficient LEA, but they won't want to join the great educational crusade unless they get a clear message that they are wanted."

The private sector doesn't want to feel loved. They want to make a profit, and the stock exchange agree that there is potential business of £350 million a year to be made from privatised education. Ms. Morris does not go into detail about the precise insights the private sector will provide, but there are educational skills which they will need and at present do not possess. The only people with these skills work in the LEAs, so the private sector goes into the market to buy them. "Top education officers are being poached by private companies in a brain drain which could provoke a crisis in the public sector." [21]

Nobody knows the gains of such a process, but the losses are immediate. There are two extra layers of cost – more pay for the officials, and profit for the companies – plus a large degree of instability, within the LEAs and beyond. And the only people with responsibility for the system, and with the powers to control it, are the government – who haven't carried out pilot studies as a test, don't have a clear rationale, but are still anxious to destabilise the system as thoroughly as possible.

While Estelle Morris works to give encouraging signals to the entrepreneurs outside, her colleague is despatched to reassure the insiders, or some of them, at least. "David Blunkett's speech to the NAHT annual conference doesn't square with the one he gave three weeks earlier at a conference The Education Network organised. Far from saying that elected councillors have no future place in schools, Mr. Blunkett congratulated the 300-plus local authority elected councillors and officers for working in parthership with both the government and schools to deliver the government's key education policies." [20]

It sounds, yet again, as if the spinning is getting in the way. Keep both sides happy, by telling them different stories, and some time later we can make up our minds. Part of the passion for dismantling LEAs is classic Woodhead impatience – "I can't be doing with all this." There's no sign that the increasing involvement of private finance has been carefully considered or costed. It's an impulsive crusade – "Let's do it, never mind about the cost."

But government has to mind. It has to be careful and constructive, to value long-term benefits above short-term gains in the polls. There has to be serious intellectual effort, to think things out and then follow them through, rather than flit between soundbites.

People in education may often feel isolated, but they are not alone. Ambulance workers and the police, nurses and social workers could swap similar tales of privatisation, limited resources and reorganisation. With the NHS the government is trying to set up a five year plan, which explicitly depends on the support of people working in the service. How long have teachers waited for an offer like that? Maybe that is because doctors have more clout than teachers, or because the government calculates that doctors have more public support. But either way real problems remain.

Blair tried to generate new momentum for the NHS reforms by admitting that the government should be "absolutely frank" about the time needed to reform the NHS. Alan Milburn, health minister, reiterated that the government would gain more respect by being "dead straight with people about the depth of problems and the amount of time to put it right." On message, and the same message – we shall be totally truthful, about how tough the problems are.

But honesty is not a tactic which can conveniently be controlled. On the day of these announcements Bernard Rebeiro, consultant surgeon, attacked the government for announcing 7,500 new consultants, when only 1,500 of those would be new posts. 200 new CT scanners had been promised, although three-quarters of those were replacements. Rebeiro objected that such spinning was raising unrealistic expectations. "The government is giving the impression the health service is going to be so much better when it isn't." [21] Honesty is a good policy, but it doesn't respond to spinning, it isn't cheap, and sometimes it can bite.


## GETTING IT RIGHT


Ministers and editors, facing criticism, will sometimes fight back with "All right then, what's your alternative?" This is a bit rich, since neither government policy nor editorial decisions have shown much interest in the views of practitioners, but it still deserves a response.

Michael Armstrong is ready for them:

"Your leader asks those of us who reject the government's vision of education to articulate an alternative.

My vision of primary education starts from a recognition that children's creative thought and action lie at the heart of educational experience from infancy and that the primary classroom, at its best, is the setting for a provocative engagement with culture, shared between a teacher and her class.

That means, among so much else, the abandonment of an over-determined curriculum which ignores the innumerable ways in which the content of every good primary classroom necessarily varies, to accommodate the developing concerns of its members. It means the rejection of testing in favour of forms of assessment based on the body of work produced within the classroom and each individual's contribution. It means giving classroom teachers rather than heads the leading role in educational management. It means redefining inspection as collaborative evaluation and reflection.

These alternatives may be outside the bounds of present possibility, granted the present orthodoxy, but please don't pretend that they don't exist. You will find them tucked away somewhere or other within the TES almost every week." [22]

I know he's right, because that is where I've found many of the examples which have encouraged me that it is worth getting involved in this discussion. So will the government consider what Armstrong says, and take it seriously? Or will it be filed away, under "Pointless progressive protest."?

Michael Fullan has been looking at changes in schools, and whether or not they last. Real changes, his team concludes, depend on the following:
- teachers working together in teams
- heads and teachers working together to focus in pupil learning
- alliances between communities and schools
- better teacher education, support of new teachers, rewards for teachers throughout their careers
- recruiting, developing and supporting school leaders
- co-ordination of policy at LEA and national level
- co-ordinated support, with systems of accountability.

"The interactive infrastructure outlined above builds in powerful 'lateral accountability', as people cannot help being influenced, energised and rewarded for their performance, or being noticed if they fail to contribute." [23]

That's impressive, but it isn't what we've got. What we've got, as Michael Barber told an audience in Washington, is a very different animal: "The sustained drive from central government is perceived as an entirely 'top down' reform with its associated pressures to conform, whereas all evidence suggests that successful reform requires a combination of 'top down' and 'bottom up' change." [24]

It's not that we don't know how to do it. School self-evaluation has been tried, and found to work. It has been developed by John MacBeath, together with the NUT, and other countries have seized on their work as a route to involvement and success.

"In healthy systems there is sharing and networking of good practice within and amongst schools on a collegial basis... It is an unhealthy system which relies on the constant routine and tensions of an external body to police its schools." [25]

It is also an unhealthy system which has to keep itself going with misleading myths about testing, teaching and the nature of learning. It is not the case that this government is gutless. On some issues, it has been prepared to face up to critics, and to fight hard. It has been resolute, for instance, in its determination to tolerate selection, extend testing, humiliate failing schools, and retain Chris Woodhead. The failure is not of nerve, but of judgement.

Blunkett is eager to stress his "vision". What's important, however, is what he hears. Does he take in what other people tell him, or does he try to do it on his own? Only a government willing to hear what people want to tell it can be fully informed, and unless it is fully informed its judgement will be impaired, and its policies mistaken.

The literacy strategy, for instance, has raised the public profile of literacy, and pressured teachers into tackling work they would not otherwise have undertaken. But one cost of that has been that this has sometime felt like an alien programme, imposed from outside, which doesn't give teachers the chance to respond to individual need. If Johnny, or Serena, hasn't grasped step 3, do I go on to step 4, or look for ways of trying to ensure that they understand? Have I got the time to do that? Is 'some step 4' better than 'understood step 3', and who is it that makes that decision? Unless the teachers feel that they control and own that process, then it's unlikely to take root in the schools.

So, how could New Labour start to put things right? If there was a change of direction, a willingness to respond, what would they need to do? My own list would go as follows:
- Stop producing new initiatives
- Stop creating new types of school
- Drop PRP, and offer a pay rise to all teachers
- Create support for young teachers, and make sure it works
- Target the least successful schools, the pupils achieving least, with professional support
- Drop the use of A-C grades as a measurement.

Compared with the list of mistakes, that's a modest start. But it would make a dramatic difference, and it would not be easy. Dropping the A-C measurement, for instance, would be controversial. It would attract media criticism, and would involve government in having to explain, to educate opinion, to defend a principle. That's not something they're used to, it will call for nerve and they will look hard for reasons why it shouldn't be taken on.

That short-term programme would be a start, but it wouldn't be enough. Beyond that we need to build an education system which isn't dependent on political gimmickry. Each time there's any development, a government minister leaps into action to write the letter, make the speech, claim the credit. So what do their opponents do? They challenge the progress, doubt the achievement, seek to undermine what's going on. Such a style doesn't guarantee lasting power for anyone, but it does ensure that schools are continually under fire.

We need a kind of consensus. In one sense we already have one, but it's about the wrong issues and it's never been proclaimed. New Labour has accepted key elements of the Tory raid – the lottery of the school market, the league tables, the focus on A/C grades. But these will not give us the progress that we need, and in many ways they represent an obstacle to it. So we need a considered, open, rational approach to establish agreed foundations for a system which will educate all our children. That won't come easily, and it certainly won't come by pretending that the challenge isn't there.

We need a more stable, less volatile atmosphere. We need pressures to bring schools together, rather than to drive them apart. We need to find ways of encouraging teachers from different schools to share their insights and experience, rather than seeing each other as rival brands. And we need less emphasis on outstanding individual heads, and more on an expanding community of good teachers. That's a tough professional programme, but it can only work with the support of resources and political will.

Government action is vital, but that is not all that needs to happen. A healthier situation will mean fuller, more mature coverage in the media. We need intelligent, adult versions of school and teachers in film and television drama. Teachers need to use their brains and imagination to provide the public with more interesting and attractive models of their work. But while all that is necessary, it is incidental to the main decisions which are being made, and currently these are being made by a small number of politicians, in ignorance or self-delusion.

Maybe I'm wrong. Maybe everything will be all right. This is, after all, a busy, committed government, which has generally had popular support. At the time he resigned, Chris Woodhead thought morale was good. David Blunkett thinks it will get better as the test scores rise. It's tempting for old teachers like me, who have worked for thirty years, and been ignored, to leave them to it. We tried to tell them, but they didn't want to know, so let them do it their way and see what happens.

But that won't do. There are plenty of teachers under fifty, doing an important job, who need a positive, realistic picture of the future. And there are kids, here and to come, who may come into a fragmented system, but will go to some kind of school. We have to think about them, and one of the things we owe them is honesty.

In my teacher-training year, I did a three week practice in a junior school. The headteacher was anxious that we should have maximum respect, and not be treated as 'students.' "I've told the children you're visiting graduate teachers", she explained. Two days later a nine year-old was looking up at me, and she wasn't fooled. "Are you going to be a teacher?" she asked.

Teachers, and politicians, like to pretend that they control what other people know. They don't, and the other people, whether pupils, teachers or citizens, can rapidly smell a lie. The evidence in this book shows that at the points where the government is most emphatic, it has simply got things wrong. People don't like to have their thinking done for them. If you insult pupils, bore them with mechanical work and insist that you know best, their potential will not be realised. If teachers are taken for granted and patronised, they will not be fully involved, and they will look for ways of expressing their resentment. That may be through retirement, letters to the TES, or by working to rule.

At the moment we are losing teachers, emotionally and practically, and the plan cannot work without them. Everything that the government wants for education would work better with the active involvement of teachers, yet what ministers do and say tells teachers that they do not matter. Until that basic relationship is honestly addressed, nothing will improve.

Things will not stay the same. Lies generate a life and momentum of their own, growing in their effects. Within the myths, the problems won't be solved. Focus groups won't repair teacher morale, and the editor of the Daily Mail can't supply the teachers that we need. For there to be a change, the truth has to be faced, and there are three ways in which that might happen. First, government starts to listen. Blunkett is a curious figure, but he can be open, honest and imaginative, even if that side of him has not always been encouraged. And there must be many people working within New Labour who know that these myths are damaging.

The second route of improvement is through pressure from outside. Every Easter the newspapers report on angry teachers, and a teachers' strike would only feed that appetite. Teachers have to be more creative about how and why they demonstrate. But they need to be part of the pressure, because if teachers seem to accept what is happening, why should anyone else consider change?

They will need, though, the support of parents and academics, of people in the media, and of the public at large. Most appropriate of all, pupils could play a role. 8 year olds at Micklefield primary school have made a start. During a year 3 test, Shane O'Neil passed his teacher a note saying he had had enough. Madeline Rampton said she was sorry, but the complaint should go to Mr. Blunkett, not to her. Pupils wrote to him, and got a sympathetic reply saying that life could be hard, but explaining why testing was important. [26] The number of pupils feeling like that is going to grow, they won't all be eight years old, and many of them will not be convinced by that reply.

Already the work done in school is duller than it was, and duller than it needs to be. Teachers who know that they can enthuse and involve pupils more fully are deciding not to do so, because they are put under pressure and have targets to meet. Young teachers coming into the profession are not encouraged to initiate courses or try out new ideas. Their job is not seen as creation, but delivery.

I started teaching English in 1967. For years pupils had performed a limited range of fairly mechanical tasks, some of them with success. There was a need for new ideas, and more varied approaches. This was partly necessary in order to involve large numbers of pupils who felt that the examination curriculum offered them nothing. It was also important, however, that those achieving success in limited exams should extend the range of what they could do, and be encouraged to develop their talents in a more creative way. These needs produced a range of materials and, through coursework, a variety of working approaches which transformed the subject. It became more interesting, more challenging to teach, and more satisfying to learn. None of that involved any lessening of standards or rigour, but it did call for intelligence, commitment and hard work.

I look now at bookshops, and at the shelves of school texts, almost all of them specifically related to passing some test or exam. The focus has narrowed, the variety has been sacrificed, and although there are lively and positive exceptions the average diet is much poorer than it was. If we are going to involve all pupils fully in their learning, then that kind of movement is going to have to happen again, but it won't be possible within the straitjackets which New Labour have been so eager to adopt.

The last scenario is the worst. This is that government listens to no one, so that we wait for events to spell out the truths they will not hear. When there are obviously, nationally, not enough teachers or heads to carry out their commands, they may then wonder if the commands are right. Each time I talk to colleagues slightly younger than me, and register the weariness and anger which accompany their commitment, I sense that nightmare scenario move one step closer.

I don't want to be a pessimist. I would love to spend my retirement watching a flourishing education system soar above anything achieved in my lifetime. It would be a delight to witness talented young people going into teaching, and to be sure that the system was ready to receive them, and make the most of their talents. So it would be good to believe that before we get to the point of no return there is a glimmer of light, a taste for honesty, which will help us towards more gradual and constructive change. That way, we can look for a future for pupils, and for education, which gets beyond the simple myths to the more complex and challenging nature of the truth about teaching, and that truth will set us free.

# POSTSCRIPT

And that was where I wanted to end. I have been writing this book for two years, and I have tried to keep it positive. I wanted to be persuasive rather than damning. I wanted to be fair, to a government which worked hard to make a difference to the quality of education. Maybe their early promise to spend no more than the Tories was simply prudence, buying them approval and time in which to be more committed later. Maybe the courting of newspaper approval was a necessary part of getting elected. Maybe as plans collapsed, because they had been rapidly imposed from the top, they would see the need to consult more widely.

I was wrong. This is a book about honesty, and I have to admit the truth. As this book has been written, the context in which English teachers work has become increasingly overcast. I say "English", because the ability of Scotland, Northern Ireland and Wales to do things differently offers more hope to teachers there, while underlining to teachers here that there are alternatives, other choices which our leaders might have made. But in England, in March 2001, this is how it looks.

There are not enough teachers. The atmosphere in schools is suffering from this fact, as work is less organised, standards of discipline less consistent, pupils' confidence undermined and the morale of teachers sapped by the constant effort to find bodies. And as usual, the impact has been worst on those schools least favoured with money, full-time staff, and local esteem. The rates of teachers suffering from stress-related illness have soared. Many teachers over fifty have simply had enough, and are desperate to retire. Pay bonuses, disputed and mishandled, were supposed to raise morale. They are increasingly seen as the gateway to a decent pension. Heads and teachers continue to leave early, because of government pressures rather than the job itself, and the current age profile of the profession suggests that the situation will get far worse before it gets better.

We don't have enough replacements. We still aren't able to produce a clear, reliable calculation of how many teachers we have, but it isn't enough. The gain of paying student teachers is offset by the damage done to those who just missed getting paid. The contortions of the fast track scheme, and the disruption it involves for other teachers not involved in it, cannot be justified by the 1500 people who have actually managed to get on it. They are just enough, as it happens, to replace the 1400 who dropped out during their first year of teaching in 1999-2000. [28] We don't need a few superkids; we need a lot of good, committed teachers.

The work of being a teacher is less interesting and less satisfying than it was. The room for initiative and creativity has been reduced, and that can't be compensated for by a rise in grades. The whole testing apparatus, from junior school to GCSE, is under massive strain. Lessons are duller than they were, resources less challenging, and increasingly pupils coming into the system present massive demands in terms of social behaviour as well as intellectual development. Many pupils suffer from mental strain, and a much larger number wish that they could do work which was more interesting, over which they had more control.

I hate writing that. It's a ready made package of doom, which could simply be lifted out of context. "SYSTEM ABOUT TO COLLAPSE says ex-teacher." I've suffered from headlines like that all my working life, and I wouldn't wish any more on the people who try to make the system work.

It isn't all the government's fault. They didn't inherit a perfect system, and some of these problems are international. There is, for instance, a worldwide shortage of teachers. On the other hand, in the long run I don't think our attempt to bribe teachers to come here from South Africa will look particularly enlightened.

What matters, though, is how New Labour react to these problems. In November 1999 experts were suggesting that it might be time to start paying trainee teachers. The Government spokesman could afford to dismiss such advice – "The reality is that we've started to turn around what was a very serious problem." But that wasn't the reality at all. The reality was that six months later they would be forced to take that advice. Estelle Morris was sure that the government's new thinking about fast-track entry would transform the situation; its effect has been minimal.

It's not just the problems that are depressing. It's the failure to face them, and to be honest about what's happening. As the election approaches government ministers warn us against cynicism, a Tory conspiracy to reduce their majority. I do feel cynical, but not as a result of a rightwing plot. There were things I believed in, like freedom of information, an ethical approach to arms, an integrated transport policy and a greater concern for the environment. Four years ago it looked as though a Labour government would take us closer to those things, but not any more. They briefly offered the illusion, and then they waved it away. And now I must add to that list of disposable dreams the belief for which I worked for 30 years – that we could have a system which offered decent education for all.

It was a nice day in February, 2001. I'm retired, a self-employed writer who can decide what he wants to do with his time. I went for a walk. On my way home, I saw the front page of the Daily Mail, displayed outside the local garage. DEATH OF THE COMPREHENSIVE, it said.

Nothing very special about that. Throughout my thirty years of teaching somebody was saying that you couldn't educate all kids, that standards were getting worse, that teachers didn't care, and the system needed shaking up before it fell to bits. And if no person was actually saying it, some newspaper would write it anyway.

What was different this time was that the paper was reporting a speech by a Labour prime minister. Tony Blair, facing an election, deliberately chose to spell out to everyone that the present pattern had failed, and that the vision of the future must involve more specialist schools, more fragmentation, a further expansion of the lottery. His press spokesman was allowed to say that the days of the bog-standard comprehensive were over.

This isn't a rational decision, based on evidence. The figures don't prove that comprehensives have failed. So far as bright pupils are concerned, comprehensives have been more successful than grammar schools. [24] The level of achievement is lower in areas where there are grammar schools than in areas without them. [28] So this isn't an argument about what works. It's a gesture, an attempt to look good by offering some parents something better than the rest.

To readers of chapter 6, that doesn't come as a big surprise. It did seem that the numbers of specialist schools were being rationed, maybe as a preliminary to the scheme being phased out, but someone changed their mind. Ten years ago we would have expected a nod in the direction of consultation – Labour party members might be asked for ideas, or senior figures in education might have offered their response. Not now. New Labour insisted that the price of electoral victory was virtual dictatorship.

So if Andrew Adonis suggests to Tony Blair that this is the way to go, and he's convinced, then that is what we'll do. Adonis is one of Blair's advisers and speechwriters. He is also an ex-Liberal Democrat with no solid record in education. As a governor, he backed the appointment of Torsten Friedag and then resigned rather than staying around to help pick up the pieces. New Labour's preference is to move on rather than see things through.

In the short term, this looks like a good move. Tactically, it could be neat. It pushes the Tories further to the right, offering schools a vague kind of freedom, a further break-up in the pattern which is already being broken up anyway. The one consolation for conservatives is that although they don't have their own personnel in power, at least their policies are being followed.

Opinion polls a week later say that a majority of Labour voters like the offer of something extra. It's selection as a prize for fund-raising, rather than a prize for passing an exam, so the apartheid is financial rather than intellectual. For the plan to work we need 60% of the population who wish to send their children to non-specialist schools, but maybe that poll result will come in later.

Some of the press are very keen. "Comprehensive education was supposed to give every pupil the same start in life. So there is a certain irony that, as Education Secretary David Blunkett rings its death knell..." [29] Norman Tebbitt told Mail on Sunday readers that he found Blunkett's development encouraging, and the Telegraph was glad to have its views confirmed: "In unveiling his five year plan for education, the Prime Minister made a welcome, implicit admission that comprehensive education has for many been a disaster." [30]

But such enthusiasm comes at a cost. This is not good news for people who work in comprehensive schools. For them, going from "education for all" to "specialist schools for 40%" is not a realistic scaling down, an adjustment of targets. It's a betrayal of a principle, and the idea of universal provision is uniquely powerful. As case studies from the third world show, you get commitment and effort in the service of that cause which you don't get simply for a rise in the league tables, or extra cash. Many teachers see this recent announcement as the last straw, the death sentence for a dream which hasn't been consistently realised, but has been passionately pursued and sporadically achieved. If the government isn't really interested any more, and their decisions, money and regulations will be slanted the other way, then what is the point of carrying on?

They have slid from "Read my lips; no more selection.." to "the many, not the few," to the outrageous suggestion that Tony Crosland would have approved this latest retreat. He would have seen it as intellectual cowardice, and he would also have been aware of its devastating impact upon the workforce. It's not been possible to calculate how far government policy has been responsible for the numbers of people leaving teaching, but I'd be very suprised if more of them want to stay on as a result of this announcement.

What can we do, those of us who believe in education for all? Those who still remain in the Labour Party can seek comfort from fellow members, many of whom retain the belief that all kids deserve a decent education. A lot of them will recall 1995, and David Blunkett's passionate reassertion of the traditional faith. On an old-fashioned straight vote this new policy would not have stood a chance. But that's not how the Labour Party works these days, and unhappy members aren't encouraged to express their unease.

Only the Liberal Democrats remain as a party with faith in the idea of an equal system, but the cynicism for which New Labour is responsible also affects their prospects. Are such ideals just a luxury of opposition? Do they have to be shed in the reality of power? In advance, you can't be sure, but while Liberal Democrat speakers may make the most sense, it's a considerable act of faith to imagine them in power.

One possibility, for those disenchanted with the whole process, is to find an imaginative way to record their disillusion. There might be a "Yes for Education" campaign, in which voters unwilling to support any of the major parties record a large tick across their ballot paper. This would be symbolically positive, yes rather than no, although New Labour would deplore it as a futile gesture. But the number of spoiled papers would be at least a message, and it's hard to see any other kind to which this government will respond.

So, what will happen? I know that there will continue to be lots of kids, with all the challenge and potential which that implies. Despite the sillier pronouncements about computers, and interesting but peripheral developments in home education, I believe that for the foreseeable future most of these kids will need to be taught in schools, and in classes. As always, the people teaching those classes will need to be resilient, imaginative and professional, and they will need to work together.

How we manage that under the present arrangements, with the policies declared by our two main political parties, I cannot see. But the build-up to the election seems the right time to raise these questions, so as to centre the debate in the detailed context of what has happened over the last four years. I don't have to have a ready-made solution, which grateful readers will authorise me to impose. But I do have a duty to tell the truth, so far as I can, and that is what I have tried to do. Whether anything follows from that is as much your responsibility as mine.

Paul Francis, Much Wenlock.   March 2001

1    Guardian 10.4.00
2    See Paul Flynn, "Dragons Led By Poodles" Politico's for the full story.
3    Kay Driver, letter to Observer 18.6.00
4    David Aaronovitch, Independent 7.4.00
5    TES 20.10.00
6    TES 20.10.00
7    Observer, 16.7.00
8    Guardian 13.10.00
9    Observer 16.7.00
10   TES 7.4.00
11   Valerie Bayliss, director of the Royal Society for Arts Opening Minds project.
12   Matthew Taylor and Joe Hallgarten, IPPR, in TES 17.3.00

13    Eileen Tracy, Guardian 21.3.00
14    Today programme, 12.4.00, quoted in Observer 16.4.00
15    Observer 16.4.00
16    Guardian 4.8.00
17    TES 5.5.00
18    Guardian 11.7.00
19    TES 6.2.98
20    Guardian 20.3.00
21    TES 20.10.00
22    Letter to Guardian 5.6.00
23    Guardian 18.10.00
24    Letter to TES, 4.2.00
25    TES 23.6.00
26    TES 21.7.00
27    TES 21.7.00
28    TES 18.8.00
29    TES 29.12.00
30    Observer 4.5.96 and Guardian 22.5.00
31    Guardian 2.11.99
32    Daily Express 13.2.01
33    Daily Telegraph 13.2.01

# NAMES AND ABBREVIATIONS

## NAMES AND POSTS of sources

Burjar Avari, principal lecturer in multicultural education, Manchester Metropolitan University

Mike Baker, BBC education correspondent

Michael Barber, London Institute, now government adviser

John Benington, professor of public management, Warwick University

Christine Blower, NUT president

David Blunkett, education minister

Patricia Broadfoot, professor of education, Bristol University; leader of QUEST

Margaret Brown, professor of education, King's College, London

Stephen Byers, former education minister, now minister for trade and industry

Kenneth Clarke, Tory education minister

David Cohen, Michigan State University

Pat Collarbone, director, London Leadership Centre, London Institute

Cary Cooper, professor of organisational psychology, UMIST

David Fontana, psychology, University of Cardiff

Michael Fullan, Dean of Education, Toronto University

Jonathan Gardner, Andrew Oswald, economists at Warwick University

David Gillborn and Deborah Youdell, policy studies, London Institute

Harvey Goldstein, professor of education, London Institute

Colin Harrison, School of Education, Nottingham University

David Hart, general secretary of NAHT

Margaret Hodge, chair of select committee, then education minister

John Howson, visiting fellow at Oxford Brookes University

Chris Husbands, professor of education, Warwick University

Judith Ireson and Susan Hallam, London Institute

Martin Johnson, president of NAS

Gareth Jones, formerly professor of organisational development at Henley Management college, now director of human resources and legal affairs, BBC

Graham Lane, Local Government Association

Dr. David Lines, business and economics lecturer, ICRA, London Institute

John MacBeath, professor of education, Strathclyde University; director of
    Quality in Education Centre.
Margaret Maden, professor of education, Keele University; head of Centre
    for Successful Schools
David Marsden, lecturer, LSE
Linda McNeil, researcher from Rice University
Anthea Millett, head of TTA
Keith Mitchell, director of Education, Durham LEA
Estelle Morris, education minister
Peter Mortimore, professor of education, London Institute
Richard Murnane, professor at Harvard
Bob Schaeffer, National Centre for Fair and Open Testing
Gillian Shephard, Tory education minister
Jacqui Smith, education minister
Alan Smithers, director of centre for education and employment research,
    Liverpool University
Sally Taverner and Vivienne Baumfield, education lecturers, Newcastle on
    Tyne
Brian Towers, Professor, Industrial Research Journal
Margaret Tulloch, secretary of CASE
Angela Valenzula, researcher from University of Texas, Austin
Mike Wallace, Professor of Education, Cardiff
Anne West, director of Centre for Educational Research, LSE
Christine Whatford, president of the Society of Education Officers
Chris Whetton, director of NFER

# ABBREVIATIONS

| | |
|---|---|
| AST | Advanced Skills Teacher |
| ATL | Association of Teachers and Lecturers |
| CASE | Campaign for the Advancement of State Education |
| CRE | Commission for Racial Equality |
| CTC | City technology college |
| DoE | Department of Education (up until 1996) |
| DfEE | Department for Education and Employment (replaced DoE in 1996) |
| FE | Further education |
| GCSE | General certificate of secondary education (exam for 16 |

|          |                                                                    |
| -------- | ------------------------------------------------------------------ |
|          | year olds)                                                         |
| HMCI     | Her majesty's chief inspector                                      |
| HMI      | Her majesty's inspector                                            |
| ICRA     | International Centre for Research on Asessment, London Institute   |
| IPPR     | Institute of Public Policy Research                               |
| KS       | Keystage ( KS1 ages 5 - 7;  KS2 7 - 11;  KS3  11-14; KS4 14-16).  |
| LEA      | Local education authority                                         |
| LSE      | London School of Economics                                       |
| MLD      | Moderate learning difficulties                                   |
| NAHT     | National Association of Head Teachers                            |
| NAS/UWT  | National Association of Schoolmasters/Union of Women Teachers    |
| NCC      | National Curriculum Council                                      |
| NFER     | National Foundation for Educational Research                     |
| NUT      | National Union of Teachers                                       |
| NFER     | National Foundation for Educational Research                     |
| NPQH     | National Professional Qualification for Headship                |
| NQT      | Newly qualified teacher                                          |
| OFSTED   | Office for Standards in Education                                |
| QCA      | Qualifications and Curriculum Authority                         |
| QUEST    | Quality of Education: Children's Experiences of Schooling in England and France |
| SAT      | Standardised Assessment Test                                    |
| SHA      | Secondary Headteachers Association                              |
| STRB     | School Teachers Review Board                                    |
| TES      | Times Educational Supplement                                   |
| TIMSS    | Third International Maths and Science Study                     |
| TSI      | Technology in Schools Initiative                               |
| TTA      | Teacher Training Authority                                     |
| TVEI     | Technical and Vocational Education Initiative                  |

# INDEX

(All abbreviations are explained in "Names and Abbreviations")